Power, Protection,

and Free Trade

Cornell Studies in Political Economy

Edited by Peter J. Katzenstein

Power, Protection, and Free Trade

INTERNATIONAL SOURCES OF
U.S. COMMERCIAL STRATEGY, 1887–1939

DAVID A. LAKE

CORNELL UNIVERSITY PRESS

Ithaca and London

First published 1988 by Cornell University Press.

International Standard Book Number 0-8014-2134-9
Library of Congress Catalog Card Number 87-47869
Printed in the United States of America
Librarians: Library of Congress cataloging information
appears on the last page of the book.

The paper in this book is acid-free and meets the guidelines for
permanence and durability of the Committee on Production Guidelines
for Book Longevity of the Council on Library Resources.

To Wendy,
with love

Contents

Preface

I began this project in the late 1970s seeking to explain the contradictory mixture of cooperation and conflict then present in the international economy. All of the advanced industrialized states were caught in the web of stagflation, oil prices were skyrocketing for the second time in less than a decade, and nontariff barriers to trade were rising. Yet the Tokyo Round of the General Agreement on Tariffs and Trade had just reduced tariff levels once again, and the leaders of the Western world were undertaking a unique and historic attempt to coordinate their macroeconomic policies. I was attracted by, but ultimately dissatisfied with, the "theory of hegemonic stability," which in many ways adequately captured the problems of the late 1970s but not the successes. What was needed was a theory that could account for both conflict and cooperation in nonhegemonic international economic systems. This book is the distant descendant of that original quest.

After developing an early version of what is now Chapter 1, I began to search for "least likely" cases that would allow for a rigorous elucidation of the theory. The problems associated with the decline of the Pax Americana no longer seemed to me appropriate to that end; examining an era of structural change in which the future is not yet known renders theory testing difficult, if not wholly meaningless. Although it possessed little intrinsic interest at first, American trade strategy in the prehegemonic era appeared to be a good "hard" case for the theory. I chose it for that reason. The deeper I delved into the case, the more fascinating it became.

In this book, I develop and test a systemic-level theory of national trade strategy, a theory that abstracts from domestic-level characteristics and focuses exclusively on how nation-states stand in relation one to another. In doing so, I deviate from classical theories of international trade, draw upon several less widely accepted literatures in international economics, and make strong generalizations. The theory is also intentionally parsimonious. As a consequence, I slight systemic variables not directly related to international trade and alternative explanations at the national and individual levels of analysis. Throughout, I seek to probe the limits of the systemic approach. This probing is not only analytically important, it is empirically fruitful as well. Applying the theory to the case of American trade strategy between 1887 and 1939 leads to an interpretation that differs from and challenges the current historiography.

I have benefited from the criticisms and support of numerous advisers, colleagues, and friends. Richard Rosecrance encouraged my interest in systemic theories of international politics and taught me the value of history for such an approach. Peter Katzenstein, first as adviser and later as editor, was an indefatigable critic whose suggestions are reflected throughout the book. Walter LaFeber, an exemplar for any young scholar, questioned my interpretations of American trade strategy and in the process led me through a voluminous history. I am grateful to all.

I had the good fortune to spend 1981–82 as a Research Fellow at the Brookings Institution with G. John Ikenberry and Michael Mastanduno. Their friendship and support made a difficult writing job easier. Much of what is now Chapter 2 was stimulated by our loud discussions in the library corridors and our subsequent collaborations. Jeffry Frieden, a good friend and colleague, has read and commented on virtually every word I have written over the last four years. In return for his efforts, I always let him win at tennis.

Robert Keohane, John Odell, and several anonymous reviewers read and commented on the complete manuscript. In addition, many colleagues have provided useful comments on various portions of the book: John Conybeare, David Dollar, Glenn Fong, Robert Gilpin, Judith Goldstein, Joanne Gowa, Lori Gronich, Stephan Haggard, Thomas Ilgen, Bruce Jentleson, Stephen Krasner, Fred Lawson, Charles Lipson, Timothy McKeown, Kenneth Oye, Ronald Rogowski, Arthur Stein, Kenneth Waltz, Beth Yarbrough, and Robert Yarbrough. Selected portions of the manuscript have been presented at annual meetings of the American Political Science Association and the International Studies Association; at the University of California, Davis; Stanford University; the University of California, Berkeley; and the Program on Interdependent Political Economy at the University of Chicago. I thank the participants in these meetings for their often enlightening comments.

I am grateful to the Peace Studies Program at Cornell University, the Institute for the Study of World Politics, the Brookings Institution, the UCLA Office of International Studies and Overseas Programs, and the UCLA Academic Senate for financial assistance. Deborah Shapiro, Joel Rothblatt, and Scott James all served as outstanding research assistants. Bess Karadenes assisted with the final proofreading. Roger Haydon guided the manuscript through the publication process with remarkable ease. Trudy Calvert greatly improved the prose. None of the individuals or institutions noted above, however, is responsible for any remaining errors.

Earlier versions of portions of this book were published as "International Economic Structures and American Foreign Economic Policy, 1887–1934," *World Politics*, vol. 35, no. 4 (July 1983), copyright © 1983 by Princeton University Press, adapted with permission of Princeton University Press; "Beneath the Commerce of Nations: A Theory of International Economic Structures," adapted from the *International Studies Quarterly*, vol. 28 (1984) with permission of the International Studies Association, Byrnes International Center, University of South Carolina, Columbia, SC 29208, USA; and "American Trade Strategy in the Pre-Hegemonic Era," *International Organization*, vol. 42 (Winter 1988), adapted with permission of the MIT Press and the World Peace Foundation.

I also thank my parents, Edward and Gloria Lake and Samuel and Sylvia Krieger, for their confidence and encouragement over the years. Although Brenden Manker Lake, whose birth coincided with the final revision of the manuscript, was too late to offer much support, his pending arrival helped bring this project to a timely conclusion. Finally, my greatest debt of gratitude is to my wife, Wendy Krieger Lake, to whom this volume is dedicated. The book is as much hers as mine, for I would never have contemplated—far less completed—this endeavor were it not for her love, support, and encouragement. This is a debt I look forward to repaying for many years to come.

DAVID A. LAKE

Los Angeles, California

Power, Protection,
and Free Trade

Introduction

In May 1930 more than a thousand members of the American Economic Association issued a petition urging Congress to vote down the tariff bill then pending in the conference committee and the president to veto the measure should it come to him for signature. One month later, Herbert Hoover signed the Smoot-Hawley Act into law. Economists have long recognized the benefits of free trade, first articulated by Adam Smith in 1776 and extended by David Ricardo in the early nineteenth century. Yet trade protection occurs and recurs, often in phases and perhaps even in cycles. Even today, after nearly forty years of strong American support for free trade in the world economy, protectionism is once again an important political issue in the United States.

The dominant explanation for protection is one of domestic political failure. Because restrictions on trade benefit relatively small groups of producers whereas the mass of consumers benefit from free trade, producers have a greater incentive to organize and influence the political process. Pressured by failing industries unwilling to bear the costs of economic change, politicians promote trade-restrictive measures that benefit the few at the expense of the many. The problem, according to this explanation, lies not in a misidentification of political objectives or in the value of economic openness but in the unwillingness or inability of politicians to adhere to the goal of free trade.[1]

[1]For classic studies of the tariff which take this view, see Frank W. Taussig, *The Tariff History of the United States*, 8th ed. (New York: Putnam, 1931); and E. E. Schattschneider, *Politics, Pressures and the Tariff* (New York: Prentice-Hall, 1935). The argument is developed more formally in the public choice literature on tariffs, also referred to as "endogenous tariff theory." See in particular Richard E. Caves, "Economic Models of Political Choice: Canada's Tariff Structure," *Canadian Journal of Economics* 9, (May 1976): 278–300;

Drawing upon an equally old historical tradition associated with Alexander Hamilton and Friedrich List, this book advances an alternative
explanation that conceives of both protection and free trade as legitimate and effective instruments of national policy. Like the early mercantilists of the seventeenth and eighteenth centuries, Hamilton and
List believed that power and wealth are proper and, in the long run,
harmonious goals of national policy; that nation-states—rather than
individuals or global society—are the most important actors on the
international stage and the appropriate unit of analysis; and that nation-
states pursue national interests defined in terms of power and wealth.[2]
Yet unlike their predecessors, who focused narrowly on the sovereign's
gold stocks, Hamilton and List recognized that the sources of national
power and wealth are many and varied and that different policies are
necessary at different stages in a country's development. Although neither Hamilton nor List set forth a fully developed theory of international trade, both attempted to identify the conditions under which free
trade and protection would best serve the national interest. Hamilton
argued that national wealth and power could be enhanced by protecting
certain "infant industries," which could not otherwise survive the rigors
of international competition.[3] List attempted a more general indictment
of free trade. Considering the practices of several European nation-
states, List denounced free trade as the instrument used by the leading
commercial power to maintain its dominance over others. To break free
from the leading power's grasp and become an international power in its
own right, List argued, a country needed to protect its economy and
stimulate the process of industrialization.[4]

Jonathan J. Pincus, *Pressure Groups and Politics in Antebellum Tariffs* (New York: Columbia
University Press, 1977); and Robert Baldwin, *The Political Economy of U.S. Import Policy*
(Cambridge: MIT Press, 1985). Many more studies are reviewed in Real P. Lavergne, *The
Political Economy of U.S. Tariffs* (New York: Academic, 1983). The only such study to focus
on the period covered here is Bennett D. Baack and Edward John Ray. "The Political
Economy of Tariff Policy: A Case Study of the United States," *Explorations in Economic
History* 20 (January 1983): 73–93.

[2]See Jacob Viner, "Power versus Plenty as Objectives of Foreign Policy in the Seven-
teenth and Eighteenth Centuries," *World Politics* 1 (October 1948): 1–29; E. F. Heckscher,
Mercantilism, trans. Mendel Shapiro, rev. 2d ed. (New York: Macmillan, 1955); and
Charles Wilson, *Profit and Power: A Study of England and the Dutch Wars* (New York:
Longmans, Green, 1957). For an alternative view that explains mercantilism as a form of
rent-seeking by societal groups, see Robert B. Ekelund and Robert D. Tollison, eds.,
Mercantilism as a Rent-Seeking Society: Economic Regulation in Historical Perspective (College
Station: Texas A&M University Press, 1981).

[3]*Documents Relating to American Economic History: Selections from the Official Reports of
Alexander Hamilton*, arr. Felix Flugel (Berkeley: University of California Press, 1929).

[4]Friedrich List, *The National System of Political Economy* (London, 1885; rpt. New York:
Kelley, 1977).

In this same spirit, Part I of this book develops a deductive, systemic-level theory of national trade interests which attempts to specify the conditions and circumstances that stimulate rational power- and wealth-seeking nation-states to pursue free trade, protection, or some combination of both. My central proposition is that the national trade interests, political choices, and ultimately trade strategies of individual countries are fundamentally shaped and influenced by the constraints and opportunities of the international economic structure. Protection and free trade, then, are not simply the result of domestic political pressures but the considered response of self-seeking nation-states to varying international structures.

A second theoretical proposition developed in Part I concerns the relationship between systemic incentives and the domestic political process. Chapter 2 addresses the question of how the constraints and opportunities of the international economic structure are communicated or translated into national trade strategies. A disaggregated conception of the state is presented in which the principal domestic political cleavage is between the foreign policy executive, concerned with national power and wealth, and the representative element of the state, responsive primarily to the rent-seeking interests of society. The clash between these two sets of interests ultimately determines trade policy. Domestic politics is not seen as unimportant, but I argue that the constraints and opportunities of the international economic structure are influential and that domestic political factors, normally granted analytic autonomy from systemic incentives, are best understood as interacting with these constraints.

AMERICAN TRADE STRATEGY

Part II of this book tests the systemic theory of international economic structures in a "hard" or least likely crucial case study of American trade strategy between 1887 and 1939.[5] During this period, the United States possessed a large domestic market, low levels of economic interdependence, an isolationist ideology, and strong societal pressure groups within a highly permeable political process. Consequently, it could be argued that American trade strategy would have been unlikely to respond to the constraints and opportunities of the international economic structure. As I demonstrate in Chapters 3 through 6, however,

[5]On least likely case studies see Harry Eckstein, "Case Study and Theory in Political Science," in Fred I. Greenstein and Nelson W. Polsby, eds., *The Handbook of Political Science*, 8 vols. (Reading, Mass.: Addison-Wesley, 1975), 7:79–137.

that strategy was shaped in important ways by these systemic incentives, thereby offering strong support for the theory.

Trade Strategy Defined

Trade strategy is a government plan or method for obtaining one or more objectives within the international economy related to the import or export of tangible goods. All trade is strategic, or characterized by interactive decision making, at the most basic level: every import is another country's export. Thus, almost by definition, trade strategy refers to government policies that are contingent upon the actions of other nation-states or intended to manipulate the preferences and policies of others.

Trade strategy has two dimensions (see Figure I.1). The first, international market orientation, indicates a country's willingness to permit the international market to control its trade flows. A liberal, open, or free trade strategy, as traditionally defined in the literature on international political economy, relies upon the market as the principal determinant of the pattern of international trade. A protectionist or mercantilist strategy, on the other hand, regulates trade flows through government fiat in the form of tariffs, nontariff barriers to trade, barter arrangements, or centrally planned trade. The second dimension, the degree of international political activity, denotes the desire of a country to influence the international economic order and the policies of others. In a passive strategy, policies are typically directed inward at the country's own domestic economy. An active strategy seeks to influence the economic order and the policies of other countries.

In the period 1887–1939, no formal statements of American trade strategy were offered on a regular or periodic basis. Rather, trade strategy must be inferred from the debates over tariff policy, the central trade issue of the era and the principal instrument through which

Figure I.1. Two dimensions of trade strategy and characteristic indicators

Liberal International Market Orientation Protectionist	low, nonnegotiable, and nondiscriminatory tariffs	low, negotiable, and nondiscriminatory tariffs
	high, nonnegotiable, and discriminatory tariffs	high, negotiable, and discriminatory tariffs

Passive   Active
Degree of international political activity

strategy was implemented.[6] Trade strategy is, however, distinct from and more general than tariff policy; two (or more) tariff acts may differ in their particulars yet reflect a single trade strategy.

Eight tariff acts were passed by Congress and signed into law during the period examined in this book.[7] Each can be classified within the dimensions of the international market orientation and degree of international political activity in two ways. Tariff policies can be categorized by their substantive legislative provisions. Three elements are of particular importance: the average rates of duty, their "negotiability," and the extent of discrimination between countries. Higher rates of duty are more protectionist, lower rates more liberal. Tariff acts that do not discriminate between countries are more liberal than those that do, although discrimination may also indicate an active trade strategy. Similarly, measures that fix rates irrespective of the actions of other countries or contain flexible provisions that are not implemented are more passive than acts that allow the legislature or the executive to bargain with other countries over duties and other provisions.

Tariff policies can also be classified by their stated purposes. Declarations of intent, especially by politicians, are often misleading. Yet during the tariff debates, policy makers appear to have been quite explicit when discussing the purposes of the legislation. In the late nineteenth and early twentieth centuries, the tariff was a politically divisive issue. The perspectives of both the "protectionists" and "free traders" were highly developed and neither group appeared to believe it necessary to disguise its objectives in passing any tariff bill. Moreover, in nearly all cases there is a close correspondence between the first and second means of classifying the trade acts. Tariff acts that sought to close the United States off from the international economy are classified as protectionist and passive. Conversely, those acts which sought to stimulate trade both at

---

[6]Because I am testing hypotheses rather than writing history, not all of the historical record is necessary. Only such information is gathered as is necessary to disconfirm or support the hypotheses developed in Chapters 1 and 2. I consulted first the public record, such as the *Congressional Record* and congressional hearings and reports, then published primary materials, including memoirs and collected papers, and finally unpublished primary material, largely private papers of the individual decision makers and government documents.

[7]These eight acts are the McKinley Tariff (1890), Wilson-Gorman Tariff (1894), Dingley Tariff (1897), Payne-Aldrich Tariff (1909), Underwood Tariff (1913), Fordney-McCumber Tariff (1922), Smoot-Hawley Tariff (1930), and the Reciprocal Trade Agreements Act (1934). The last was not a completely new tariff act but an amendment to the 1930 act. Tariff bills are named for the chairman of the House Ways and Means Committee, who is principally charged with writing the bill, and in some cases, the chairman of the Senate Finance Committee, if the Senate revises the measure substantially. For the Smoot-Hawley bill, the normal order is reversed because of the Senate's important role in nearly rewriting the entire bill.

home and abroad are classified as liberal and active. The specific reasons for the classification of each of the eight bills are discussed in Part II.

Historical Overview

Rapid and dramatic changes occurred in American trade strategy in the period 1887–1939. After the Civil War and before 1887, the United States was a relatively passive and highly protectionist nation-state. Tariffs were high, nonnegotiable, and nondiscriminatory. During World War II, the United States shed the last vestiges of its nineteenth-century strategy. By 1945, it had emerged as an active world leader strongly supportive of universal free trade. The transition from America's passive protectionism of the mid-nineteenth century to its active liberalism of the mid-twentieth is the substantive focus of this book. Within this period, four phases can be identified.

President Grover C. Cleveland, a northern Democrat, broke the dominant post–Civil War protectionist consensus in his 1887 Annual Message to Congress by calling for duty-free status for raw materials. In the ensuing debate, the tariff was internationalized or reconceptualized as a more active instrument for promoting exports. Although maintaining the essential structure of protection at home, both the McKinley Act of 1890, passed under the Republican administration of Benjamin Harrison, and the Wilson-Gorman Tariff of 1894, enacted during Cleveland's second term, pursued special trading relationships with the countries of Latin America by lowering duties on a selected and limited number of raw materials. Both parties hoped these relationships would expand American exports to the region at the expense of British and other European traders. Thus the United States sought and, as will be seen in Chapter 3, easily obtained both protection for imports and expansion of exports.

Between 1897 and 1912, the second phase of American trade strategy, the United States continued to pursue highly protectionist policies and became more active in the international economic arena. Specifically, the strategy of bilateral bargaining first adopted in the McKinley Act was expanded to include the increasingly protectionist countries of continental Europe. In the Dingley Act of 1897, the United States offered the continental Europeans reciprocal reductions in duties for the first time and threatened penalty duties against selected Latin American countries unless they granted trade concessions to American exporters. Reflecting new confidence in the ability of the United States to compete on equal terms in world markets, the Payne-Aldrich Act of 1909 granted lower duties to all countries that did not unduly discriminate against American goods. Despite their differences, however, both tariff acts rejected liberal free-trade principles and actively sought to exploit the national trade strategies of other countries.

Between 1912 and 1930, the United States departed from its historic policy of protection. The Underwood Act, passed under the leadership of President Woodrow Wilson in 1913, drastically lowered tariff rates and endorsed the principle of freer international trade. A decade later, in an international economy still unsettled by the war, the United States increased its tariff moderately in the Fordney-McCumber Act of 1922. Nonetheless, tariff rates remained far below those of earlier phases. This modest increase from the low levels of 1913 was partially offset by a more active trade strategy and adoption of the nondiscriminatory most-favored-nation principle. Throughout this third phase of trade strategy, then, American policy was characterized by tariff restraint and a high degree of international activism.

Finally, during the period from 1930 to 1939, the United States took a dramatic turn toward renewed protection in the Smoot-Hawley Act of 1930, only to reverse course and adopt the liberal and extremely active Reciprocal Trade Agreements Act in 1934. Although the latter signaled an important departure in American trade strategy, it was not a radical break with past practice. Rather, the 1934 act was intended as a complement to protection, enabling the United States to reopen foreign markets to its exports. Not until after 1945 did the United States fully endorse the principle of free trade at home and abroad.

Chapters 3 through 6 examine these four phases of American trade strategy. Each chapter analyzes the constraints and opportunities the United States confronted in the international economic structure; how these constraints and opportunities shaped the national trade interest and, in turn, trade strategy; and the role of the foreign policy executive in the policy-making process. The Conclusion summarizes the strengths and weaknesses of the theory as revealed in the case study.

THEORETICAL OVERVIEW

American trade strategy between 1887 and 1939 is typically explained by a combination of interest-group politics and competition among political parties. The interest-group argument is well-known. Producers have concentrated interests in protection, and consumers have diffuse interests in free trade. As a result, producers organize more easily and bring greater pressure to bear on the political process. The decentralized and relatively open American political process, moreover, contains many points of access for motivated petitioners, ensuring that their voices will be heard. At least in the omnibus tariff acts passed by Congress in the period examined here, the almost infinitely divisible nature of the tariff, which often allowed duties to be tailored to specific producers, created a norm of mutual noninterference and a process of legislative logrolling in which virtually all claimants could be satisfied. As a result, the American tariff tended toward equality and uniformity in duties and universality in application.[8]

The role of political parties is often superimposed on this interest-group explanation. The Republicans, with an electoral base in the Northeast and Midwest, are identified as the party of protection, and the Democrats, drawing on the traditionally trade-dependent South, the party of free trade. Fluctuations in tariff rates, in this view, are explained by changes in party dominance.[9]

These explanations are widely accepted, but they appear inadequate. As discussed in more detail in Part II, the industrial structure of the American economy did not change in tandem with trade strategy. The dependence of American manufacturers on exports rose dramatically over the 1890s, yet the tariff remained highly protectionist. This dependence increased only slightly before World War I, but the tariff was drastically lowered in 1913. American dependence on exports and foreign investment continued to rise during the war, but tariffs were increased in 1922. Explanations of trade strategy based on political parties are also open to question. In the early 1890s, there were important commonalities in policy despite changes in party. Conversely, party platforms changed significantly over time, even though the electoral bases remained similar. These anomalies should not necessarily lead us to dismiss the importance of interest groups and political parties, but they should call into question the narrowness of explanations derived entirely from domestic political factors.

The most important international alternative to this domestic-level explanation is the theory of hegemonic stability, although it focuses principally on international economic regimes and is never applied to

[8]See Schattschneider, *Politics, Pressures and the Tariff*; and Theodore J. Lowi, "American Business, Public Policy, Case-Studies, and Political Theory," *World Politics* 16 (July 1964): 667–715. On interest groups see William H. Becker, *The Dynamics of Business-Government Relations: Industry and Exports, 1893–1921* (Chicago: University of Chicago Press, 1982); and Joan Hoff Wilson, *American Business and Foreign Policy, 1920–1933* (Boston: Beacon, 1973).

[9]Tom E. Terrill, *The Tariff, Politics, and American Foreign Policy, 1874–1901* (Westport, Conn.: Greenwood Press, 1973), presents the clearest argument on the importance of party competition. Party competition is also important to Taussig (*Tariff History*); and Edward Stanwood, *American Tariff Controversies in the Nineteenth Century* (Boston: Houghton Mifflin, 1903).

American trade strategy before World War I.[10] There are two principal
variants of this theory. The first, associated with Charles P. Kindleberger, focuses on the provision of the collective good of international
stability, with instability defined as a condition in which small disruptions (for example, the 1929 stock market crash) have large consequences (the Great Depression). Assuming that markets are inherently
unstable—or nonhomeostatic systems—and tend toward stagnation
and fragmentation, Kindleberger argues that the international economy will be stable only if a single leader is willing to assume responsibility for "(a) maintaining a relatively open market for distress goods;
(b) providing counter-cyclical long-term lending; and (c) discounting in
a crisis."[11] Kindleberger has subsequently added that the leader must
also undertake to "manage, in some degree, the structure of foreign
exchange rates and provide a degree of coordination of domestic monetary policies."[12]

The second variant, found in the writings of Robert Gilpin and Stephen D. Krasner, attempts to explain the strength and content of international economic regimes. Both authors share Kindleberger's assumption that markets are nonhomeostatic systems. Yet according to this
view, liberal international economies collapse not only as a result of
inherent flaws in the self-regulating international market mechanism
but also because nation-states pursue goals other than aggregate national income and welfare. Krasner posits three additional goals: social
stability, political power, and economic growth.[13] Gilpin takes a similar
position, arguing that "other than in a few . . . exceptional circumstances, societies throughout history have placed much greater emphasis on security values such as social stability or self-sufficiency than
on income gains from the free operation of markets."[14] The political
tasks in this variant, therefore, involve not only curing market dysfunc-

[10]This label was coined by Robert Keohane in "The Theory of Hegemonic Stability and
Changes in International Economic Regimes, 1967–1977," in Ole Holsti, Randolph Siver-
son, and Alexander L. George, eds., *Change in the International System* (Boulder: Westview,
1980), pp. 131–62.
[11]Charles P. Kindleberger, *The World in Depression, 1929–1939* (Berkeley: University of
California Press, 1973), p. 292.
[12]Charles P. Kindleberger, "Dominance and Leadership in the International Economy:
Exploitation, Public Goods, and Free Rides," *International Studies Quarterly* 25 (June 1981):
247.
[13]Robert Gilpin, *U.S. Power and the Multinational Corporation: The Political Economy of
Foreign Direct Investment* (New York: Basic Books, 1975); "Economic Interdependence and
National Security in Historical Perspective," in Klaus Knorr and Frank N. Trager, eds.,
Economic Issues and National Security (Lawrence: Regents Press of Kansas, 1977); and
Stephen D. Krasner, "State Power and the Structure of International Trade," *World Politics*
28 (April 1976): 317–47.
[14]Gilpin, "Economic Interdependence," p. 22.

tion through hegemonial intervention but also creating an international order that meets the security needs of nation-states so that they can pursue the gains from freer trade. Both Gilpin and Krasner argue that strong liberal international economic regimes are most likely to be created when a single hegemonic leader dominates the international economy.

With the growing popularity of the theory of hegemonic stability, the views of these three authors have been reduced to a simpler and more deterministic form which draws a direct and causal link between hegemony, regime stability, and economic openness. Robert Keohane, for example, states that the theory "holds that hegemonic structures of power, dominated by a single country, are most conducive to the development of strong international regimes whose rules are relatively precise and well obeyed. According to the theory, the decline of hegemonic structures of power can be expected to presage a decline in the strength of corresponding international economic regimes."[15] This simplified version of the theory of hegemonic stability, which draws heavily upon the example of Britain's hegemonic decline in the late nineteenth and early twentieth centuries, has been subjected to several varied tests, with mixed results.[16] Most important, the continued openness of the international economy in the 1970s and early 1980s despite America's declining hegemony has been widely perceived as a major shortcoming or anomaly of the theory.

Since its "discovery," this anomaly has guided several important research projects in the field of international political economy. The recent volume on international regimes edited by Krasner and Keohane's *After Hegemony* both use this shortcoming as a rationale for studying international regimes. Likewise, Judith Goldstein argues that the continued openness of the United States is a result of the frozen or rigid American state structure created through past success.[17]

[15]Keohane, "Theory of Hegemonic Stability," p. 132.

[16]For example, Timothy J. McKeown, "Hegemonic Stability Theory and Nineteenth Century Tariff Levels in Europe," *International Organization* 37 (Winter 1983): 73–91; Arthur A. Stein, "The Hegemon's Dilemma: Great Britain, the United States, and the International Economic Order," *International Organization* 38 (Spring 1984): 355–86; Peter F. Cowhey and Edward Long, "Testing Theories of Regime Change: Hegemonic Decline or Surplus Capacity?" *International Organization* 37 (Spring 1983): 157–88; and Fred Lawson, "Hegemony and the Structure of International Trade Reassessed: A View from Arabia," *International Organization* 37 (Spring 1983): 317–37.

[17]A special issue of *International Organization* 36 (Spring 1982); Robert Keohane, *After Hegemony: Cooperation and Discord in the World Political Economy* (Princeton: Princeton University Press, 1984); Judith Goldstein, "A Re-examination of American Trade Policy: An Inquiry into the Causes of Protectionism" (Ph.D. diss., University of California, Los Angeles, 1983); and "Ideas, Institutions, and American Trade Policy," *International Organization* 42 (Winter 1988).

Rather than reject the theory of hegemonic stability or supplement it through the analysis of additional variables, I seek to remain within the analytic framework of the theory but to refine and extend its logic. The theory of international economic structures presented here differs from the theory of hegemonic stability in its definition of the international structure, its ability to explain the political economy of nonhegemonic as well as hegemonic structures, and its conclusions and predictions on the degree of openness likely to be found in nonhegemonic structures. In particular, the theory seeks to shed the "hegemonic obsession" of much of the current literature. By failing to distinguish between the structurally derived interests of nonhegemonic nation-states, past studies have been unable to discern differences between nonhegemonic international economic structures. Differentiating between such structures is, I believe, necessary for a proper understanding of the politics and processes of the international economy.

Despite the similarities in their conclusions, Kindleberger, Gilpin, and Krasner define the international economic structure differently. Kindleberger employs the single dimension of relative size, which he divides into three categories: small, middle, and large-sized countries. Gilpin defines the structure by political-military power and relative efficiency. He also identifies three categories of nation-states within the international political economy: hegemonic powers, peripheral states, and growth nodes. Like Gilpin, Krasner uses two dimensions but focuses on the degree of equality (or inequality) in both the level of development and the size of nation-states and posits six hypothetical distributions of potential economic power.[18]

For reasons explained in Chapter 1, I define the international economic structure as the configuration of nation-states within the two dimensions of relative size and relative labor productivity. Within these two dimensions, seven categories of actors are identified, each with a specific trade policy preference ordering. This preference ordering and the strategic interaction between categories create constraints and opportunities for individual nation-states which, in turn, shape the national trade interest. Thus, by examining the international economic structure, the position of a country within it, and changes in the structure over time, it is possible to explain and predict national trade strategies. Throughout, the emphasis is on developing a rigorous, deductive, and systemic-level theory specific enough to be open to empirical testing through an examination of the trade strategies of individual countries.

[18]Kindleberger, "Dominance and Leadership," pp. 249–51; Gilpin, "Economic Interdependence," p. 22; Gilpin, *U.S. Power*; Krasner, "State Power," p. 323.

In the process, necessary and sufficient conditions for economic open-ness under alternative international economic structures are identified.

The chapters in Part II do not attempt to test the relative explanatory power of the theory of international economic structures against the prevailing domestic explanations of interest-group politics and competi-tion between political parties. Rather, these chapters attempt to develop the strongest possible support for the theory of international economic structures and to discern the limits of a systemic approach in explaining trade strategy in a single country. This is a necessary first step toward conducting a meaningful debate on the relative efficacy of domestic and international explanations. Each chapter in Part II, however, does briefly summarize the anomalies raised for the domestic approach by the interpretation of American trade strategy presented here, and the final chapter presents some tentative conclusions on the complementary nature of domestic and international explanations of trade strategy.

The theory of international economic structures set forth in Chapter 1 is clearly associated with the growing school of structural or neo-Realism in international relations. Although structural Realist theories have gained wide visibility over the last decade, they are open to at least one of the criticisms leveled against Realist theories of the 1950s and 1960s. Both Realists and structural Realists "black box" domestic politics. Al-though most Realists do not assert that the international system is wholly determining and are aware that domestic politics exert an impact upon policy, the relationship between the systemic and national levels of analysis in this literature remains ambiguous. This problem can be ignored with relative impunity by many systemic theories. Both Ken-neth Waltz's *Theory of International Politics* and the theory of hegemonic stability, for instance, seek to explain systemic processes and outcomes such as balances of power or regime stability as a result of systemic features. Within this approach there is considerable room for individual deviancy: the failure of one country to balance or adhere to the regime does not disconfirm the theory.[19] In seeking to develop a systemic theory of the behavior of individual nation-states, however, the question of how systemic constraints and opportunities are communicated into

---

[19]Kenneth Waltz, one of the most important neo-Realist theorists, is careful to circum-scribe his argument in *Theory of International Politics* (Reading, Mass.: Addison-Wesley, 1979); Waltz notes repeatedly throughout the book that he is writing a theory of interna-tional relations, not foreign policy. Waltz, for instance, does not state that all countries will balance, only that balancing behavior will be selected out through evolution and emulated through socialization. See also his essay "Reflections on Theory of International Politics: A Response to My Critics," in Robert Keohane, ed., *Neorealism and Its Critics* (New York: Columbia University Press, 1986), pp. 322–45.

policy becomes central. In other words, it is no longer possible to abstract from domestic politics.

In Chapter 2, I attempt to unpack the black box of domestic politics and determine how the constraints and opportunities of the international economic structure are recognized and acted upon within the domestic sphere so as to result in observable trade strategies. I argue that the state can be decomposed into at least two sets of conflicting actors: the foreign policy executive and the representative element. The latter aggregates and articulates the interests of the politically mobilized groups within society. The former—typically facing a national electorate and mandated to protect and enhance the power and wealth of the nation-state—identifies the constraints and opportunities of the international economic structure and seeks to ensure the adoption of policies consonant with its demands. Because of the relative rather than absolute nature of power, and to the extent that collective action is difficult within society, the interests articulated by the foreign policy and representative elements of the state must differ. This conflict prevents the foreign policy executive from acting unilaterally; to a greater or lesser extent, it must bargain with the representative element and society. This bargaining process, in turn, is influenced by the structure of the state and executive or presidential leadership. Particular attention is paid in Part II to executive strategies for gaining influence within and access to the congressionally dominated tariff-making process.

At the most basic level, the theory of international economic structures, like all systemic theories, can be confirmed or disconfirmed only by the behavior of nation-states. The theory does not contain any conception of political process, so the way nation-states arrive at policy is an unanswerable and unimportant question. All that is needed, at this level, is a correlation between the behaviors predicted by the theory and those observed in reality. This simple test is sufficient if actual strategy does in fact coincide with the predictions, or if one is examining a large number of cases and therefore can tolerate a certain number of anomalies. The framework for understanding the domestic political process developed in Chapter 2, however, allows for testing the systemic theory in a single case without denying the importance of domestic politics. By specifying who should be especially sensitive to systemic incentives, the theory of international economic structures can be confirmed if the foreign policy executive articulates preferences and pursues policies consistent with the predicted constraints and opportunities, even if the final policy does not fully coincide with the national trade interest. Of course, the larger the gap between the national trade interest and the trade strategy actually pursued, the less useful the theory of international economic structures will be. In addition, the theory will be falsified if a country's trade strategy is inconsistent with the constraints and opportunities of the international economic structure *and* the foreign policy executive fails to advocate and pursue the predicted policies.

Following these criteria, and given the least likely nature of the case examined, this book offers relatively strong support for the theory of international economic structures. With only a few exceptions, American trade strategy did conform to the constraints and opportunities of the international economic structure. Moreover, state officials within the foreign policy executive were normally sensitive to the systemically generated national trade interest and advocated appropriate strategies.

CONCLUSION

This Introduction closes with two cautionary notes. First, the theory of international economic structures is not intended as either a deterministic or a unicausal explanation of trade strategy. I seek to push a systemic theory to its practical limits, but I am under no delusions that it provides a completely satisfying explanation. Other factors, including ideology, business cycles, and the sheer weight of history, are also important. In the end, all constraint-based theories will be underdetermining; this one is no exception. Second, unlike the modern mercantilists and many present-day trade economists, I eschew normative conclusions. I desire merely to explain the trade strategies of individual countries; whether the policies actually pursued are, by some definition, optimal is a question I leave to others.

Although I seek to avoid judgments on the value of specific policies, I have not altogether ignored practical concerns. Since its inception, the United States has been torn between the wish to retreat into the home market and the desire to trade in the international economy. The first tendency reached its apogee in the period between the Civil War and 1887, the second, during the post-1945 Pax Americana. During the period 1887–1939, neither the desire for protection against imports nor the wish to expand exports clearly predominated in American politics. Confronted with a growing desire to participate in the international economy and reap the advantages of its steadily increasing productivity, the United States altered its traditional strategy of high tariff protection and international passivity after 1887. As the previous consensus declined, America had to decide how and to what extent to trade in an international economy it could not control. Today, the United States faces a similar decision. With the decline in American power, the United

States is now only the most influential nation-state within a fairly large group of relative equals. Although it is "still an extraordinary power,"[20] it can no longer unilaterally lead the international economy in accordance with its own desires. By reexamining America's prehegemonic era, new light can be shed on the problems and choices likely to face the United States in the years ahead.

Concern has also been raised over the implications of America's declining hegemony for the maintenance of the current liberal international economic regime. Many fear that with the waning of American power, the Pax Americana will follow the path of the Pax Britannica into a new phase of protectionism and economic conflict. By recognizing the critical role played by nonhegemonic nation-states within the international economy, the often assumed parallel between the decline of the Pax Britannica and the decline of the Pax Americana becomes questionable. As I try to demonstrate throughout this work, the analogy is misleading. Despite several important similarities, America's decline need not and will not follow the path blazed by Britain earlier in this century. Rather than portending a future of decay in the international economic order, the decline of American hegemony actually presents new opportunities for international cooperation.

[20]Susan Strange, "Still an Extraordinary Power: America's Role in a Global Monetary System," in Raymond E. Lombra and William E. Witte, eds., *The Political Economy of International and Domestic Monetary Relations* (Ames: Iowa State University Press, 1982); see also Bruce Russett, "The Mysterious Case of Vanishing Hegemony; or, Is Mark Twain Really Dead?" *International Organization* 39 (Spring 1985): 207–31.

Part I

STRUCTURE AND STRATEGY

CHAPTER ONE

A Theory of International Economic Structures

Many statesmen have been introduced to the benefits of free trade in undergraduate economics courses or, in earlier periods, through the writings of Adam Smith and David Ricardo. But over the last two centuries, the teachings of liberal trade economists have been followed only sporadically. The law of comparative advantage is one of the basic tenets of economics. Yet in perhaps no other area is the gap between economic theory and political practice so large.

As noted in the Introduction, the most widely accepted explanation of this anomaly is interest-group or, in public choice parlance, endogenous tariff theory. Government leaders, this theory maintains, are under pressure from highly organized, rent-seeking societal groups. Dependent upon such groups for support, politicians have little choice but to grant protection to claimants, thereby benefiting selected producers at the expense of consumers. This theory is attractive, and I build on it in Chapter 2.

Yet even within the advanced industrialized democracies, governmental forms vary in their degree of centralization and autonomy—factors that should allow for differential insulation from society and rent-seeking pressures.[1] All of the major economic powers have maintained extensive protectionist systems at some stage in history despite clear differences in domestic structures. Great Britain in the seven-

---

[1]Peter J. Katzenstein, ed., *Between Power and Plenty: Foreign Economic Policies of Advanced Industrialized States* (Madison: University of Wisconsin Press, 1978). For approaches that examine various institutions within the United States, see Judith Goldstein, "A Re-examination of American Trade Policy: An Inquiry into the Causes of Protectionism" (Ph.D. diss., University of California, Los Angeles, 1983), and Robert E. Baldwin, *The Political Economy of U.S. Import Policy* (Cambridge: MIT Press, 1985).

teenth and eighteenth centuries, the United States in the late eighteenth and nineteenth centuries, France and Germany in the late nineteenth century, and Japan in the twentieth century have all vigorously pursued protectionist policies. These same countries, with the possible exception of Japan, have all pursued free trade at other times with almost equal vigor and often without a significant change in domestic structure.

Moreover, politicians and political economists have articulated important rationales for protection based on the "public interest." Jean Baptiste Colbert's mercantilism, Alexander Hamilton's "infant industry" argument, the German historical school, and MITI technocrats in Japan all maintain that protection is in the national interest at certain stages in a country's economic development. This economic philosophy has often dominated the political agenda in the past and may do so again in the future. At other times, the teachings of economic trade theorists have gained prominence and greater support. The current allegiance of politicians in the United States to the principle of free trade (but not necessarily the practice) provides ample evidence: even protectionist policies have to be couched in liberal rhetoric and framed in terms of reciprocity, or the opening of foreign markets to American exports. In each case, protection or free trade has been generally espoused as being in the "national interest."

Finally, free trade and protection appear to be contagious and cyclical. The brief era of European free trade in the mid-nineteenth century rapidly gave way to near universal protectionism by the end of the century, only to be superseded by a period of free trade among the advanced industrialized democracies following World War II. Specific explanations for each country's policy vary widely: France adopted free trade in 1860 in an attempt to secure British support for its northern Italy policy,[2] the United States maintained its highly protectionist system because Republicans, who formed the dominant party after the Civil War, had declared themselves to be the "party of protection,"[3] and so on. As Kenneth Waltz has persuasively argued in a slightly different context, this proliferation of explanations indicates the need for a systemic-level theory of trade policy which abstracts from national-level characteristics.[4]

From Adam Smith on, economists have struggled to make the real

---

[2]A. A. Iliasu, "The Cobden-Chevalier Commercial Treaty of 1860," *Historical Journal* 14 (March 1971): 67–98.

[3]Tom E. Terrill, *The Tariff, Politics, and American Foreign Policy, 1874–1901* (Westport, Conn.: Greenwood, 1973).

[4]Kenneth N. Waltz, *Theory of International Politics* (Reading, Mass.: Addison-Wesley, 1979).

world of trade policy conform to their model, with limited success. In doing so, they have often ignored the systemic incentives for free trade and protection and the very real political issues at stake. I start here with the assumption that the political process is at least partly rational, that means relate to ends, and that the beliefs of statesmen have some basis in reality. Accordingly, I seek to explain the trade strategies adopted by nation-states. Furthermore, given the apparent presence of contagion and cyclical processes, the wide variance in unit-level explanations of national trade policies, and the public interest rationales developed by both protectionists and free traders, I attempt to build a systemic-level theory of national trade interests and strategy.

INTERNATIONAL POLITICS AND INTERNATIONAL TRADE

The international system is anarchic and based upon the principle of self-help.[5] This is the basic fact of modern international relations.[6] Anarchy is defined here as the absence of any centralized political authority higher than the nation-state. The absence of central authority does not necessarily indicate a lack of "order" within the international system.[7] Anarchy is also compatible with strong international regimes, defined as "principles, norms, rules, and decision-making procedures around which actor expectations converge,"[8] or other patterns of behavior recognized as legitimate by the community of nation-states. Regimes and order, however, are problematic under anarchy. Nation-states themselves must choose whether to participate in the global arena and what rules they will observe. In a self-help system, nation-states are responsible only to themselves. They are, in other words, the sole judge of their national interests.

Anarchy renders the construction of a stable, liberal, and open international trading order difficult. In the construction of free markets within countries, governments must provide the basic economic in-

---

[5]Ibid.

[6]Like all "facts," however, the permanence of anarchy is open to several interpretations. Richard Ashley has argued that Realists assume the nature of the units or states when this concept should be conceived of as a variable and made endogenous to the theory ("The Poverty of Neorealism," *International Organization* 38 [Spring 1984]: 225–86). Although Ashley's point is correct and important for "grand theory," a middle-range theory such as that developed here can safely ignore "first principles."

[7]Hedley Bull, *The Anarchical Society: A Study of Order in World Politics* (New York: Columbia University Press, 1977).

[8]Stephen D. Krasner, ed., *International Regimes* (Ithaca: Cornell University Press, 1983), p. 1.

frastructure, for example, property rights, transportation networks, and a stable currency, and they must coerce or induce the compliance of citizens whose interests are harmed or at least not benefited by the functioning of market processes.[9] Governments succeed at home because their authoritative nature is backed by a monopoly of the legitimate use of violence.[10] Within a society, for instance, thieves are imprisoned, taxes are levied for highway construction, and disadvantaged groups are compensated. In the international arena, nation-states must also provide a basic infrastructure and obtain the compliance of countries that gain less from free trade than others.[11] Yet, in the absence of centralized authority, nation-states face a problem of collective action: each prefers that others bear the burden of providing the infrastructure and coercing or compensating the relatively disadvantaged. Free riding, for reasons developed below, can be overcome only by large and possibly middle-sized countries.

Anarchy and the principle of self-help also shape national interests in a second way. Self-help implies, first, that countries are concerned only with their national advantage and not with global welfare. The gains and losses to their own country capture the attention of central decision makers. Thus the reliance on self-help necessitates what Friedrich List termed a "political" rather than a "cosmopolitical" economy.[12]

Self-help also implies that a country will be concerned not only with its own absolute gain from trade but also with its relative gain, or the difference between its gain and the gains of others. Power, the pursuit of which follows from anarchy, is a relational concept. To the extent that one country is strong, others must be weak. Wealth, on the other hand, is an absolute trait. All countries gain from free trade, but—as John Stuart Mill first demonstrated—not necessarily to the same degree or extent. This simultaneous concern with both absolute and relative gains from trade and the contradiction between them has three implications for trade strategy. First, those countries that gain absolutely and relatively

<hr>

[9]See Douglas North, *Structure and Change in Economic History* (New York: Norton, 1981); Karl Polanyi, *The Great Transformation: The Political and Economic Origins of Our Time* (Boston: Beacon, 1957).

[10]This is the distinguishing characteristic of the state. See Max Weber, *Economy and Society*, 2 vols., ed. Guenther Roth and Claus Wittich (Berkeley: University of California Press, 1978), 1:56.

[11]The attributes of the international infrastructure are noted in the Introduction to this book and discussed in Charles P. Kindleberger, *The World in Depression, 1929–1939* (Berkeley: University of California Press, 1973), esp. p. 292, and "Dominance and Leadership in the International Economy: Exploitation, Public Goods, and Free Rides," *International Studies Quarterly* 25 (June 1981): 247.

[12]Friedrich List, *The National System of Political Economy*, trans. Sampson S. Lloyd (London, 1885; rpt. New York: Kelley, 1977).

from free trade will have a stronger interest in such trade than those that gain only absolutely. Second, countries that gain absolutely and relatively will seek to construct regimes or other mechanisms of control to reinforce their advantageous positions. Third, disadvantaged countries will seek to strengthen their relative positions within the international division of labor and may be willing to bear considerable short-term absolute costs to accomplish this aim.

This chapter makes two other assumptions regarding the character of the "units" or nation-states.[13] First, it is assumed that nation-states are unitary actors, that is, they act within the international system as single individuals. Thus, this chapter abstracts up from divisions within the state, between the state and society, and within society. This assumption is relaxed in Chapter 2 and the case study below. Second, it is assumed that nation-states are rational, that they make means-ends calculations and choose the policy with the greatest net return. This assumption has engendered a wave of legitimate criticism in the broader international relations and social science literatures.[14] It has been proposed that nation-states, like individuals, may be satisficers or cybernetic decision makers.[15] Individuals and, even more, nation-states are clearly not rational; few are able to make the means-ends calculations necessary for full or partial rationality to hold. Yet the assumption of rationality is useful and adopted here because it is the only decision principle that allows explanations or predictions to be derived from the international system without examining the internal decision processes of the individuals involved and the nation-state more generally (for example, the threshold of the satisficer and the order in which she encounters options, or the variables the cybernetic decision maker is tracking). Thus, despite its shortcomings, the assumption of rationality remains the only alternative available for the construction of systemic-level theories of international politics. Of course, to the extent that the predictions of systemic theories are incorrect, it may then be appropriate to introduce questions of misperception and cognition.[16] Nonetheless, the assump-

[13]For a general discussion of these assumptions, see Robert O. Keohane, "Theory of World Politics: Structural Realism and Beyond," in Ada W. Finifter, ed., *Political Science: The State of the Discipline* (Washington, D.C.: American Political Science Association, 1983), pp. 503–40.

[14]For a recent and relevant version of this critique, see Timothy McKeown, "The Limitations of 'Structural' Theories of Commercial Policy," *International Organization* 40 (Winter 1986): 43–64.

[15]Herbert Simon, *Models of Man: Social and Rational* (New York: Wiley, 1957), pp. 241–60, and John Steinbrunner, *The Cybernetic Theory of Decision: New Dimensions of Political Analysis* (Princeton: Princeton University Press, 1974).

[16]Robert Jervis, *Perception and Misperception in International Relations* (Princeton: Princeton University Press, 1976).

tion of rationality remains useful as a first approximation. When the unitary actor assumption is waived in Chapter 2, this rationality assumption is also partly relaxed.

LESSONS FROM INTERNATIONAL ECONOMICS

Classical international trade theories demonstrate that nearly all countries are absolutely better off under free trade than in autarky or under protection.[17] Adam Smith criticized the mercantilist trade restrictions predominant in his era for restricting the market, raising prices, and interfering with the division of labor, but he did not possess a fully developed theory of international trade. It was in the early nineteenth century that David Ricardo first demonstrated that the gains from trade did not depend upon absolute differences in productivity between countries, as was commonly believed. Even if one country is more productive in the manufacture of all goods (absolute advantage), Ricardo showed that as long as commodity prices differ in autarky, two countries will still gain from trade by specializing in the production of those goods in which they are relatively most productive (comparative advantage) and exchanging through international trade. The Heckscher-Ohlin theory of international trade confirms Ricardo's insights but relates comparative costs and prices and, in turn, the pattern of trade to differences in factor (typically capital and labor) endowments. Accordingly, a country will export goods relatively intensive in the use of those factors it possesses in relatively abundant supply. Thus we can predict that a capital-rich country will specialize in capital-intensive goods and export them in exchange for relatively labor-intensive commodities, thereby increasing its welfare. Within this theoretical framework, any government intervention that inhibits the free exchange of goods across national boundaries reduces the gains from trade, introduces social deadweight losses into the economy, and decreases the utility of the country.

As all countries are believed to benefit from free trade, classical theories of international trade offer little guidance for a systemic theory that seeks to explain variations in national trade strategies across countries and over time. Moreover, although the propositions on the pattern of trade are relatively robust,[18] the conclusion that all countries maximize

---

[17]See virtually any text on international trade theory, for instance Richard E. Caves and Ronald W. Jones, *World Trade and Payments: An Introduction*, 2d ed. (Boston: Little, Brown, 1977), and at a more advanced level, Jagdish N. Bhagwati and T. N. Srinivasan, *Lectures on International Trade* (Cambridge: MIT Press, 1983).

[18]"Robustness" here refers to the sensitivity of a theory's conclusions to minor alter-

their welfare over time under free trade is based on several restrictive assumptions. This classical model, though insightful, does not necessarily yield a complete understanding of the complex reality of international trade and trade policy making. Three more recent schools of thought relax the assumptions of classical theories, however, and provide an alternative view of the optimality of free trade.

First, the classic arguments in support of free trade assume that all countries are equally small "price takers," or cannot affect the prices of the goods they buy and sell. In the real world, however, some countries are "price breakers" and others "price makers." Optimal tariff theory, which has recently been subsumed under discussions of strategic trade policy,[19] posits that a relatively large country can shift the terms of trade to its advantage (increase the ratio of its export to import prices) and capture a larger share of the total gains from trade by imposing a tariff. With an optimal tariff, the large country's demand for the imported product falls, thereby lowering the world price, while the difference between the new lower world price and the now higher domestic price is retained by the government as tariff revenue. If the world price falls far enough, the large country will be better off with its optimal tariff than under free trade, despite the reduction in global welfare and the introduction of social deadweight losses into its own economy.[20]

Other countries may retaliate, however, and attempt to recapture the gains from trade by imposing their own optimal tariffs. The success of retaliation depends upon the relative sizes of the countries involved.[21] If two countries are of equal size, both lose from the imposition of optimal

---

ations in its assumptions. The predictions of the Heckscher-Ohlin theory on the pattern of trade are not very sensitive; altering the assumption of constant returns to scale to include increasing returns to scale industries does not dramatically affect the pattern of specialization. The composition and pattern of goods trade, for instance, is no longer fully determined by factor endowments, but it is possible to predict net trade in factor services as embodied in goods, which in practice is very similar to the traditional predictions of Heckscher-Ohlin. Under increasing returns, capital-rich countries specialize in and export goods that intensively use the services of capital. The converse holds for labor- and land-abundant countries. See Elhanan Helpman and Paul R. Krugman, *Market Structure and Foreign Trade: Increasing Returns, Imperfect Competition, and the International Economy* (Cambridge: MIT Press, 1985).

[19]See Avinash Dixit, "Strategic Aspects of Trade Policy," mimeo, Princeton University, January 1986; and Gene M. Grossman and J. David Richardson, "Strategic Trade Policy: A Survey of Issues and Early Analysis," in Robert E. Baldwin and J. David Richardson, eds., *International Trade and Finance*, 3rd ed. (Boston: Little, Brown, 1986), pp. 95–114.

[20]See Dixit, "Strategic Aspects of Trade Policy"; and Harry G. Johnson, "Optimum Tariffs and Retaliation," *Review of Economic Studies* 21 (1954): 142–53.

[21]Johnson, "Optimum Tariffs"; Raymond Riezman, "Tariff Retaliation from a Strategic Viewpoint," *Southern Economic Journal* 48 (January 1982): 583–93; and John Whalley, *Trade Liberalization among Major World Trading Areas* (Cambridge: MIT Press, 1985), p. 239.

tariffs after retaliation is taken into account. A large country imposing an optimal tariff against a smaller nation-state, however, may be better off even after retaliation than under free trade. Small countries can effectively retaliate against a large country only through collective action, but because retaliation also imposes costs on the small countries a free rider problem emerges. Relatively large countries, then, may possess optimal tariffs greater than zero following retaliation.

The second school of importance is the "new mercantilism," founded on the Keynesian and neo-Marxist analyses of the balance of trade. From at least the age of mercantilism in the sixteenth century to the present, statesmen have believed in the salubrious effects of balance-of-trade surpluses (that is, exports exceed imports). Mercantilists perceived surpluses as the most effective means of augmenting the gold stock and expanding the money supply.[22] The recent export-led growth strategies of the Federal Republic of Germany and others are contemporary manifestations of this old adage. Even today, trade deficits are commonly seen as a political problem which governments should rectify, whereas trade surpluses are generally desired.

In classical international trade theories imports and exports are always assumed to be instantaneously balanced. Accordingly, many economists dismiss the political emphasis on trade surpluses as antiquated "mercantilist" thought. As John Maynard Keynes wrote, however, "We, the faculty of economists, prove to have been guilty of presumptuous error in treating as a puerile obsession what for centuries has been a prime object of practical statecraft." Starting with Keynes, the new mercantilists have argued that trade surpluses and the pursuit of a competitive edge in international trade do benefit a nation-state in the long run by stimulating profits, domestic investment, technical progress, and—ultimately—growth.[23]

The new mercantilist literature suggests two complementary goals for nation-states. Drawing upon several centuries of experience and the beliefs of statesmen, it is recommended that countries seek a trade surplus. It is also argued that countries need to obtain a competitive edge in international trade, although this would have to extend to a

[22]John Maynard Keynes, *The General Theory of Employment, Interest and Money* (New York: Harcourt, Brace and World, 1964), chap. 23.

[23]Ibid., p. 339; Michal Kalecki, *Selected Essays on the Dynamics of the Capitalist Economy, 1933–1970* (Cambridge: Cambridge University Press, 1971), pp. 15–25; Joan Robinson, *Contributions to Modern Economics* (Oxford: Blackwell, 1978), pp. 201–12; J. B. Burbidge, "Post-Keynesian Theory: The International Dimension," *Challenge*, November–December 1978, pp. 40–45; Hans O. Schmitt, "Mercantilism: A Modern Argument," *Manchester School of Economic and Social Sciences* 47 (June 1979): 93–111; and David Vines, "Competitiveness, Technical Progress and Balance of Trade Surpluses," *Manchester School of Economics and Social Studies* 48 (December 1980): 378–91.

substantial cross-section of industries to have a significant effect. By stimulating exports, such an edge is sufficient to set off a virtuous cycle of growth.[24]

Critically important to this view is the open economy multiplier, which highlights the differential effects of imports and exports. Most simply, spending on imports puts income into foreign but not domestic hands; like savings, imports create a leakage out of the domestic income cycle. Like investment, however, increased exports provide a net injection into the domestic economy, stimulating an increase in national income the magnitude of which is determined by the marginal propensities to save and import. Increased exports or a reduction in the marginal propensity to import (conditions often reflected in a trade surplus but not necessarily so by definition), as a result, create virtuous cycles of growth whereas decreased exports or a higher marginal propensity to import can initiate vicious cycles.

The third new school focuses on increasing returns to scale. The conclusions of the Ricardian and Heckscher-Ohlin theories depend upon the assumption of constant returns to scale. Yet increasing returns to scale are "an indisputable fact of life."[25] Increasing returns or economies of scale are of two general types. First, internal economies are specific to the plant or firm and are clearly present as the expanded division of labor within the modern firm suggests, but limited, as indicated by the general absence of monopoly. Second, and more important, external economies or positive externalities apply to the sector or country. Here, increased production over time improves the quality of labor, develops entrepreneurship, expands intrafirm specialization in the production of intermediate goods, increases growth of technical knowledge and research and development, and enhances the national infrastructure. Positive externalities are generalized "spin-offs" of the production process.[26] The presence of positive externalities is indicated by the tendency of production to concentrate around geographic centers within countries (cities) and within the international economy more generally (core countries).[27] Increasing returns (both internal and external) are also the best explanation for the recent growth of "intraindustry" trade between the advanced industrialized countries.[28]

[24]This debate is summarized and extended in Vines, "Competitiveness."

[25]Miltiades Chacholiades, "Increasing Returns and Comparative Advantage," *Southern Economic Journal* 37 (October 1970): 157. See also Nicholas Kaldor, *Economics without Equilibrium* (Armonk: M. E. Sharpe, 1985), p. 70.

[26]Johan Galtung, "A Structural Theory of Imperialism," *Journal of Peace Research* 8, 2 (1971): 81–109.

[27]Kaldor, *Economics without Equilibrium*, p. 69.

[28]Helpman and Krugman *Market Structure and Foreign Trade*, esp. chap. 6. Edward E. Leamer, *Sources of International Comparative Advantage: Theory and Evidence* (Cambridge:

Increasing returns occur naturally in some industries and are often created by technical change in others.[29] They can be static or, more central to the analysis developed here, dynamic and cumulative (that is, each technological innovation that increases returns begets a second round of innovation and change). Increasing returns tend to be associated with industries that intensively use physical and human capital. Labor-intensive products are typically agricultural and primary commodities or manufactured goods in the last stages of their product cycles. They generally produce little value added, are made with existing technology, and create relatively few positive externalities. Capital-intensive goods, on the other hand, are usually high value-added manufactured items early in their product cycles. Because of their relative "infancy," internal economies are often not completely exhausted. And through learning or by stimulating innovation, capital-intensive production often creates significant external economies. The founding of the first steel mill eases the way for a second. Likewise, the training of a semiskilled or skilled labor force benefits all potential entrepreneurs in the region. Although debate continues on the magnitude of these and other external economies, capital-intensive production clearly appears to generate greater spin-offs than labor-intensive production. The best, and perhaps simplest, indicator of dynamic economies of scale is relative labor productivity (output per worker-hour) across industries or, at the level of aggregation used here, countries at any given moment, or within industries and countries over time (see Appendix).[30] High relative labor productivity reflects both the capital intensity of production and, more directly, the larger increases in output that result from increasing returns production.

Making the more realistic assumption of varying returns across industries alters the clear predictions of the Ricardian and Heckscher-Ohlin

MIT Press, 1984), provides an empirical discussion of the factor similarities between developed countries.

[29]"Industry" here primarily refers to production techniques. Automobiles, for instance, can either be made largely "by hand" or mass produced. Obviously, only the latter method is characterized by substantial increasing returns.

For a discussion of the role of positive externalities, the antebellum cotton textile industry, and trade policy see Paul A. David, "Learning by Doing and Tariff Protection: A Reconsideration of the Case of the Ante-Bellum United States Cotton Textile Industry," *Journal of Economic History* 30 (September 1970): 521–601; Jeffrey G. Williamson, "Embodiment, Disembodiment, Learning by Doing, and Returns to Scale in Nineteenth-Century Cotton Textiles," *Journal of Economic History* 32 (September 1972): 691–705; and Paul A. David, "The Use and Abuse of Prior Information in Econometric History: A Rejoinder to Professor Williamson on the Antebellum Cotton Textile Industry," *Journal of Economic History* 32 (September 1972): 706–27.

[30]The argument in this chapter is developed only for cross-national comparisons at a single moment in time. The case study in Chapters 3 through 6 employs both cross-national and longitudinal comparisons.

theories. With increasing returns in some sectors and constant returns in others, it is difficult to make any generalizations because much depends on the type and extensiveness of the economies of scale and whether the production possibilities frontier retains its traditional concave shape or becomes convex.[31]

Most important, free trade may not be the optimal long-term policy in the presence of dynamic increasing returns. Under the assumption of constant returns to scale all industries are, in a very real sense, equal. It is immaterial whether a country possesses a comparative advantage and specializes in agriculture, textiles, or steel. When some industries yield increasing returns, however, this equality diminishes. The long-term benefits to countries that specialize in industries with dynamic increasing returns will be greater than those for countries concentrating on constant returns sectors. Because both internal and external economies are greater, countries of relatively high labor productivity enjoy a disproportionate share of the long-term gains from specialization and trade. Some measure of protection designed to "capture" a larger share of the world's increasing returns industries may be warranted.[32] This point is developed in more detail below.

The effects identified by these three new schools of international economics on national trade interests and strategy can be arrayed along the two dimensions of relative size, important for optimal tariffs and—as will be seen below—the policy implications of the open economy multiplier, and relative labor productivity, an indicator of differential returns to scale.

THE INTERNATIONAL ECONOMIC STRUCTURE

The central proposition of this book is that the international economic structure and the position of nation-states within it create constraints

[31]The literature on increasing returns to scale and trade is fairly large. See, among others, R.C.O. Matthews, "Reciprocal Demand and Increasing Returns," *Review of Economic Studies* 17, 2 (1949–50): 149–56; Jan Tinbergen, *International Economic Integration*, 2d ed., rev. (Amsterdam: Elsevier, 1954), Appendix 2; Murray C. Kemp, *The Pure Theory of International Trade* (Englewood Cliffs: Prentice-Hall, 1964), chap. 8; T. Negishi, "Marshallian External Economies and Gains from Trade between Similar Countries," *Review of Economic Studies* 36 (January 1969): 131–35; Raveendra Batra, "Protection and Real Wages under Conditions of Variable Returns to Scale," *Oxford Economic Papers* 20 (November 1968): 353–60; and Arvind Panagariya, "Variable Returns to Scale in General Equilibrium Theory Once Again," *Journal of International Economics* 10 (November 1980): 499–526.
[32]See Helpman and Krugman, *Market Structure and Foreign Trade*; and Paul R. Krugman, ed., *Strategic Trade Policy and the New International Economics* (Cambridge: MIT Press, 1986).

STRUCTURE AND STRATEGY

Figure 1.1. Seven categories of international economic actors

Relative size (percentage of world trade)	Low	1.0	High
Large — 15.0	Imperial leaders (IL)		Hegemonic leaders (HL)
Middle — 5.0	Spoilers (SP) Free trade free riders (FTFR)		Opportunists (OP)
Small	Protectionist free riders (PFR) Free trade free riders (FTFR)		Liberal free riders (LFR)

Relative labor productivity

and opportunities that shape the trade strategies of countries in important and predictable ways. The international economic structure is defined here as the configuration of nation-states within the two dimensions of relative size and relative labor productivity.[33] Relative size is determined by each country's proportion of world trade (exports plus imports). Relative labor productivity is defined and measured by national output per worker-hour relative to the average national output per worker-hour in the other middle and large-sized countries (see Appendix).

Neither of these two dimensions is entirely distinct from the national trade strategies I seek to explore. A country's proportion of world trade, for instance, is affected by prior policy decisions. A protectionist trade policy will reduce a country's share of world trade, but so will the policies of other countries, localized depressions, changes in exchange rates, and a host of other factors. Because of the numerous factors that influence a country's relative size and labor productivity, it is possible to assume, for reasons of simplicity, that the causal relationship is unidirectional and specifically from the international economic structure to trade strategy.

Within the two dimensions of relative size and relative labor productivity, it is possible to identify at least seven categories of nation-states.[34] These seven categories are defined graphically in Figure 1.1.

[33]This theory is intentionally parsimonious. Relative size and relative labor productivity are the common dimensions underlying the several international trade theory literatures discussed above. I have purposely excluded other possible explanatory factors from the theory, including national security considerations, macroeconomic conditions, trade patterns, international monetary and financial regimes and processes, and levels of trade dependence.

[34]The reasons for the overlap between spoilers and protectionist free riders, on one

30

Table 1.1. The international economic structure, 1870–1938: Proportion of world trade (PWT) and relative labor productivity (RLP)

Year	United States		United Kingdom		Germany		France	
	PWT	RLP	PWT	RLP	PWT	RLP	PWT	RLP
1870	8.8[a]	1.22	24.0[a]	1.63	9.7[a]	.66	10.8[a]	.65
1880	8.8[b]	1.29	19.6[b]	1.50	10.3[c]	.64	11.4[b]	.69
1890	9.7[d]	1.37	18.5[d]	1.45	10.9[d]	.69	10.0[d]	.63
1900	10.2[e]	1.42	17.5[e]	1.30	11.9[e]	.74	8.5[e]	.65
1913	11.1[f]	1.56	14.1[f]	1.15	12.2[f]	.73	7.5[f]	.68
1929	13.9[g]	1.72	13.3[g]	1.04	9.3[g]	.66	6.4[g]	.74
1938	11.3[h]	1.71	14.0[h]	.92	9.0[h]	.69	5.2[h]	.82

[a]Mulhall data, 1870, 1880, in Simon Kuznets, *Modern Economic Growth* (New Haven: Yale University Press, 1966), p. 306.

[b]League of Nations data, 1876–80, League of Nations, *Industrialization and Foreign Trade* (League of Nations, 1945), pp. 157–67.

[c]Mulhall data, 1880, 1889, in ibid., p. 306.

[d]League of Nations data, 1886–90, in Kuznets, *Modern Economic Growth*, p. 307.

[e]League of Nations data, 1896–1900, in ibid.

[f]League of Nations data, 1911–13, in ibid.

[g]League of Nations, *Review of World Trade,* 1927–29.

[h]Ibid., 1936–38.

Relative productivity data derived from Angus Maddison, "Long Run Dynamics of Productivity Growth," *Banca Nazionale del Lavoro Quarterly Review* 128 (March 1979): 43.

The empirical demarcations between categories are guided by the theory of hegemonic stability (see Introduction) but, in the end, remain somewhat tentative. The division between small and middle-sized nation-states is placed at 5.0 percent of world trade. Over the last one hundred years, no more than five nation-states were in the middle- and large-sized categories at any one time. For these categories to be meaningful, they should be limited to countries that do or can exert a major influence over the international economy or the policies of others. Nearly all of the nation-states traditionally regarded as major or important actors within the international economy have been above this 5.0 percent level. Raising the threshold between small and middle-sized countries by 1 or 2 percent would not dramatically affect the composition of the latter category (see Table 1.1). Reducing this cutoff point by 1 or 2 percent, however, would greatly expand the number of nation-states within the middle-sized category. A division of 15.0 percent of

hand, and free trade free riders, on the other, are made clear below. They are distinguished by the size of the domestic market, a nonsystemic attribute which is nonetheless essential for understanding their systemic trade preferences. The categories are arrayed here, however, only along their systemic dimensions.

world trade between middle- and large-sized countries places the United Kingdom from the eighteenth century until the early twentieth century and the United States from World War II until the mid-1960s in the large category. This is largely congruent with the theory of hegemonic stability and was chosen for that reason.[35] Most countries have been well below the 15.0 percent level. The precise division between the large and middle-sized categories is important here only for dating the transition of the United Kingdom from the former to the latter level. Given the rapid rate of decline in the British position before World War I (see Table 1.1), shifting the cutoff point between categories slightly in either direction would not have a major impact upon the analysis.

The relative labor productivity of each country is calculated by dividing that country's absolute labor productivity by the average absolute labor productivity in the other middle- and large-sized nation-states (see Appendix). The 1.0 level, the demarcation between high and low relative labor productivity, indicates that labor productivity in one nation-state is exactly equal to the average of the others. A level below 1.0 indicates that the nation-state's labor productivity is less than average; a level greater than 1.0 indicates that the country's labor productivity is higher than average. The 1.0 division between nation-states of high and low relative labor productivity is intuitively meaningful and accurately reflects the second theoretical dimension discussed below.

Although all countries within a category share a common trade interest, the two dimensions of relative size and relative labor productivity are continuous. It is possible, as a result, to have variations within categories. The further to the right a nation-state lies on the horizontal axis within any specific category, for instance, the greater its interest in free trade will be relative to other members of that same category.

It is also important not to reify the demarcations between categories: they are clearly artificial constructs and are not intended to reflect how actual statesmen understand the world around them. Nor should they be taken too literally. The United States, for instance, accounted for 13.9 percent of world trade in 1929 and 15.3 percent in 1960, and even though the difference is only 1.4 percent I classify the United States as an opportunist in the first period and a hegemonic leader in the second (see Tables 1.1 and 1.2). More important for understanding America's trade interests, however, is the configuration of nation-states within the international economic structure as a whole. In 1929 the United States

---

[35]Kindleberger, *World in Depression*, dates the period of potential American hegemony from the mid- to late-1920s, but he is primarily concerned with monetary and financial power. Any level of trade that would classify the United States as hegemonic during this period would be theoretically meaningless. See Table 1.1.

Table 1.2. The international economic structure, 1950–1977: Proportion of world trade (PWT) and relative labor productivity (RLP)

Year	United States		Federal Republic of Germany		France		Japan		United Kingdom	
	PWT	RLP	PWT	RLP	PWT	RLP	PWT	RLP	PWT	RLP
1950	18.4	2.77	4.5	.66	5.9	.80	1.7	.25	13.1	1.15
1960	15.3	2.28	9.3	.95	5.7	.87	3.7	.31	9.6	.98
1970	14.4	1.72	11.2	1.06	6.4	.96	6.7	.55	7.2	.86
1977	13.4	1.45	13.5	1.15	6.5	1.07	7.3	.64	5.9	.77

SOURCES: Relative productivity data derived from Angus Maddison, "Long Run Dynamics of Productivity Growth," *Banca Nazionale del Lavoro Quarterly Review* 128 (March 1979): 43. Proportion of world trade data for 1950 from Statistical Office of the United Nations, *Direction of International Trade*, Ser. T, 5, 8. For 1960, 1970, and 1977, proportion of world trade from United Nations, *Monthly Bulletin of Statistics,* selected years.

shared its dominant position with Great Britain, which possessed 13.3 percent of world trade. In 1960, the United States's share was nearly twice that of Great Britain, still its nearest competitor. The categorizations should be treated skeptically; although they are more formalized than other definitions of the international economic structure,[36] assigning cutoff points between categories does not wholly substitute for judgment and intuition.

Relative Size

The relative size of a country is important for three unrelated reasons. Because the international infrastructure necessary to regulate foreign commerce and stabilize the international economy approximates a collective good, relatively large countries bear a disproportionate share of the costs of providing the infrastructure. In addition, relatively large countries possess international market power and may also enjoy an optimal tariff greater than zero. Finally, the ability of governments to manipulate the open economy multiplier is determined by their relative size within the international economy.

As in domestic political economies, an international infrastructure must be established to facilitate trade. The international infrastructure is composed of two separate dimensions: a set of regimes governing

[36]Ibid.; Robert Gilpin, *U.S. Power and the Multinational Corporation: The Political Economy of Foreign Direct Investment* (New York: Basic Books, 1975); Stephen D. Krasner, "State Power and the Structure of International Trade," *World Politics* 28 (April 1976): 317–47; and the other sources cited in the Introduction.

international transactions and international economic stability. For substantial trade to arise between countries, three tasks must be fulfilled, and they can be most easily accomplished through international regimes. First, a monetary system must be created specifying reserve assets and exchange rates. For the same reasons that money within a country is created as a store of value and a medium of exchange, an international reserve asset is necessary. International monetary relations, however, are complicated by the need to exchange one national currency for another, requiring rules governing such transactions. The content of this international monetary regime is less important: reserve assets have changed over time from gold, gold and silver, gold and United States dollars, to dollars and Special Drawing Rights (an international monetary unit created by the International Monetary Fund [IMF]); likewise, exchange rates have been fixed, or officially tied to the reserve asset, or floating, when prices are set by international market forces.[37] It is important to have some common rules. In the absence of an international monetary regime, countries will be dependent upon barter—an inefficient form of exchange.

The second task is to ensure freedom of transit for trade, just as property rights must be enforced within domestic political economies. Both buyers and sellers must be confident that the goods they contract for will reach their destination with minimal interference. Traditionally, freedom of transit has been equated with "freedom of the seas," a legal construct first developed under Dutch hegemony in the seventeenth century and continued by British and American leadership thereafter.[38] Today, the expanded use of trucks and railroads for intracontinental transport and airplanes for rapid delivery has greatly expanded the subjects covered by the international transit regime.

Finally, an international financial regime must be constructed to facilitate capital flows between countries.[39] Foreign finance accelerates the long-term economic expansion of less-developed markets. Some investment in local production or warehousing and distribution facilities may also be required to sustain a high volume of trade in goods. Most important, short-term credit is necessary to facilitate current trade in goods and to ease temporary balance-of-payments constraints. Without the necessary short-term credits, or unless markets clear instantaneously, trade is inhibited.

The specific content is often less important than the existence of some

[37]Robert O. Keohane and Joseph S. Nye, *Power and Interdependence: World Politics in Transition* (Boston: Little, Brown, 1977), pp. 63–162.
[38]Ibid.
[39]See Charles Lipson, *Standing Guard* (Berkeley: University of California Press, 1985).

rules governing international monetary, transportation, and financial issues. Strong regimes will also, as Robert Keohane has argued, reduce transaction costs, provide information, and lower uncertainty,[40] not only allowing international trade to occur but facilitating its expansion.

International economic stability, the second dimension of the international infrastructure, is also a necessary requirement for an open, liberal trading order. Societies seek homeostasis.[41] When the international economy is unstable, or characterized by widely fluctuating exchange rates, prices, and, in turn, patterns of trade, countries are more likely to insulate themselves from this potentially disruptive force.[42] Historically, protection has been a key instrument of insulation, but protection creates social deadweight losses. Only when the benefits of insulation exceed the costs of protection will countries withdraw from the international economy.

International infrastructure approximates a public good.[43] Regimes can be exclusive (for example, the dominant naval power can ignore privateers who prey only on ships flying the flag of a particular country) or partial (for example, the Soviet bloc has generally been excluded from the IMF and General Agreement on Tariffs and Trade). Yet, in practice, excluding specific countries from international economic regimes is difficult and self-defeating because it undermines the very purpose of the regimes. Excluding countries from the benefits of international economic stability is even more difficult. Thus, although the infrastructure of international trade is not a "pure" public good, countries do possess an incentive to free ride on the efforts of others, and a collective action dilemma emerges.

Insofar as the international infrastructure approximates a collective good, the insights of Mancur Olson and Richard Zeckhauser, first developed to explain the unequal sharing of burdens in alliances, become

---

[40]Robert O. Keohane, *After Hegemony: Cooperation and Discord in the World Political Economy* (Princeton: Princeton University Press, 1984).

[41]See Polanyi, *Great Transformation*, for a classic statement of this assumption.

[42]Constructing a theory of instability is beyond the scope of this study. Such a theory would need to specify the causes of instability and identify threshold effects of instability on the relevant political variables. I do neither here. In Chapter 5 the issue of instability becomes central to the analysis, and I compare price and exchange rate fluctuations in the eras before and after World War I. Prices and exchange rates are the principal determinants of international trade patterns and so are highly appropriate indicators. Yet one can only conclude that fluctuations were greater after 1919 than before.

[43]John A. C. Conybeare, "Public Goods, Prisoners' Dilemmas, and the International Political Economy," *International Studies Quarterly* 28 (March 1984): 8–9, argues that free trade is not a collective good. I agree. The argument put forth here focuses only on the intermediate product of international infrastructure and not the final product of free trade.

35

helpful. In the provision of any collective good in a political economy in which members differ in size, these authors argue, there is a strong tendency for the largest members of the group to bear a disproportionate share of the burden of providing the good. The larger countries, in Olson's earlier terminology, form a "privileged" group who value the collective good enough to provide it for themselves, even though they cannot prevent others from enjoying it as well.[44] Following this logic, larger countries can and will bear a greater share of the costs of providing the international infrastructure.

Charles Kindleberger argues that because international economic cooperation is unstable, only a single hegemonic nation-state can lead an international economy. "With a duumvirate, a troika, or slightly wider forms of collective responsibility," he states, "the buck has no place to stop."[45] There is no doubt that cooperation is more difficult to achieve in nonhegemonic systems. At the very least, the gains from cooperation must be larger to offset the additional costs of negotiating and enforcing agreements among the parties, and the results have been unstable historically.[46] Yet Kindleberger's conclusion has no grounding in collective goods theory; privileged groups need not be limited to one actor, although such a group is unlikely to exist in a system in which there are many equally small actors. Given the wide disparity in size in the international system even without hegemony, there is no a priori reason to conclude that international cooperation under a nonhegemonic system is impossible, but cooperation in the absence of hegemony will be most likely to occur between the middle-sized nation-states.[47]

The willingness and ability of nation-states to stabilize the international economy is also influenced by the resources available to them for regulation relative to the size of the disturbance(s) they must control. The present theory treats instability as an external shock to the international economic structure. The type and magnitude of economic disturbances may be related to the international economic structure, but several important types of disturbances, such as the accelerating pace of technological advance which led to the rapid decline in prices during the

[44]Mancur Olson and Richard Zeckhauser, "An Economic Theory of Alliances," *Review of Economics and Statistics* 58 (August 1966): 266–79; Olson, *The Logic of Collective Action* (Cambridge: Harvard University Press, 1971).

[45]Kindleberger, *World in Depression*, pp. 299–300.

[46]On the problem of enforcement costs see Beth V. Yarbrough and Robert M. Yarbrough, "Free Trade, Hegemony, and the Theory of Agency," *Kyklos* 38 (1985): 348–64; and "Cooperation in the Liberalization of International Trade: After Hegemony, What?" *International Organization* 41 (Winter 1987): 1–26.

[47]Duncan Snidal, "The Limits of Hegemonic Stability Theory," *International Organization* 39 (Autumn 1985): 579–614, makes a parallel argument.

late nineteenth century or the condition of global agricultural surplus in the late 1920s and 1930s, span several different international economic structures and, as a result, can be safely treated as exogenous to this structure.

The ability of nation-states to regulate disturbances successfully is determined by two factors: the absolute level of resources available to them for regulation and the efficiency with which they use these resources.[48] Each of these factors may compensate for the other. A single country with large resources, such as the United States at its hegemonic zenith, may be able to regulate a disturbance successfully even though the application of its resources is inefficient. Conversely, a nation-state with fewer resources may successfully regulate a similar disturbance if it uses these resources more efficiently. Two or more nation-states, particularly if they are middle-sized, are likely to possess greater collective resources than a single hegemonic leader. The combined shares of world trade of the United States and the United Kingdom, two middle-sized nation-states after 1912, were 25.2 percent in 1913 and 27.2 in 1929, compared with the United Kingdom's 24.0 percent at the peak of its hegemony in 1870. Likewise, the United States, Federal Republic of Germany, and France accounted for 33.4 percent of world trade in 1977, whereas the United States alone held only 18.4 percent in 1950. Two or more nation-states, however, will be unlikely to use their combined resources as efficiently as a single hegemonic leader. At the very least, there will be costs involved in organizing the joint intervention necessary for the successful regulation of disturbances in the international economy.

Because disturbances can differ in magnitude, and assuming that nation-states differ in their resources and ability to manage them, it is not axiomatic that a hegemonic leader will be successful in regulating or stabilizing the international economy. This may have been the case during the Great Depression of 1873–96, when the United Kingdom's international leadership faltered and the international economy moved toward greater closure.[49] If hegemony does not guarantee stability, it is equally true that nonhegemonic nation-states may be able to cooperate

---

[48]For a discussion of the concept of regulation, see Richard N. Rosecrance, *Action and Reaction in World Politics: International Systems in Perspective* (Westport, Conn.: Greenwood, 1977), pp. 220–27.

[49]Peter A. Gourevitch, "International Trade, Domestic Coalitions, and Liberty: Comparative Responses to the Crisis of 1873–1896," *Journal of Interdisciplinary History* 8 (Autumn 1977): 281–313. Gourevitch dismisses international structural explanations in this article because Britain's power position had not significantly declined. He does not develop the concept of regulation used here.

and successfully stabilize the international economy under appropriate circumstances.

To summarize, large countries, and to a lesser extent middle-sized nation-states as well, possess incentives voluntarily to provide the infrastructure necessary for a liberal international economy. As a result, they will bear a disproportionate share of the burden of providing this quasi-collective good.

Relative size also affects the trade interests of individual countries in a second manner, discussed above in reviewing the literature on optimal tariffs. Trade barriers always reduce global welfare, yet large countries have an incentive to impose optimal tariffs because they increase national welfare. By adopting a tariff, the large country reduces its demand for the imported product, lowers the world price of the good (if the elasticity of supply is great enough), and—in this static model—turns the terms of trade to its advantage. This relationship is continuous: the larger the country, the greater are its incentives to impose optimal tariffs.

John Conybeare has argued that optimal tariff theory militates against the theory of hegemonic stability because large countries benefit not from free trade, as the latter theory posits, but from optimal tariffs.[50] Yet it is difficult to draw any specific generalizations on this point. Whether or not a country's postretaliation optimal tariff is greater than zero depends not only on its own relative size but also on the sizes of its trading partners. Even a hegemon is unlikely to benefit from protection if its trading partners are also substantial—or at least middle-sized in the terminology adopted above—and retaliatory. The relative size of a country by itself indicates little about the incentives for imposing optimal tariffs. More important is the relative size of the country's trading partners, which requires examining the international economic structure as a whole.

For at least the last century, the international economic structure has always consisted of several middle-sized nation-states and, in two relatively brief periods, a single hegemonic leader (see Tables 1.1 and 1.2). All of these countries are likely to have possessed some market power, although this depends more precisely on the composition of trade and the various elasticities of supply. The circumstances under which optimal tariffs would be highest, or when a single hegemonic leader confronted a large number of poorly organized small countries, have been historically rare. Although large countries and, to a lesser extent, mid-

---

[50]Conybeare, "Public Goods"; and *Trade Wars: The Theory and Practice of International Commercial Rivalry* (New York: Columbia University Press, 1987), chap. 2.

dle-sized countries may still possess postretaliation optimal tariffs greater than zero, these duties are not likely to be as great as sometimes estimated.[51] Consequently, the static welfare gain from optimal tariffs may be offset over time by the third effect of relative size.

Relative size also influences the ability of governments to manipulate the open economy multiplier for political ends. The new mercantilists do not dispute the classical contention that global welfare is maximized by free trade. They do argue, however, that individual countries gain more from exports than from imports because of the multiplier effect. As J. B. Burbridge summarizes, "From the point of view of one nation, exports tend to increase employment, output, and profits; imports tend to reduce them." Moreover, welfare gains from imports are static, but gains from exports are dynamic and cumulative. "Higher levels of profit, in turn, provide the finance to expand capacity and install still more efficient equipment, which tends to make their competitive advantage all the stronger."[52] Thus virtuous and vicious cycles of growth are set in motion in which export "success leads to success and failure engenders failure."[53]

The presence of virtuous and vicious cycles opens the possibility of national gains through political manipulation of exports and the marginal propensity to import. All countries enjoy the multiplier effect, but their ability to influence it varies with their size. The demand for a small country's exports is exogenously determined and, for practical purposes, independent of its trade policies.[54] Although a country might gain a temporary advantage from export subsidies, such payments are likely to bankrupt its national treasury or be countered by similar measures abroad. Import protection, on the other hand, can reduce the marginal propensity to import and, as a result, the drain on the national income cycle without damaging the small country's exogenously set exports. At any given level of exports, the open economy multiplier will then be larger. And by shifting consumption from imported to domestic goods, protection will also stimulate investment and, consequently, growth. This is not necessarily an argument in favor of domestic protec-

---

[51]Whalley, *Trade Liberalization*, estimates that postretaliation tariffs for the United States, European Economic Community, and—to a lesser extent—Japan "may well be higher than 50 percent" and notes that tariff levels during the early 1930s might actually have been "optimal" (p. 246). Given the welfare losses associated with the Smoot-Hawley and other tariffs during this period, this estimate clearly appears too high.

[52]Burbridge, "Post-Keynsian Theory," p. 41.

[53]Joan Robinson, quoted in ibid., p. 42.

[54]Technically, any reduction in imports must reciprocally reduce exports, but for small countries the effect of a reduction in imports is so diffuse that we generally consider exports to be exogenous. This is not so for large countries.

tion for small countries. Protection reduces the gains from trade and, by raising prices for goods, creates social deadweight losses. It does demonstrate, however, that protection is not an unmitigated evil for small countries.

The efficacy of export subsidies and import protection is reversed in large countries. In large countries, exports are not determined exogenously, but rather are partly a function of levels of imports and government export policies. Large countries are able to influence world prices of goods and may stimulate exports through subsidies. Any significant reduction in a large country's imports, however, reduces the ability of other countries to purchase its exports. As a result, protection in large countries reduces both imports and exports. The loss of the export stimulus may be offset by increased domestic investment, but the net result is indeterminate. Moreover, the dynamic gains from the open economy multiplier may vitiate the static gains reaped by large countries through optimal tariffs; the terms of trade effect may increase welfare in the short run, but reduced exports may decrease welfare by an even larger amount in the long run. Whatever the precise effect, however, large countries are less effective than small countries in using protection to reduce the marginal propensity to import and thereby stimulate growth. This is an important disparity between small and large countries, with middle-sized countries occupying an intermediate position, which becomes more important in the discussion of relative labor productivity.

Relative Labor Productivity

Statesmen have traditionally believed that countries gain from industrialization and the expansion of manufacturing plant and that in the long run protection is an effective instrument in pursuit of this goal. Even today, industrialization and not specialization in agricultural, primary, or craft production is the goal of many statesmen in the Third World. And the economic success of Japan and the newly industrializing countries of East Asia has reinforced this belief. The problems arising from specialization in traditional industries and the dynamic advantages from industrialization are highlighted by Joan Robinson in her reexamination of Ricardo's classic example of free trade between England and Portugal. "In reality," she writes, "the imposition of free trade in Portugal killed off a promising textile industry and left her with a slow-growing export market for wine, while for England, exports of cotton cloth led to accumulation, mechanization and the whole spiralling growth of the industrial revolution."[55]

---

[55]Joan Robinson, *Aspects of Development and Underdevelopment* (Cambridge: Cambridge University Press, 1979), p. 103.

Yet, according to classical trade theories, countries are best off specializing in goods that intensively use their most abundant factor. It is immaterial, in the terms of these theories, whether a country specializes in wine or textiles, raw material extraction or high-tech industry—a conclusion again at odds with practical statecraft. Two characteristics of classical trade theories need to be reassessed to reconcile them with political practice.

First, classical theories are static and based upon the existing productivity of current resources. Recent theoretical work has argued and historical experience has demonstrated, however, that comparative advantage is not fixed or immutable, but rather open to political manipulation. By intervention in the market, and particularly through protection of infant industries, industrial targeting, selective credit policies, and state-sponsored research and development, governments can reshape their economies creating comparative advantage, or what John Zysman and Laura Tyson refer to as "competitive advantage," in new areas.[56]

Second, both Ricardo and Heckscher-Ohlin assume that internal and external returns to scale are constant, and the conclusion that the area of specialization is irrelevant follows from this simplification. In actuality, some industries are characterized by diminishing returns, others by constant returns, and still others by increasing returns. The latter industries are relatively intensive in the use of human and nonhuman capital and, accordingly, are marked by relatively high labor productivity. Consequently, capital-rich countries will tend to specialize in industries with increasing returns, as reflected in their high relative labor productivity, whereas land- or labor-abundant countries will specialize in industries with constant or diminishing returns to scale, as indicated by their low relative labor productivity.

With differentiated returns, a country's area of specialization is no longer unimportant. Countries that specialize in increasing returns industries enjoy greater spin-offs or positive externalities. And—in conjunction with the effects of the open economy multiplier—a consistent bias is introduced over time in the distribution of the gains from trade in favor of relatively productive countries. "In this . . . case," Nicholas Kaldor writes, "it is not the differences in the relative prices of factors that are important, but relative differences in labor productivities (measured in terms of a common currency) which, even in the absence of any differences in capital productivities (in the amount of capital employed per unit of output) will make the country with the higher productivity a favorable one for exports and a relatively unfavorable one for imports. It will therefore tend to have [*ceteris paribus*] a surplus of exports over

[56]John Zysman and Laura Tyson, eds., *American Industry in International Competition: Government Policies and Corporate Strategies* (Ithaca: Cornell University Press, 1983).

imports. In the other . . . [countries] with which it trades, the opposite
will take place." Goods produced by increasing returns industries, in
other words, tend to become relatively cheaper as production expands
whereas the products of industries with constant or diminishing returns
become comparatively more expensive. As exports increase, a country
with relatively high labor productivity will grow more rapidly over time
than others. "Its productivity growth will be accelerated and unless its
domestic absorption (meaning its domestic consumption and investment) keeps pace with its faster productivity growth, its export surplus
will reappear, giving rise to another push, making for faster growth
rates for itself and slower growth rates for the others." Thus increasing
returns and expanding exports combine to create a doubly virtuous
cycle of accelerating relative growth. "This," Kaldor concludes, "is the
principle of cumulative causation whereby some regions gain at the
expense of others, leading to increasing inequalities" within the international economy. This is also the process referred to as "backwash" by
Gunnar Myrdal, "polarization" by Albert Hirschman, and—in a slightly
different context—"unequal exchange" by Arghiri Emmanuel.[57]

All countries continue to gain from trade in a world of nonconstant
returns, but over time and in the presence of increasing returns countries with relatively high labor productivity gain disproportionately as a
result of the doubly virtuous cycle. Because of these unequal gains, free
trade is no longer the optimal policy. A country *may* be able to improve
its condition by adopting protection and shifting domestic production
toward the increasing returns good, thereby moving down its cost curve
and, perhaps, manifesting an underlying comparative advantage it
could not otherwise have obtained because of the entrenched position of
existing competitors. This is the classic "infant industry" argument first
put forth by Alexander Hamilton. In increasing returns production,
however, external economies are created only over the long run; thus
the period of "infancy" may be extended. In addition, if the positive
externalities are large enough, it may still be beneficial to protect a
specific industry even if it never outgrows its infancy. Thus "infant
industry protection" is a misnomer and the term "increasing returns
protection" is used here instead.

The increasing returns argument for protection applies equally to
countries of both high and low relative labor productivity, although the
height and extensiveness of the trade barriers should differ consider-

---

[57] Kaldor, *Economics without Equilibrium*, pp. 72–75; Gunnar Myrdal, *Economic Theory and
Under-developed Regions* (London: Duckworth, 1957), pp. 23–38; Albert O. Hirschman,
The Strategy of Economic Development (New Haven: Yale University Press, 1958), pp. 183–
90; and Arghiri Emmanuel, *Unequal Exchange* (New York: Monthly Review Press, 1972).

ably. Countries with high relative labor productivity already possess a comparative advantage in increasing returns industries and gain both absolutely and relatively from trade. As a result, they possess a strong interest in free trade abroad. This allows the highly productive country to expand its exports and thereby to enjoy the fruits of the doubly virtuous cycle, and limits the ability of others to create a comparative advantage in competitive increasing returns industries. Free trade abroad, in other words, expands the virtuous cycle and reinforces the favored position of countries with high relative labor productivity at the top of the international division of labor.

Even though countries with higher than average labor productivity gain from free trade abroad, they may still use protection to compete with one another for larger shares of the world's increasing returns industries.[58] But because the doubly virtuous cycle depends upon exports leading imports, relative size also becomes important here. As noted above, in small and, to a lesser extent, middle-sized countries exports are set exogenously and domestic protection will have little or no effect on foreign demand. In large countries, however, exports are a function, at least in part, of imports. Consequently, domestic protection—of whatever form, including increasing returns protection—creates an impediment to exports. Large countries with relatively high labor productivity, as a result, will be less likely to adopt increasing returns protection than their small or middle-sized counterparts.

Countries with low relative labor productivity gain from international trade but typically reap fewer benefits than highly productive nation-states. Less productive countries, therefore, have a strong incentive

---

[58]I recognize that trade restrictions are a "second best" policy for stimulating increasing returns protection. Because of the presumed positive externalities, social returns are greater than private returns and some government intervention is necessary to stimulate production. Subsidies might be the optimal intervention instrument, but tariffs or other trade restrictions have been more commonly used. Several reasons can be suggested for this paradox. Tariffs are a diffuse indirect tax on consumers and a source of revenue for the government. Subsidies are a direct payment to producers and therefore more transparent and a drain on government revenues. The diffuse and opaque nature of trade restrictions makes them less likely to generate political opposition from nonbeneficiaries. Also, because trade restrictions alter market incentives for all relevant entrepreneurs and subsidies are direct "rewards" to specific producers, the former are typically perceived as less "interventionist" and more consistent with a policy of laissez-faire than the latter. In this case, however, the reality may be quite different. Trade restrictions, at least for small and middle-sized states, expand tendencies toward trade surplus, further reinforcing the virtuous cycle discussed above. Finally, states vary in the policy instruments available to them (see Katzenstein, ed., *Between Power and Plenty*). By their definition (see Chapter 2), however, all states possess the ability to regulate interactions with foreigners, even though they may lack the more refined and sectorally specific instruments, such as subsidies, available to other, "stronger" states.

43

created by their concern over the relative gains from trade to adopt an extensive policy of protection designed to stimulate increasing returns industries, disrupt the existing pattern of comparative advantage, and raise their position in the international division of labor over time, while continuing to export in areas of traditional or previously created comparative advantage. The ability of less productive nation-states to adopt a protectionist increasing returns strategy, however, is largely conditioned by the size of the domestic market, an admittedly nonsystemic but nonetheless indispensable factor.[59] Countries with small domestic markets cannot realize economies of scale in production in the absence of international trade. Although they fail to gain to the same extent as more productive countries, less productive nation-states with small domestic markets may not be able to improve upon their free-trade utility. Protection will not significantly expand production or stimulate growth but will only introduce inefficiencies into the economy, and subsidizing production may be prohibitively expensive. Less productive countries with large domestic markets, on the other hand, can gain in the long run from stimulating increasing returns industries within their borders. Rather than specializing in the constant returns commodity, as a less productive economy would typically do under free trade, the country diversifies its economy, realizes economies of scale, and—if successful— creates a new comparative advantage in the increasing returns industry raising its level of relative labor productivity. The social deadweight loss from protection is offset, in this view, by the increased growth stimulated by the combination of export growth and increasing returns.

Structure and Interests

The effects of relative size and relative labor productivity on national trade strategies can be summarized by the following propositions: (1) Relatively large countries bear a disproportionate share of the burden of creating and maintaining the international infrastructure. This role may be provided by a single hegemonic leader, although it is not certain that even here such a leader will possess the necessary ability. Even though negotiating and enforcement costs will be higher, middle-sized countries may also be able to provide the international infrastructure through cooperative leadership. (2) Relatively large countries may possess optimal tariffs greater than zero, but this depends on the size and retaliatory proclivities of their trading partners and the dynamic effects of the open economy multiplier. (3) Countries with high relative labor

[59]See Kaldor, *Economics without Equilibrium*, pp. 65–67, on the importance of market size for increasing returns industries.

productivity possess a strong interest in free trade abroad, although they may still use domestic protection to compete for greater shares of the world's increasing returns production. Countries with low relative labor productivity and small domestic markets can do little to improve upon their free-trade utility. While also desiring to export goods in their areas of traditional or created comparative advantage, countries with relatively low labor productivity and large domestic markets can gain by stimulating increasing returns production. Consequently, they possess a strong interest in domestic protection.

These three propositions are interactive. Drawing upon each proposition, I derive trade policy preference orderings for the seven categories of nation-states identified above (see Figure 1.1). Ambiguities and plausible alternative preference orderings are noted where appropriate. Even though protection and free trade are continuous concepts, the choices available to a nation-state are simplified for purposes of analysis to greater free trade (FT) or greater protection (P) for itself (first term) and all others (second term). In this notation, for example, P/FT represents a preference for protection at home and free trade abroad. It should be emphasized that this notation does not necessarily imply policies of complete free trade or protection. A free-trade strategy can countenance some measure of protection for selected industries, and a protectionist policy may still leave some sectors open to international competition. The two choices merely refer to the general thrust or central tendency of policy.

As defined above, there are three categories of nation-states with high relative labor productivity. In order of increasing size, they are liberal free riders (LFRs), opportunists (OPs),[60] and hegemonic leaders (HLs). Countries within all three categories share a strong interest in free trade abroad as a result of their high relative labor productivity. Free trade in other countries allows liberal free riders, opportunists, and hegemonic leaders to export and, by inhibiting the development of comparative advantage in competing increasing returns industries, preserve their favored positions within the international economy. Their incentives for optimal tariffs and increasing returns protection, which differ according to relative size, however, are contradictory. The larger the country, the greater is the likelihood that its postretaliation optimal tariff will be

---

[60]In several earlier articles I referred to this category of nation-states as "supporters." As the theory evolved, this label became something of a misnomer and a source of confusion. The term "opportunist" better reflects the exploitive behaviors expected of middle-sized, relatively productive nation-states. When a hegemonic leader is present they free ride; when two or more exist they restrain protectionism in one another; when only one exists, it may precipitate the closure of the system.

greater than zero. Conversely, the smaller the country, the more effica-cious increasing returns protection will be over time.

Hegemonic leaders have a strong preference for universal free trade (FT/FT) when they confront at least middle-sized and retaliatory part-ners. In this case, their optimal tariffs will be low, if still greater than zero, and increasing returns protection will inhibit exports, thereby reducing the open economy multiplier. Even in the absence of free trade abroad, hegemonic leaders still possess few incentives to adopt domestic protection, which will only further restrict their exports. This suggests a dominant hegemonic strategy of free trade at home regardless of the policies of others. If hegemonic leaders do adopt protection, they are likely to prefer that others remain open for their exports. This yields a trade policy preference ordering of FT/FT > FT/P > P/FT > P/P. If, however, all of a hegemonic leader's trading partners are small and its optimal tariff with retaliation is significantly greater than zero, a second preference ordering is suggested: P/FT > FT/FT > P/P > FT/P. The conditions underlying the first preference ordering are more typical, and that ranking is used in the analysis which follows. Interested readers can easily substitute the second ranking where appropriate. The United Kingdom in the mid-nineteenth century and the United States in the mid-twentieth century are the only two post–Industrial Revolution ex-amples of hegemonic leaders.[61]

Opportunists, or middle-sized, relatively productive nation-states, possess less market power than large countries and, typically, face re-taliatory trading partners. As a result, their optimal tariff is normally close to zero. Given their limited market power, however, exports are determined exogenously and their incentives for increasing returns protection are substantial. Although the protection/free trade dicho-tomy overstates their interests in domestic protection, the preferences of opportunists can be ranked as P/FT > FT/FT > P/P > FT/P.

Because opportunists possess only moderate influence within the in-ternational economy, their mixed interests create the tendency and their middle size the ability to free ride when a hegemonic leader is present to maintain a liberal international economy. The hegemon's dominant strategy of free trade at home not only creates incentives for an opportu-nist to adopt increasing returns protection confident that its exports will

---

[61]Christopher Chase-Dunn, "International Economic Policy in a Declining Core State," in William P. Avery and David P. Rapkin, eds., *America in a Changing World Political Economy* (New York: Longmans, 1982), argues that the Netherlands was a hegemonic power in the seventeenth century. Insufficient data exist to classify the Netherlands within the dimensions of the international economic structure specified here. For this reason, the examples and analysis are confined to the post–Industrial Revolution period.

remain robust, but may actually encourage the latter to pursue its albeit relatively low optimal tariff by removing the fear of retaliation. During periods of hegemonic decline, as we shall see, opportunists become critical in determining the openness or closure of the international economy.

The United States was an opportunist from at least the early nineteenth century until World War II. After a brief two decades as a hegemonic leader, the United States returned to this category in the mid-1960s. The Federal Republic of Germany and France joined the United States within this category in approximately 1965 and 1975 respectively (see Table 1.2). If past trends continue, Japan will also become an opportunist within the next decade.

Liberal free riders, although smaller, possess interests similar to those of opportunists. Their optimal tariffs are very low but, like those of their middle-sized counterparts, are offset by the desire to stimulate increasing returns production through protection. Thus the preferences of liberal free riders are ordered as $P/FT > FT/FT > P/P > FT/P$. Belgium and Sweden today would be classified as liberal free riders.

Corresponding to the categories of liberal free riders, opportunists, and hegemonic leaders are several categories of nation-states with low relative labor productivity. Like countries of high relative labor productivity, these nation-states all favor free trade abroad. International openness facilitates exports, hinders other less productive countries from fostering increasing returns industries, and prevents highly productive nation-states from sheltering their increasing returns industries.

Assuming that they possess large domestic markets, as might be expected, imperial leaders (ILs)—relatively large countries with less than average labor productivity—can increase their long-run relative gains from trade by stimulating increasing returns industries through domestic protection. This interest in protection derived from relative labor productivity reinforces tendencies in imperial leaders created by their large size to impose optimal tariffs. As a result, the question of retaliatory trade partners affects only the cardinal and not the ordinal preference rankings. The preferences of imperial leaders can be ordered as $P/FT > P/P > FT/FT > FT/P$. Imperial leaders, as a result, will pursue protection at home regardless of the policies of other nation-states unless induced or coerced to do otherwise.

The international trading system would be quite different under imperial than hegemonic leadership. Imperial leaders might still bear a disproportionate share of the costs of providing an international economic infrastructure, but the component regimes would be substantially weaker and most likely based on some form of administered trade. Since

47

the Industrial Revolution, no imperial leaders have existed within the international economy.[62]

Even though small and middle-sized countries with low relative labor productivity have optimal tariffs close to zero they may still be extremely protectionist. Domestic market size will vary, however, and exert important effects.

As noted above, countries with low relative productivity and small domestic markets, referred to here collectively as free trade free riders (FTFRs), can do no better than to adopt free trade at home. Their preferences, as a result, are $FT/FT > FT/P > P/FT > P/P$. At first glance, this ranking appears somewhat paradoxical, because free trade free riders have stronger preferences for free trade than the more productive opportunists or liberal free riders. Free trade free riders, however, have little chance to expand their share of the world's increasing returns industries, whereas the latter already have a comparative advantage in this area and compete for even larger shares. Free trade free riders, as a result, have few options and little opportunity to improve their relative condition. Although the concept of domestic market size is difficult to operationalize,[63] many Third World nation-states and several of the less productive European countries today would be considered free trade free riders. Historically, countries with less than average labor productivity and small domestic markets have also been relatively small within the international economy. As a result, although their interests coincide with those of hegemonic leaders, they have generally played an inconsequential role in creating or maintaining an open international economy.

Small and middle-sized countries with less than average labor productivity and large domestic markets, referred to here as protectionist free riders (PFRs) and spoilers (SPs) respectively, have ordinally ranked

---

[62]Readers of earlier drafts of this chapter have suggested that the Soviet Union might be classified as an imperial leader within the Communist bloc trading system. If the Soviet bloc is considered as an autonomous subsystem, the Soviet Union would appear to fit both the structural definition and the policy predictions for an imperial leader. The Soviet bloc is not an autonomous subsystem, however, but a grouping of countries only loosely integrated into the larger international economy. Although it may be useful to apply the theory developed here at the regional level, the theory's ability to generate testable hypotheses collapses when it is recognized that regions are also situated within the global system and that trade policy is made with consideration to the larger economy. I prefer, therefore, to limit the applicability of the theory to the international economy as a whole. In this approach, the Soviet Union is classified as a protectionist free rider.

[63]Domestic market size is best measured by gross national product, population, or other such aggregate indicators. The absence of a precise definition and operationalization does not create significant problems for this analysis because the concept does not play a role in the case study of Part II.

preferences identical to those of imperial leaders: P/FT > P/P > FT/FT > FT/P. Although their optimal tariffs are considerably lower than those of imperial leaders, they have the same potential for stimulating increasing returns production through trade protection. Because of their middle size and protectionist preferences, spoilers can play a critically disruptive role within the international economy. France and Germany in the late nineteenth century and France and Japan throughout most of the post–World War II era are the principal examples of this category.

Structure and Strategy

International economic structures are distinguished by the number of middle- and large-sized nation-states present in the international economy and the categories into which they are classified. Changes in the international economic structure are of two kinds: changes within a structure and changes of a structure.[64] Changes within a structure occur within specific categories. A hegemonic leader's willingness and ability to stabilize the international economy, for example, is affected as its relative size increases or decreases, even though it may remain in a position of hegemony. More important, changes of structure occur when any middle- or large-sized nation-state changes category. The decline of a hegemonic leader into an opportunist, the rise of a protectionist free rider into a spoiler, or the transformation of a spoiler into an opportunist would each constitute a change of structure. Since the mid-nineteenth century there have been six distinct international economic structures: two of hegemony (United Kingdom, until 1912, and United States, 1945–65), two of bilateral opportunism (United States and United Kingdom, 1912–32, and United States and Federal Republic of Germany, 1965–75), one of multilateral opportunism (United States, Federal Republic of Germany, and France, 1975–   ), and one of unilateral opportunism (United States, 1932–45).[65] Each structure has its own processes for resolving the conflicting preferences of nation-states.

---

[64]Robert Gilpin, *War and Change in World Politics* (Cambridge: Cambridge University Press, 1981), makes similar distinctions between types of international change; see pp. 39–49.

[65]The data series on relative labor productivity used for this book ends in 1977 (see Tables 1.1 and 1.2). Projecting from existing trends and drawing upon productivity growth rates available from other sources, it appears that the United States and the Federal Republic of Germany are securely placed as opportunists within the international economic structure. France's position is more difficult to assess; it appears to have maintained its slightly higher than average relative labor productivity and, therefore, its position as an opportunist.

A hegemonic international economic structure is depicted in Figure 1.2. As in all game-theoretic matrices, the row player's (in this case, the OPs, LFRs, SPs, PFRs, and FTFRs) payoffs are given first and the column player's (HL) payoffs second. The payoffs are represented on an ordinal scale of one to four, with four being the most preferred outcome, three the second most preferred outcome, and so on. The Nash equilibrium cell is the one in which each player receives its highest payoff obtainable given the actions of the other. A dominant strategy exists when any actor would adopt the same policy regardless of what the other does.

As can be seen in Figure 1.2, a hegemonic structure will not axiomatically lead to a liberal international economy: universal free trade (FT/FT) is the Nash equilibrium only for hegemonic leaders and free trade free riders. In every interaction between a hegemonic leader and opportunists, liberal free riders, spoilers, or protectionist free riders, the equilibrium is FT/P (or P/FT from the perspective of the small and middle-sized countries; this lies in the southwest cell of matrices a and b). In each of these cases, the hegemonic leader must impose (offer) greater or lesser positive or negative sanctions (side payments) to obtain the nation-states' compliance with universal free trade.[66] In other words, the hegemonic leader must directly alter the costs and benefits of free trade that spoilers, protectionist free riders, opportunists, and liberal free riders face as a result of their positions within the international economic structure.

The sanction imposed (offered) by the hegemonic leader for compliance with a liberal international economy must be at least equal to if not greater than the difference between the best payoff obtainable by nation-states in the absence of compliance and the free trade payoff. In the cases of protectionist free riders, spoilers, liberal free riders, and opportunists the size of the sanction (or the price of compliance) must be equal to or greater than P/FT − FT/FT. The price of compliance is likely to be high for spoilers and protectionist free riders (difference between first and third choices) and moderate for opportunists and liberal free riders (difference between first and second choices).

[66]Arthur A. Stein, "The Hegemon's Dilemma: Great Britain, the United States, and the International Economic Order," *International Organization* 38 (Spring 1984): 355–86; and Timothy J. McKeown, "Hegemonic Stability Theory and Nineteenth Century Tariff Levels in Europe," *International Organization* 37 (Winter 1983): 73–91. Both argue that there is little evidence that either Britain or the United States acted in the manner predicted here. McKeown specifically notes the lack of evidence that Britain effectively manipulated other countries to secure free trade. For a counterargument, see Scott C. James and David A. Lake, "The Second Face of Hegemony: Britain and the American Walker Tariff of 1846," paper presented to the Conference Group on Political Economy, Chicago, Illinois, September 3–6, 1987.

Figure 1.2. A hegemonic international economic structure

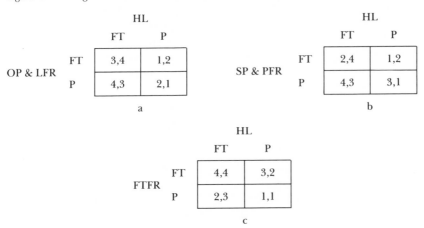

HL = FT/FT > FT/P > P/FT > P/P
OP & LFR = P/FT > FT/FT > P/P > FT/P
SP & PFR = P/FT > P/P > FT/FT > FT/P
FTFR = FT/FT > FT/P > P/FT > P/P

The sanctions imposed (offered) by the hegemonic leader can take the form of threatening to close its market to the goods of the noncomplying country, absorbing the costs of adjustment, or accepting a measure of protection in some areas to secure cooperation in others. Historically, hegemonic leaders have also drawn upon their political-military power to ensure compliance by others to a free-trade regime. The United Kingdom's role as the "balancer" of the nineteenth-century European state system and Napoleon III's need for British support for his Italian policy, for example, may have induced France to adopt a free-trade policy in the Cobden-Chevalier Treaty of 1860.[67] Likewise, America's military presence in Europe has been a critical influence on the Federal Republic of Germany's liberal orientation toward the international economy during the postwar era.[68]

In addition to paying the price of compliance, a hegemonic leader must also provide the necessary international infrastructure. This requires that relatively strong monetary, transit, and financial regimes be created or maintained and that the international economy be stabilized. The cost of providing these necessary conditions of international openness is referred to as the *price of infrastructure* (PI) and can vary over time.

[67]Iliasu, "Cobden-Chevalier Commercial Treaty."
[68]Michael Mastanduno, "Between Economics and Security: The Western Politics of East-West Trade" (Ph.D. diss., Princeton University, 1985), examines the relationship between America's economic and political hegemony in the post–World War II era.

Establishment or maintenance of a liberal international economy depends on the price of infrastructure and on the resources of the hegemonic leader available for influencing other nations relative to the sum of the individual prices of compliance. The total resources available to the hegemonic leader are limited to the difference between the outcome derived from the independent decisions of opportunists, liberal free riders, spoilers, and protectionist free riders (FT/P) and the free trade outcome (FT/FT). These resources, less the price of infrastructure, must be equal to or greater than the sum of the individual prices of compliance, or

$$(FT/FT - FT/P)_{HL} - PI \geq \Sigma (P/FT - FT/FT)_{OP, \ LFR, \ SP \ \& \ PFR}$$

for universal free trade to be established. It is not axiomatic that hegemony lead to a liberal international economy. In an international economic structure composed only of a hegemonic leader and spoilers, for example, the price of compliance would most likely exceed the benefits of universal free trade received by the hegemonic leader. Similarly, even if the hegemonic leader can pay the price of compliance, it may fail to regulate international instability successfully. Even in the absence of hegemony, some international openness will exist as free trade free riders pursue their dominant strategies of free trade at home.

The constraints and opportunities of a hegemonic international economic structure are relatively unambiguous; each actor possesses clear interests within the structure. The hegemonic leader will pursue free trade at home and abroad until the costs of doing so exceed the benefits. Free trade free riders will also adopt a liberal trade policy, although their actions will have little effect on the international economy as a whole. Opportunists, liberal free riders, spoilers, and protectionist free riders will protect their domestic economies while taking advantage of the openness provided by the hegemonic leader. They will deviate from this course only when coerced or induced to do so by the hegemonic leader.

An international economic structure of bilateral opportunism is shown in Figure 1.3.[69] When two or more opportunists exist in an

---

[69]Bilateral and multilateral opportunism are identical except in the following manner: two-person iterated prisoner's dilemma can potentially lead to cooperation in the northwest cell of the matrix. N-person prisoner's dilemma eventually breaks down with the introduction of the possibility of free riding. Although the dynamics of the game change, it may not constitute a practical problem for the circumstances under discussion here. The number of opportunists never has been and never will be very large. Some free riding may go undetected, but most will be caught and punished. Thus, some cooperation may occur, although it will be less stable than under bilateral opportunism. For a general discussion of N-person games see Morton D. Davis, *Game Theory: A Nontechnical Introduction*, rev. ed. (New York: Basic Books, 1983), pp. 163–228.

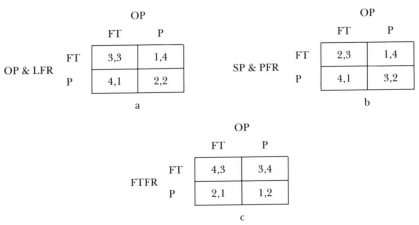

Figure 1.3. An international economic structure of bilateral opportunism

OP & LFR = P/FT > FT/FT > P/P > FT/P
SP & PFR = P/FT > P/P > FT/FT > FT/P
FTFR = FT/FT > FT/P > P/FT > P/P

international economy, they confront a classic prisoner's dilemma. If each opportunist attempts to maximize its individual gains (P/FT), the net outcome will be suboptimal (P/P). Opportunists have a high incentive to cooperate, however. Opportunists and liberal free riders possess strong interests in free trade abroad, although the latter will only marginally influence support for free trade within the international economy as a whole. Consequently, the cost of not cooperating (P/P − FT/FT) is likely to be significantly greater than the gain that would be obtained by protecting selected industries (P/FT − FT/FT).

Moreover, drawing upon the recent literature on prisoner's dilemma, there are at least two reasons for expecting the cooperative or universal free trade (FT/FT) outcome to occur. First, trade relations between nation-states approximate an iterated game. Trade policy making is a continuous process and tariff systems are periodically revised. Consequently, any defection by one party can be easily punished by others. When two actors participate in an iterated prisoner's dilemma and, in Robert Axelrod's terminology, the "shadow of the future" is large "tit-for-tat" or conditional cooperation is the maximizing strategy.[70] In other words, when actors value future returns highly enough it is ra-

---

[70]Robert Axelrod, *The Evolution of Cooperation* (New York: Basic Books, 1984). In "tit-for-tat" a player cooperates on the first move and then does whatever his or her opponent did on the previous move. Thus it reciprocates cooperation, punishes defection, and forgives.

tional and possible for them to cooperate and accept their second best outcomes rather than attempt to achieve their most preferred outcomes.

It is also possible to identify the conditions under which cooperation will fail to arise in an iterated prisoner's dilemma. Tit-for-tat is stable only if the shadow of the future is sufficiently large. International economic instability, and particularly fluctuations in the exchange rates and prices that determine the pattern of international trade, will increase the discount rate. In other words, instability changes a nation-state's evaluation of the future trading system, leading it to place greater weight on present returns and devaluing possible but uncertain future gains. Thus opportunists are less likely to cooperate (adopt FT/FT) and more likely to pursue narrow short-term interests (P/FT) during periods of international economic instability.

Tit-for-tat is also unstable when an end point for the game exists or is perceived to exist. Defection (or protection in this case) is rational on the last play of the game. Knowing this, each player has an incentive to defect on the next to last move, and so on. Once an end point is perceived, it is extremely difficult to maintain cooperation. If an opportunist is believed to be changing or about to be changing categories within the international economic structure, an end point is effectively created. The shadow of the future diminishes and the structure of cooperation will rapidly break down. Thus if the international economic structure is perceived to be changing, each opportunist can be expected preemptively to defect from free trade and adopt P/FT.

Second, cooperation can emerge within prisoner's dilemma by formal or informal agreements or "contracts" between the parties.[71] Arthur Stein has identified prisoner's dilemma as a subset of "dilemmas of common interest." Such dilemmas, Stein argues, can be and have been resolved historically through "collaborative regimes" which constrain the self-seeking behavior of nation-states and allow for cooperation through highly formalized sets of rules which "specify what constitutes cooperation and what constitutes cheating" and procedures by which each party can be "assured of its own ability to spot others' cheating immediately." Likewise, Robert Keohane has argued that once created, regimes will be respected because they serve the useful purposes of reducing uncertainty and providing information. Cooperation is thereby reinforced by the presence of a regime. As they provide a "good" in and of themselves, regimes will tend to persist even after the

---

[71] Russell Hardin, *Collective Action* (Baltimore: Johns Hopkins University Press, 1982), pp. 125–230.

underlying national interests that brought them into being have changed.[72]

Thus, cooperation can be expected to occur in prisoner's dilemma when multiple plays of the "game" are possible and the shadow of the future is large, and/or when the parties are able to structure a regime to constrain their self-seeking behavior. Interestingly, the two arguments supporting the possibility of cooperation under prisoner's dilemma reach different conclusions about the likelihood of cooperation persisting when underlying interests change. For those who focus on the iterative nature of the relationship, changing interests are likely to prompt preemptive defection. For at least some regime theorists, however, cooperation can be expected to persist for at least a relatively short period of time despite such change. The case study developed in Part II supports the former conclusion.

If two or more opportunists agree to cooperate and provide free trade among themselves, they still face the same costs as does a single hegemonic leader if they desire to expand or maintain free trade in the international economy as a whole. Figure 1.3c indicates that opportunists will exploit free trade free riders by adopting domestic protection. In this case, the crude dichotomization between freer trade and greater protection used in the game matrices proves misleading. Free trade free riders typically specialize in constant returns industries in areas of traditional comparative advantage, so their exports will not impinge upon the increasing returns industries protected in opportunists. The more likely equilibrium in these dyadic relationships, as under hegemony, is universal free trade (FT/FT). In their relations with spoilers and protectionist free riders, on the other hand, opportunists must be willing and able to pay the price of compliance demanded by others and the price of infrastructure. In addition, the opportunists will incur *negotiating costs* (NC) in orchestrating the joint interventions necessary to bring about a liberal international economy. These costs may be considerable, precisely because the negotiations aim to constrain or alter national behavior from what it would be in the absence of cooperation. These negotiating costs are likely to escalate as the number of opportunists increases. Although the aggregate gains from trade will increase as well, reaching a mutually acceptable agreement among a large number of actors will be difficult. As the number becomes large, and perhaps even

---

[72]Arthur A. Stein, "Coordination and Collaboration: Regimes in an Anarchic World," *International Organization* 36 (Spring 1982): 312; Robert Keohane, "The Demand for International Regimes," *International Organization* 36 (Spring 1982): 325–55; and *After Hegemony*. See Stephen D. Krasner, "Regimes and the Limits of Realism: Regimes as Autonomous Variables," in Krasner, ed., *International Regimes*, pp. 355–68.

as it approaches five or six, the problem of free riding among the opportunists may become insurmountable.

A liberal international economy will arise in bilateral opportunism only when the net benefits of free trade for the opportunists, less the costs of negotiation, and less the price of infrastructure, exceeds the price of compliance of the other nation-states. In other words, universal free trade will occur in a structure of bilateral opportunism only if

$$\Sigma(FT/FT - P/P)_{OP} - NC - PI \geq \Sigma(P/P - FT/FT)_{SP, \, PFR \, \& \, LFR}.$$

Thus the absence of hegemony does not necessarily mean the absence of leadership; under these conditions, effective collective leadership of a liberal international economy is possible and, indeed, probable.

The national trade interests revealed by a structure of bilateral opportunism are more ambiguous than those of a hegemonic structure. As under hegemony, free trade free riders will adopt liberal trade policies, while spoilers, protectionist free riders, and liberal free riders pursue protection at home and free trade abroad unless coerced or induced to do otherwise by powers with stronger interests in universal free trade. It is the mixed interests of the opportunists themselves which introduces the ambiguity into the system. The policies pursued by the opportunists and particularly their willingness to cooperate will be strongly influenced by the degree of instability within the international economy—making their efforts to control this instability even more problematic—and their perceptions on the likelihood of the present structure enduring into the future.

An international economic structure of unilateral opportunism is depicted in Figure 1.4. The most important difference between bilateral and unilateral opportunism is that the constraints on domestic protection imposed upon an opportunist by the need for cooperation are absent. The relationship between an opportunist and liberal free riders is similar to that in bilateral opportunism. Because of their small size, however, it is unlikely that liberal free riders can resist the temptations of free riding or supply the necessary constraints upon the opportunist to prevent it from adopting protection. Likewise, the dominant strategy of protection at home possessed by protectionist free riders and spoilers will fail to restrain protectionism in the opportunist. Only in its relations with free trade free riders does a single opportunist face incentives for free trade.

A single opportunist with a strong interest in free trade abroad may be able to exert a moderating influence upon protectionism in the international economy. The ability and willingness of a single opportunist to

Figure 1.4. A international economic structure of unilateral opportunism

a

LFR \ OP	FT	P
FT	3,3	1,4
P	4,1	2,2

b

SP & PFR \ OP	FT	P
FT	2,3	1,4
P	4,1	3,2

c

FTFR \ OP	FT	P
FT	4,3	3,4
P	2,1	1,2

OP & LFR = P/FT > FT/FT > P/P > FT/P
SP & PFR = P/FT > P/P > FT/FT > FT/P
FTFR = FT/FT > FT/P > P/FT > P/P

construct or maintain a liberal international economy will be determined by the benefits of universal free trade less the price of infrastructure, relative to the sum of the individual prices of compliance, or

$$(FT/FT - P/P)_{OP} - PI \geq \Sigma(P/P - FT/FT)_{SP,\ PFR\ \&\ LFR.}$$

Given the magnitude of the task and the limited resources of the opportunist, it is not likely that a liberal international economy can be either constructed or maintained, although it remains a possibility. To the extent that the opportunist can induce or coerce others to adopt a measure of free trade, it may be able to obtain a partial success and create or maintain a modicum of openness within the international economy.

A paradox emerges in unilateral opportunism, however. Under conditions of international economic openness, which may exist temporarily as the legacy of a previous international economic structure, and high international economic instability, which will increase the desires for protection in all countries, the single opportunist may actually undermine the liberal order instead of moderating protectionism in the international economy and attempting to create at least a measure of free trade abroad. A single opportunist can achieve its highest payoff (P/FT) only by preempting the protectionist policies of spoilers and

STRUCTURE AND STRATEGY

protectionist free riders, thereby creating a higher relative level of protection approximating its first choice. By preemptively adopting a
higher level of protection, the opportunist channels imports formerly
absorbed by its market toward other countries (which are now relatively
more open) while, in the short run and to the extent that these now
diverted goods are noncompetitive with the exports of the opportunist,
not significantly reducing its foreign markets. The opportunist, as a
result, obtains greater protection at home than it would have otherwise
achieved and maintains its exports. This strategy, however, will quickly
lead to a tariff war in which, through a pattern of action and reaction,
the opportunist and spoilers build higher and higher tariff walls around
their economies. As a result, this strategy will create benefits for the
opportunist only if implemented preemptively. If the opportunist waits
until other nation-states have increased their levels of protection, it will
lose its export markets and fail to gain additional protection for its own
economy. This strategy is logical only if greater protection abroad is
imminent and is likely to occur in the transition from some other structure to one of unilateral opportunism. Because the opportunist gains
from openness in the international economy and its preemptive protection will clearly act as a catalyst for closure, acting too soon or before
protection abroad is imminent will cause an undue loss of exports for the
opportunist. Achieving maximum benefits, therefore, requires precise
timing. Even with such timing, the strategy will provide benefits to the
opportunist only in the short run, defined as the time it takes other
nation-states to retaliate.

Once tariff levels reach heights that prohibit international trade and
nation-states become locked into the extreme P/P outcome, the interests
of the opportunist will be best served by a return to greater free trade
abroad. Any reduction in foreign tariffs then benefits the opportunist.
Although it most likely cannot lead the international economy effectively, the opportunist will benefit from even limited bargaining with
other countries over tariff reductions. Because the influence of a single
opportunist will be limited, the bargaining will most likely center on the
exchange of tangible concessions between countries, and the actual
reductions are likely to be moderate.

Like bilateral opportunism, the constraints and opportunities of unilateral opportunism are more ambiguous than under hegemony.
Whereas under normal conditions a single opportunist will seek free
trade abroad, it is influenced by the preexisting international economic
structure and the level of stability. During the transition from an international economic structure of hegemony or bilateral opportunism, and
particularly if it coincides with a period of high international economic

58

instability, the single opportunist is likely to seek preemptive protectionism, a paradoxical strategy. If it does so, however, the opportunist will soon return to a strategy of seeking to build free trade abroad.

In summary, hegemony is neither a necessary or sufficient condition for the creation or maintenance of a liberal international economy. If the price of compliance and/or the price of infrastructure exceeds the benefits of universal free trade, the hegemonic leader will be both unwilling and unable to lead the international economy toward greater openness. Conversely, two or more opportunists, and in some cases even a single opportunist, may be willing and able to construct or maintain a liberal international economy if the conditions specified above are met. Thus it is important to distinguish between different nonhegemonic international economic structures. Each possesses distinctive politics and processes important for understanding the international economy.

In conclusion, it should be emphasized that the theory of international economic structures developed here does not contain within it a theory of change. There is no mechanism endogenous to the international economic structure which drives change at the systems level from one structure to the next or at the country level from one category to another. On the basis of the theory sketched above, however, it is possible to suggest a tentative model of change. Robert Gilpin and others see hegemony as fragile, ultimately insecure, and doomed to decay. "From a political perspective," Gilpin writes, "the inherent contradiction of capitalism is that it develops rather than that it exploits the world. A capitalist international economy plants the seeds of its own destruction in that it diffuses economic growth, industry, and technology, and thereby undermines the distribution of power upon which that liberal, interdependent economy has rested."[73] In practice, this is correct. In the theory developed above, however, successful hegemony, bilateral opportunism, or (rarely) unilateral opportunism is self-reinforcing. To the extent that a hegemonic leader, or one or several opportunists, is successful in creating a wholly open international economy, their positions will be strengthened and others weakened by limitations placed on the latters' ability to create a comparative advantage in the increasing returns production upon which dominance rests. The "tragedy" of hegemony or opportunism is that it is never entirely successful. With the onset of the Great Depression of 1873–96, Great Britain failed to take any active measure to preserve openness in Europe or the United States and, instead, took the easier route of turning inward upon its empire.[74]

[73]Gilpin, *U.S. Power*, p. 260; see also Stein, "Hegemon's dilemma."
[74]E. J. Hobsbawm, *Industry and Empire: The Making of Modern English Society*, Vol. 2, *1750 to the Present* (New York: Pantheon, 1968), pp. 110–26.

Similarly, the United States, preoccupied with Cold War concerns, compromised on its newly found free-trade principles during the 1950s so as to rebuild Western Europe and Japan. In both cases, protectionist competitors did create comparative advantage in increasing returns industries, ultimately undermining the economic base of the hegemon.

THE INTERNATIONAL ECONOMIC STRUCTURE
AND AMERICAN TRADE STRATEGY

The constraints and opportunities of the international economic structure are manifested at two levels. Depending upon the long-term benefits of free trade for various countries, price of infrastructure, and negotiating costs (for two or more opportunists), greater free trade or protection will result in the international economy as a whole. This chapter has focused on these necessary and sufficient conditions for openness or closure in the international economic system.

Individual nation-states, however, also face constraints and opportunities created by the international economic structure. Two or more opportunists, for instance, cannot simultaneously obtain protection at home and free trade abroad. Conversely, an opportunist can free ride on the international economic openness provided by hegemonic leadership. Stated more formally, the constraints and opportunities of the international economic structure create opportunity costs, defined as the relative costs and benefits of alternative trade strategies, for individual countries. The international economic structure, in other words, creates differing rewards and punishments for alternative policies. Any nation-state that acts against or ignores the constraints and opportunities of the international economic structure will receive less than the maximum reward and will be less well off than it otherwise could have been. The policy alternative with the highest reward (lowest punishment) can be thought of as the "national trade interest."[75]

This book examines the systemic-level theory of international economic structures in the case of American trade strategy between 1887 and 1939. Rather than attempting to analyze the constraints and opportunities of the international economic structure at the level of the inter-

[75]Stephen D. Krasner, *Defending the National Interest: Raw Materials Investments and U.S. Foreign Policy* (Princeton: Princeton University Press, 1978), has partially resuscitated the use of the term "national interest." This is a positive development for Realist international relations and international political economy. Yet Krasner defines the national interest inductively, thereby limiting the usefulness of his approach. Having worked backward from policy to establish interests, Krasner cannot then use the concept of the national interest to explain policies. To his credit, Krasner avoids this tautology. This book posits national interests deductively and can, as a result, use them to explain policy.

national economy as a whole, they are examined at the level of an individual nation-state. Problems of operationalization and data availability would make the former approach difficult, although perhaps not impossible. By focusing on a specific country, the behavior of other nation-states can be used as proxies for the costs and benefits of free trade for the hegemonic leader, the price of infrastructure, and the price of compliance. Thus, much of what would be problematic if the theory were to be tested at the level of the international economy can be treated descriptively in a case study of trade strategy in a single nation-state. I am not attempting to explain the trade strategies of countries other than the United States in the case study. When I refer to Great Britain as a hegemonic leader, for instance, I am not purporting to explain British policy as a function of its structural position. I am merely using the label as a shorthand for the syndrome of policies associated with hegemony and pursued by Britain at this time.

The case of American trade strategy between 1887 and 1939 was chosen for three reasons. Four distinct international economic structures existed during the period (see Figure 1.5). An international economic structure of British hegemony existed from the late eighteenth century until approximately 1897. At that date, America's relative labor productivity finally exceeded Britain's and a change within the structure occurred. Although Britain's position within the international economy had been gradually declining since approximately 1870, the period after 1897 is referred to as one of declining hegemony because Britain was no longer the largest *and* most productive country. In 1912, a structure of bilateral opportunism emerged, with the United States and the United Kingdom as the two opportunists. This structure lasted until approximately 1932, when Britain declined into a spoiler, creating a structure of unilateral opportunism. Thus there is significant variation in the international economic structure during the fifty-two years covered. Each of these four structures is associated with a major change in American trade strategy. Specific propositions and expectations are outlined in the four chapters in Part II.

The United States was chosen also because it approximates a least likely critical case study for the systemic theory developed here. Its large domestic market, low level of international economic dependence, domestically oriented ideology, and strong social groups should have enabled it to ignore the constraints and opportunities of the international economic structure if any nation-state could. To the extent that American trade strategy reflects the constraints and opportunities of the international economic structure, this constitutes strong support for the theory.

Finally, the case is important for the insights it can yield into the

Figure 1.5. The international economic structure, 1870–1938

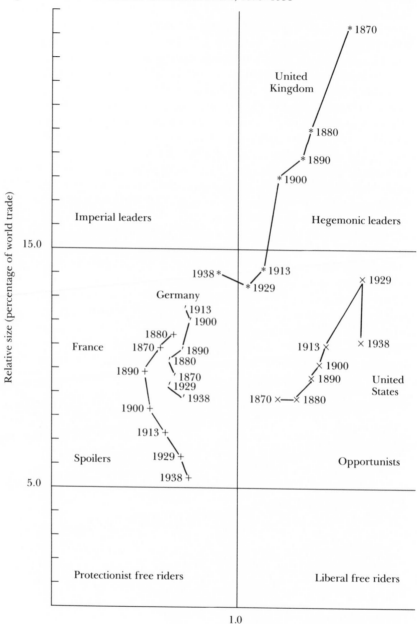

present era of declining hegemony. A simplistic analogy is often drawn between the decline of the Pax Britannica and the decline of the Pax Americana. By differentiating between nonhegemonic international economic structures, the theory outlined in this chapter invalidates this analogy. During the late nineteenth and early twentieth centuries the international economic structure evolved from hegemony, into bilateral opportunism, and finally into unilateral opportunism. The international economy experienced its greatest strains during the transition between the second and third structures, ultimately breaking down into a series of regional trade and currency blocs in the early 1930s. The Pax Americana, on the other hand, appears to be evolving from hegemony, into bilateral opportunism, and into multilateral opportunism—where it is likely to remain for the foreseeable future. This is a much more stable evolutionary path, and multilateral opportunism allows for considerable international economic cooperation and openness (discussed in more detail in the Conclusion). If the theory developed above is correct, the best historical analogy for the present is the period from immediately before World War I until the late 1920s, the only other era of either bi- or multilateral opportunism. By studying the problems and potentials of trade policy making in this earlier period, perhaps some pitfalls can be avoided within the present international economic structure.

Methodological Considerations

One strategy for assessing the utility of the theory of international economic structures would be to model empirically America's national trade interest and the relevant counterfactuals deduced from the theory. Although this approach would surely be revealing, it would require an extremely sophisticated model of the United States economy and an even more rigorously specified and operationalized theory than presented here. Because of the inherent difficulties of such an exercise, particularly at the early stage of theoretical development reached in this book, and my own inclinations and skills, this approach is not pursued. Rather, the costs and benefits of free trade or protection are treated by assertion as if the theory developed above has indeed identified *the* national trade interest. Thus the focus of the analysis is not on whether the United States maximized its long-term national income, but whether national policy makers chose trade strategies and conducted affairs in pursuit of the national trade interest identified by the theory.[76] From

[76]Thus I cannot claim to have identified *the* national trade interest but only a systemically derived goal referred to here as the national trade interest.

the viewpoint of a political scientist, at least, the latter is the more interesting question.

Even when focusing on policy choice, however, substantiating a structural argument like the one developed here is difficult. Any nation-state can choose to contravene its systemically derived national trade interest. Indeed, countries are subject to multiple domestic and international pressures. Although the nation-state as a whole may lose by acting against the constraints and opportunities of the international economic structure, groups and interests within the country may benefit. These groups may seek to pressure the government into adopting policies that fulfill their narrow interests at the expense of the national trade interest (this possibility is developed further in Chapter 2). Likewise, a country's dependence on the international economy, a nonsystemic attribute, influences the choice of trade strategy. In short, the constraints and opportunities of the international economic structure may simply be overwhelmed by other pressures within the policy-making process. To determine when the constraints and opportunities of the international economic structure will be followed and when they will be overwhelmed would require a theory of political economy which integrated all of these sometimes complementary and sometimes competing pressures. A first step is taken in this direction in Chapter 2, but the field of international political economy does not possess the necessary theory at the present time.

In light of the anarchic nature of the international system and the consequent need to ensure national survival in a competitive environment, it is hypothesized that nation-states will normally give priority to the constraints and opportunities of the international economic structure. Their trade strategies should therefore reflect, at least in part, the national trade interest as identified here. Furthermore, to the extent that any nation-state chooses to contravene its national trade interest, it is hypothesized that central decision makers will be cognizant of the trade-offs between this interest and other political pressures. The existence of competing pressures does not, in the end, pose a major problem for the theory: in the case study the constraints and opportunities of the international economic structure are reflected in trade strategy with only a few exceptions, indicating the high salience attached to systemic considerations.

Not only do competing pressures exist, but the causal linkages postulated in structural theory are often difficult to observe in specific cases. The constraints and opportunities of the international economic structure do not force a nation-state to adopt any particular policy; they only make some options more attractive and other options less so. The theory posits only constraints and not determinants of behavior. Structures are like strainers that filter out otherwise viable options. Excluded possibilities—or the counterfactuals—are not easy to define. Conversely, since favored options are seldom rationalized simply on structural grounds, heightened possibilities are difficult to discern as well.

As a first step, supporting or disconfirming evidence can be obtained by establishing the empirical relationship between the international economic structure and the substantive policy choices. Was the final policy as adopted and implemented congruent with the constraints and opportunities of the international economic structure as defined above? Consistently supporting evidence would affirm the theory.

It is also possible to make a stronger argument in favor of the theory and establish the actual presence of the constraints and opportunities of the international economic structure through two additional modes of analysis. By establishing a baseline trajectory or course of action which might have been followed in the absence of the structural constraints and opportunities it is possible to identify the effects of the international economic structure by assessing the magnitude of the policy deviations that occurred and that were predicted by the theory. Given the importance normally attached to pressures from domestic interest groups on trade strategy, the case study assumes that these pressures would have created the central thrust of policy if the constraints and opportunities of the international economic structure had not been present. It may also be possible to isolate favored and suppressed policy options through "process tracing," or a detailed analysis of the policy-making process and the terms of political discourse. The argument set forth in Chapter 2, which states that the executive should be most responsive to the demands of the international economic structure and the legislature most responsive to domestic or societal pressures, facilitates this task by defining which domestic political actors *should* adopt which political viewpoint. All three forms of analysis are adopted in the case study.

CHAPTER TWO

Structure, the State, and Trade Strategy

The systemic theory set forth in Chapter 1 identifies the constraints and opportunities of the international economic structure. It argues that this structure creates a systemically "best" trade strategy, referred to as the national trade interest, for all countries. Given the need for national survival in an anarchic and competitive international environment, the conclusion posits a primacy for systemic concerns and argues that the trade strategies of nation-states will generally conform to the constraints and opportunities of the international economic structure.

This theory posits that countries have a strong stimulus to follow the incentives of the international system, but it is mute on the domestic process or mechanism by which these constraints and opportunities are communicated and translated into specific policies. The theory of international economic structure, like the Realist and neo-Realist traditions from which it is drawn, treats domestic politics as a "black box" in which a rational and unitary state exists. This chapter attempts to elucidate the insides of the black box to identify the agent and process by which the constraints and opportunities of the international economic structure are recognized and acted upon within the domestic political sphere so as to result in observable trade strategies.

In this chapter, I present a simplified conception of the interaction of the domestic and international political systems. I posit a state inclusive of the central government, functionally differentiated in its parts, and differing in the degree of autonomy possessed by its constituent parts. Following from this conception, I isolate two categories of actors within the state: the representative element, which serves as the basic link of the state to society and, as a result, primarily reflects the interests of society, and the foreign policy executive, which seeks to promote the power and wealth of the nation-state within an anarchic international system. Because of its concern with national power and wealth, the foreign policy executive, I argue, is particularly sensitive to the constraints and opportunities of the international economic structure and acts as a conduit through which these systemic incentives pass into the sphere of domestic politics. The foreign policy executive cannot act unilaterally, however, and must bargain with the politically mobilized groups within society and the representative element of the state. This bargaining process, in turn, is influenced by the structure of the state, which creates a particular pattern of political action which endures over time, and by executive or presidential leadership. The second half of this chapter provides an overview of the domestic political process in the United States in the period 1887–1939.

THE INTERNATIONAL SYSTEM, THE STATE,
AND DOMESTIC POLITICS

Following Max Weber, the state is defined as a "compulsory organization with a territorial basis" which monopolizes the legitimate use of force.[1] As such, it is "a relation of men dominating men"[2] and the sole source of authoritative decisions within a society. In short, the state is a governing apparatus which is distinct from and superordinate to society.

The state-society distinction embedded in this definition is useful because it emphasizes the hierarchical nature of government. Hierarchy exists within the state and between the state and society. Unlike pluralist conceptions of politics, which find the origins of all government actions in societal demands,[3] this approach allows for a more independent role for the state in the formulation of public policy. If societal approaches explain policy from the demand side, employing the state-society distinction allows for an investigation of the supply side.[4]

Yet the state itself does not exist in actuality. Like the very concept of a "system" central to the argument of Chapter 1, the state is merely an analytic notion, a useful fiction. Depending upon the larger theoretical

[1]Max Weber, *Economy and Society*, 2 vols., Guenther Roth and Claus Wittich, eds. (Berkeley: University of California Press, 1978), 1:56.

[2]Alfred Stepan, *The State and Society: Peru in Comparative Perspective* (Princeton: Princeton University Press, 1978), p. xii.

[3]The most developed "societal" explanations of tariff policy are found in the public choice literature; see note 1, in the Introduction.

[4]The distinction between demand- and supply-side explanations is made in Timothy McKeown, "Firms and Tariff Regime Change: Explaining the Demand for Protection," *World Politics* 36 (January 1984): 216.

context in which it is embedded, the concept of the state can vary along three interrelated and often confused dimensions. The state can be limited to central decision makers or nearly synonymous with government. It can be an instrument of society, relatively autonomous from society, or even wholly autonomous. And the state can be understood as a unified actor with a single set of interests, or an actor composed of hierarchically arranged but functionally differentiated parts possessing individual interests. The state, in this book, is assumed to be inclusive of the central government, functionally differentiated in its parts, and differing in the degree of autonomy obtained across its constituent parts.

The state has been conceived as both narrow, limited to only the central decision makers of the government who are relatively well insulated from domestic political pressures (the president and the secretary of state in the United States),[5] and extensive, as broad as the government.[6] These two perspectives appear to derive from different interpretations of the authoritative nature of the state. The first conception defines authoritative as "imposed," or not merely reflective of the interests of any group in society. Here, the composition of the state is problematic: only those decision makers who are or can be autonomous are included. Thus the state can vary in size and membership over time and across issue areas.

In this book I adopt an extensive definition of the state in which authoritative is defined as "binding"; decisions are legitimately enforced by the coercive power of the state whether or not they reflect the interests of some group(s) in society. In this conception, all parts of the governing apparatus—including the legislature and executive agencies highly permeated by societal groups—are seen as participating in the making of authoritative or legally binding political decisions. Here, the autonomy of the state is problematic: rather than equating autonomous decision makers and the state, this conception recognizes that states may differ in their degree of autonomy.

Although scholars have not commonly done so, this conception of the state also allows for it to be disaggregated into its various but nonetheless hierarchically arranged parts.[7] The foreign policy bureaucracy, for in-

---

[5] This perspective is taken most clearly in Stephen D. Krasner, *Defending the National Interest: Raw Materials Investments and U.S. Foreign Policy* (Princeton: Princeton University Press, 1978).

[6] For examples from a variety of theoretical perspectives, see Eric A. Nordlinger, *On the Autonomy of the Democratic State* (Cambridge: Harvard University Press, 1981); Theda Skocpol, *States and Social Revolutions* (New York: Cambridge University Press, 1979); and Martin Carnoy, *The State and Political Theory* (Princeton: Princeton University Press, 1984).

[7] The conception of the state developed here reintroduces a degree of bureaucratic and

stance, may possess a different mandate and purpose than the agricultural bureaucracy, but both are responsible to the chief executive. Similarly, the legislative and executive functions are conceptually distinct in nearly all countries, although the organizational relationship between them may differ cross-nationally. By disaggregating the state, this conception also allows for differences in autonomy across the various parts of the state, depending upon the function each performs. In nearly all advanced industrialized democracies, for example, the legislature is typically the least and the central bank the most independent component.

In the analysis of trade policy, the state can be simplified into two basic categories: the representative and the foreign policy elements.[8] The representative element includes the legislature, which serves as the principal link of the state to society, and the "constituent" agencies, such as the Departments of Agriculture, Commerce, and Labor in the United States. Although in some countries the legislature serves only to ratify and legitimize decisions made in other parts of the state, its more important function is to aggregate and channel societal interests into the political decision-making process. It is assumed here that legislators are primarily motivated by the desire for reelection and are therefore responsive to societal demands.[9] Thus individual members of the legislature, in one form or another, represent constituencies organized on a

---

"intrabranch" politics into the study of the state. On the former, see Graham T. Allison, *Essence of Decision* (Boston: Little, Brown, 1971); and Morton H. Halperin, *Bureaucratic Politics and Foreign Policy* (Washington, D.C.: Brookings, 1974). For the latter, see Robert A. Pastor, *Congress and the Politics of U.S. Foreign Economic Policy, 1929–1976* (Berkeley: University of California Press, 1980).

[8]Another important element of the state may be the economic agencies, such as the Treasury Department and the Federal Reserve Bank in the United States. As compared to the constituent agencies, the economic agencies possess broad, societywide institutional mandates. Whether focusing on the macroeconomy or economic development, these broader mandates allow the economic agencies to avoid capture by particularlistic interests, rendering the agencies at least relatively autonomous. Their concern for the economic performance of the nation-state makes the economic agencies sensitive to the international economy but not necessarily to the constraints and opportunities of the international economic structure. Although they are also unconcerned with the power of the nation-state, economic agencies charged with overseeing long-term economic development are an exception to this rule and may also demonstrate a regard for the relative gains from trade. The underlying motivation, however, remains domestic economic performance and not international power. In the period studied here, the economic agencies did not play an important role in the tariff-making process. As a result, they are excluded from the analysis. Today, their role is much greater and an examination of their interests and actions would be necessary.

[9]Central to Anthony Downs, *An Economic Theory of Democracy* (New York: Harper, 1957), this is now a widely accepted assumption in rational choice models of politics. See also David Mayhew, *Congress: The Electoral Connection* (New Haven: Yale University Press, 1975).

geographic basis. If the legislature is organized into substantive committees, these subunits will also represent functional societal interests.

Constituent agencies serve a similar function as the legislature. Possessing narrow institutional mandates, these agencies are easily "captured" by the interests they are designed to serve.[10] Capture can occur directly, through the appointment of interested personnel, or indirectly, as decision makers come to identify their own career interests and success with the well-being of their constituents. As the principal link between state and society, the representative elements are the least autonomous parts of the state. Indeed, they can be understood as merely reflecting the interests of society.

It is assumed here that individuals, who ultimately constitute society, pursue their material interests, defined as the maximization of their economic well-being. As these interests are pursued, society and the representative state elements are dominated by the politically mobilized groups within society. Latent or unformed groups can influence the political process only with great difficulty. Their one point of access to the political arena is the direct election of legislators, but it is nearly impossible to signal support for specific policy positions through them except perhaps in economically homogeneous electoral districts (such as rural agricultural areas). As Mancur Olson and others have demonstrated, groups have differing incentives to form and mobilize for political action. Small, homogeneous, and geographically concentrated groups, for instance, are more likely to form than large, variegated, and geographically dispersed groups. As a result, individuals and the groups they form possess differential access to the policy-making arena.[11] The representative elements of the state, in other words, are not truly "representative" of all societal interests. Rather, they principally reflect the interests of only those manifest groups that have successfully overcome problems inherent in taking collective action.

The foreign policy executive constitutes a second component of the state. Defined as executive officials, who typically face a national electorate, and high-ranking bureaucrats charged with the overall conduct of defense and foreign affairs, the foreign policy executive sits at the intersection of the domestic and international political systems and regulates the interaction between the two.[12] Most important, the foreign

[10] On bureaucratic capture, see Marver H. Bernstein, *Regulating Business by Independent Commission* (Princeton: Princeton University Press, 1955); and Grant McConnell, *Private Power and American Democracy* (New York: Knopf, 1967), pp. 246–97.

[11] Mancur Olson, *The Logic of Collective Action* (Cambridge: Harvard University Press, 1971).

[12] This point was first made by Otto Hintze in "Military Organization and the Organization of the State," in Felix Gilbert, ed., *The Historical Essays of Otto Hintze* (New York: Oxford University Press, 1975).

policy executive is the sole authoritative maker of foreign policy and the only national actor mandated to preserve and enhance the position of the nation-state within the anarchic and competitive international system. It is charged, in other words, with husbanding the nation-state's wealth and power given the interests and actions of other countries.[13] It is this unique position of the foreign policy executive which renders it particularly sensitive to the national trade interest and, in turn, to the international economic structure that shapes this interest.

The societal pressure brought to bear on the policy-making process through the representative element of the state must differ from the national trade interest of the foreign policy executive for three reasons. First, societal interests cannot aggregate into the national trade interest as defined here. A country's position within the international economic structure is determined by economic and political aggregates for the nation-state as a whole. All industries and producers are reflected in the measure of relative labor productivity and all importers and exporters are summed into the measure of relative size (see Chapter 1). Thus if problems inherent in collective action exist, as they surely do, and only some groups mobilize or become manifest, there is no reason to assume that the "bottom-up" interests of society will be identical to the "top-down" national trade interest of the foreign policy executive. Indeed, the greater the problems of collective action within society, the more these two interests must diverge.

Second, producer groups possess relatively narrow interests. They support protection when facing competition from imports in their own markets and oppose it only if threatened with retaliation against their products abroad. Groups have little incentive to oppose protection on their own products if another industry is likely to bear the costs of foreign retaliation. In the pursuit of national wealth and power, and in responding to its national rather than regional electorate, the foreign policy executive must take these trade-offs into account and make judgments about what is good for society as a whole. It must also make appropriate choices on the means to obtain these goals in the face of opposition or resistance from foreign national and state actors.

Third, to the extent that the executive's national trade interests are shaped by considerations of relative advantage over other countries, as might be expected within an anarchic and competitive international

[13]Although the individuals who constitute the foreign policy executive may be motivated by personalistic (career enhancement) and bureaucratic (budget maximization) concerns, it is assumed that their ability to fulfill these desires depends at least in part upon the development and implementation of "successful" foreign policies, with success defined as satisfying their institutional mandate or preserving and enhancing national wealth and power.

environment, the interests of the representative and foreign policy elements of the state must also diverge. In the pursuit of material interests, no group in society—even encompassing coalitions—has any incentive to maximize the relative resources or power of the nation-state. Group interests may, at times, complement this power interest, but they possess very different roots.

Parochialism

This is not to argue that the executive is entirely free from societal constraints. Presidents and prime ministers must periodically stand for election. Yet whereas the representative element of the state can be best understood as acting in the interests *of* society, to use Vilfredo Pareto's famous distinction, the executive acts in the interests *for* society.[14] The executive is responsible to all of society, charged with responsibility for foreign affairs, and, as a result, specifically concerned with the constraints and opportunities of the international economic structure.

Because competing trade interests exist within the domestic political arena, the foreign policy executive will rarely be able to translate its systemically derived policy preferences directly and unilaterally into trade strategy. In few countries is trade policy entirely within the purview of the foreign policy executive. Trade strategy affects society, and the representative element of the state can be expected to block or at least partially undermine foreign policy initiatives. Consequently, foreign policy leaders are dependent upon the support or at least the acquiescence of society and the representative element of the state. Support from society, and particularly from politically mobilized groups within society, is needed even in the most totalitarian countries. Coercion can substitute for societal consent, but it becomes extremely costly and decreasingly effective at high levels of state-society divergence. Such conflict will also be reflected in the state, as the representative and foreign policy elements split along functional lines, thereby rendering the effective use of coercion by the state problematic.

For the constraints and opportunities of the international economic structure to be transformed into public policies, they must pass through a bargaining process between the foreign policy executive and the politically mobilized groups in society as manifested in the representative element of the state. Resolution of the conflict between these sets of interests—whether in favor of one, the other, or both—is ultimately determined by many contextual factors. Two intervening variables, however, are important in the case study discussed in Part II.

Most fundamentally, the bargaining process is influenced by the distribution of authority within the state as codified into existing laws and

[14]Pareto is cited in Krasner, *Defending the National Interest*, p. 12.

72

institutions and referred to here as state structure. This structure forms
a continuum from near anarchy, in which competing centers of political
authority vie for leadership as in present-day Lebanon, to totalitarian-
ism, in which almost all forms of political control and influence are
centralized in the highest reaches of the state. Although this continuum
is not open to precise gradations, differences across countries can nonetheless be found. Among the advanced industrialized democracies,
Japan and France possess relatively centralized states and the United
States a relatively decentralized state.[15] State structure may also vary by
issue area. Because trade affects groups differentially and has direct
implications for national power, many societal and state actors will be
involved, and authority is likely to be torn between the representative
and foreign policy elements of the state. Monetary policy, on the other
hand, has relatively symmetrical effects and does not mobilize social
groups into the political process to the same extent as does trade. Thus
the overall autonomy of the state will be higher and authority will be
more concentrated.[16]

The structure of the state does not necessarily determine the outcome
of the bargaining process between the representative and foreign policy
elements. But by specifying which elements of the state possess authority over an issue and which actors can legitimately be involved in the
political process, the structure of the state does create a set of constraints
within which the bargaining process occurs. As argued below, the decentralized structure of the American state and the constitutional delegation of authority over international commercial policy to Congress
magnified the importance of society and the representative element of
the state in the United States during the nineteenth and early twentieth
centuries. The principal task for the foreign policy executive was to gain
legitimacy in and access to the trade policy-making arena. The state's
structure also conditions the bargaining strategies and resources open to
the representative and foreign policy elements. The foreign policy executive, for instance, can use its position at the intersection of the

---

[15]Peter J. Katzenstein, "Conclusion: Domestic Structures and Strategies of Foreign
Economic Policy," in Katzenstein, ed. *Between Power and Plenty: Foreign Economic Policies of
Advanced Industrial States* (Madison: University of Wisconsin Press, 1978), p. 324.

[16]See Stephen D. Krasner, "United States Commercial and Monetary Policy: Unravel-
ling the Paradox of External Strength and Internal Weakness," in Katzenstein, ed., *Between Power and Plenty*, pp. 51–87; Theodore J. Lowi, "American Business, Public Policy,
Case-Studies, and Political Theory," *World Politics* 16 (December 1964): 677–715; Joanne
Gowa, "Public Goods and Political Institutions: Trade and Monetary Policy Processes in
the United States," *International Organization* 42 (Winter 1988); and Stephen G. Walker
and Pat McGowan, "U.S. Foreign Economic Policy Formation: Neo-Marxist and Neo-
pluralist Perspectives," in William P. Avery and David P. Rapkin, eds., *America in a
Changing World Political Economy* (New York: Longman, 1982), pp. 207–24.

domestic and international political systems to redefine issues and build transnational coalitions to bind the nation-state. It can also mobilize new or existing societal groups with complementary interests into the political system so as to gain access to the representative element of the state.

At a more proximate level, presidential or executive leadership is also important in explaining the outcome of the bargaining process between the representative and foreign policy elements. Executives bring to office differing conceptions of appropriate executive-legislative roles and varying degrees of political acumen. Although it is difficult to generalize about this idiosyncratic factor, a president who has a strong view of his policy-making role or highly developed political skills is clearly more likely to obtain his wishes when faced with legislative opposition.

DOMESTIC POLITICS AND
AMERICAN TRADE STRATEGY, 1887–1939

Society

For an investigation of trade strategy, society can be conceptually divided into four broad and not necessarily homogeneous or exclusive groups: manufacturers (capitalists and workers), financiers, farmers, and consumers.[17] Measuring the protectionist or free-trade inclination of groups is always difficult. Nonetheless, it would appear that the domestic political position and interests of each group changed in important ways over the period 1887–1939.

The political importance of industry grew dramatically over the era. In 1890, 65 percent of the United States population resided in rural

[17]Despite the attention placed on interest groups in past studies of the tariff, surprisingly few studies have rigorously measured the size and material interests of various segments of society. Neither Becker nor Wilson, for instance, presents any empirical evidence on the influence or interests they ascribe to the manufacturing groups they examine. Rather, both rely solely on statements made by the leadership of selected organizations. See William H. Becker, *The Dynamics of Business-Government Relations: Industry and Exports, 1893–1921* (Chicago: University of Chicago Press, 1982); and Joan Hoff Wilson, *American Business and Foreign Policy, 1920–1933* (Boston: Beacon, 1971).

Bennett D. Baack and Edward John Ray test a more disaggregated interest-group explanation of American tariffs for 1870, 1910, and 1914. Although derived from within the tradition of endogenous tariff theory, several of their findings parallel the arguments developed here. They find no support for partisan political considerations as an explanation of tariff policy; a positive relationship between basic industries—which might be expected to possess considerable positive externalities—and tariffs; and a positive (but insignificant) relationship between tariffs and skill intensity of production and capital/labor ratios ("The Political Economy of Tariff Policy: A Case Study of the United States," *Explorations in Economic History* 20 [January 1983]: 73–93).

areas where little manufacturing activity occurred. By 1930, rural dwellers had declined to 44 percent of the population. Similarly, manufacturing's share of national income increased from 18.2 percent between 1889 and 1899 to a high of 21.9 percent between 1919 and 1929. Although not direct measures, these figures do indicate the growing political strength of industrial interests in the United States.

Export dependence provides a useful proxy for measuring the trade interests of industry.[18] Any industry with substantial markets abroad is likely to favor free trade for two reasons: in the absence of extraordinary export subsidies it is at least competitive with foreign rivals, and it may fear retaliation abroad for protection at home. Levels of export dependence for all of American manufacturing, disaggregated into fifteen sectors, are presented in Tables 2.1 and 2.2.

In 1889, the first census year in the period studied here, only the chemicals sector, which made up 4.5 percent of American manufacturing by value, exported more than 10 percent of its production (see Table 2.2).[19] The largest manufacturing sector of the economy, food and beverages, was moderately dependent, exporting 9.7 percent of its output. All other sectors exported less than 5 percent of their products. By 1899, two years after the passage of the protectionist Dingley Act, moderately export-dependent sectors more than doubled in value to 52.9 percent of American manufacturing. Although chemicals remained the only highly export-dependent industry, food and beverages

[18]Import penetration, or imports as a percent of the value of manufacturing, might be the best measure, but it would certainly give misleading results in an economy with moderate to high levels of protection and, more important, in which levels of protection fluctuated dramatically. Using export dependence yields more accurate results with one important qualification: it magnifies the importance of the non-export-dependent industries, which are otherwise assumed to be protectionist, by lumping the non-traded-goods industries and import-penetrated industries together. This is offset, in part, by those competitive industries which choose not to export heavily, perhaps because the domestic market is not yet saturated. For a similar approach, see Glenn R. Fong, "Export Dependence versus the New Protectionism: Constraints on Trade Policy in the Industrial World" (Ph.D. diss., Cornell University, 1983); and Helen Milner, "Resisting the Protectionist Temptation: Industry and the Making of Trade Policy in France and the U.S. in the 1970s," paper presented at the Annual Meeting of the American Political Science Association, August 28–31, 1986.

[19]These figures and the data displayed in Tables 2.1 and 2.2 should be treated skeptically. I consider them to be only estimates of the level of export dependence. No single source presents both manufacturing output and trade flows for this period, nor was there any standard classification for industries. As a result, the disaggregated trade data had to be combined into categories resembling the fifteen industries listed in the census. Definitions of categories were often incomplete in both sources, so there may be errors in the classifications. Redefinitions of categories over time create a second problem. Agricultural implements, for instance, were classified as miscellaneous until 1919 and as machinery thereafter. As long as the data are treated with the proper caution, however, I do not believe the errors are debilitating.

Table 2.1. Export dependence of American manufacturing, 1887–1939 (sectors measured by value of manufacturing and grouped by level of exports)*

Year	Low exports < or = 5 percent of sectoral production	Medium exports > or = 5.1 percent and < or = 10.0 percent of sectoral production	High exports > or = 10.1 percent of sectoral production
1889	71.8	23.6	4.5
1899	42.4	52.9	4.7
1909	36.4	63.6	0.0
1919	38.0	25.2	36.8
1929	63.8	30.9	5.3

*Rows may not sum to 100 because of rounding.
SOURCES: U.S. Bureau of the Census, *Abstract of the Twelfth Census of the U.S., 1900* (Washington, D.C.: U.S. Government Printing Office [GPO], 1904), Table 156, p. 324; U.S. Bureau of the Census, *Abstract of the Fourteenth Census of the U.S., 1920* (Washington, D.C.: GPO, 1922), Table 26, p. 1054; U.S. Bureau of the Census, *Abstract of the Fifteenth Census of the U.S., 1930* (Washington, D.C.: GPO, 1933), Table 6, p. 760; U.S. Treasury Department, *Foreign Commerce and Navigation, Immigration, and Tonnage of the U.S. for the Year Ending June 30, 1890* (Washington, D.C.: GPO, 1891), Table 10, pp. 404–10; U.S. Treasury Department, *Foreign Commerce and Navigation of the U.S. for the Year Ending June 30, 1900*, Vol. 1. (Washington, D.C.: GPO, 1900), Table 8, pp. 749–53; Bureau of Statistics, U.S. Department of Commerce and Labor, *Foreign Commerce and Navigation of the U.S. for the Year Ending June 30, 1910* (Washington, D.C.: GPO, 1911), Table VII, pp. 71–76, and Table 8, pp. 838–45; Bureau of Foreign and Domestic Commerce, U.S. Department of Commerce, *Foreign Commerce and Navigation of the U.S. for the Calendar Year 1919* (Washington, D.C.: GPO, 1920), Table VII, pp. xxix–xxxix, and Table X, pp. liii–lvii; Bureau of Foreign and Domestic Commerce, U.S. Department of Commerce, *Foreign Commerce and Navigation of the U.S. for the Calendar Year 1929*, Vol. 1 (Washington, D.C.: GPO, 1929), Table XII, pp. xviii–xl, and Table XVIII, pp. lxx–lxxi.

now exported 9.3 percent of its output, nonferrous metals 9.2 percent, iron and steel 6.8 percent, and miscellaneous industries—covering everything from agricultural implements to dental goods, to glue, musical instruments, and toys—5.6 percent. In 1909, no sector exported more than 10 percent of its output. Chemical exports as a proportion of total output declined, and chemicals joined the four sectors just noted and leather in the moderately export-dependent category. These industries now constituted approximately 63.6 percent of American manufacturing. Thus over the period 1889 to 1909, American manufacturers became relatively more export-dependent and, by implication, liberal, although the movement in this direction after the turn of the century was not strong.

As a result of increased foreign demand in wartime, the export dependence of American manufacturers expanded. In 1919, 25.2 percent of

Table 2.2. Export dependence (XD) of American manufacturing, by sector and value of manufacturing (VM)

Sector	1889 VM	1889 XD	1899 VM	1899 XD	1909 VM	1909 XD	1919 VM	1919 XD	1929 VM	1929 XD
Chemicals	4.54	19.21	4.68	25.15	7.54	8.56	6.25[a]	7.94[a]	5.43	4.58
Petroleum	-	-	-	-	-	-	3.76	15.74	5.27	14.35
Food and beverages	23.64[a]	9.75[a]	22.84[a]	9.29[a]	22.79[a]	5.62[a]	20.95	15.08	17.38[a]	4.03[a]
Iron and steel	13.68	2.23	15.18	6.80	15.64	5.66	9.68	10.02	10.32	4.12
Machinery	-	-	-	-	-	-	7.84	10.67	10.18	8.70
Leather	5.83	2.55	4.94	4.68	4.91	5.30	4.29	11.61	2.75	3.18
Forest products	10.50	3.23	8.72	3.83	7.85	4.76	5.12	5.52	5.19	5.17
Miscellaneous	7.72	4.59	8.50	5.63	6.59	8.74	4.92	4.33	4.95	3.35
Rubber	-	-	-	-	-	-	1.87	4.92	1.61	6.89
Tobacco	2.53	1.83	2.39	2.12	2.06	1.15	-	-	-	-
Nonferrous metals	3.79	2.19	6.34	9.20	6.13	8.72	4.14	8.03	5.20	6.72
Paper and printing	5.33	0.70	5.13	1.54	5.83	1.40	4.95	2.95	7.32	1.38
Stone, glass, and clay	2.75	0.98	2.48	1.89	2.63	2.06	1.83	4.86	2.26	4.18
Textiles	15.09	1.00	13.86	1.84	15.25	1.43	15.14	4.40	13.36	1.44
Vehicles	4.60[b]	1.26[b]	4.93[b]	1.73[b]	2.78	3.67	9.25[b]	4.65[b]	8.74	9.72

[a] Includes wines.
[b] Includes shipbuilding.
SOURCES: See Table 2.1.

United States industry exported between 5 and 10 percent of its output and 36.8 percent exported more than 10 percent of its production. Because the ratio of low-export-dependent industries remained relatively constant, it is clear that the dramatic increase in highly export-dependent industries came largely at the expense of the middle category. Industries that did not export significantly before the war were similarly disadvantaged during and after the hostilities. By 1929, after a decade of relative domestic prosperity, levels of export dependence had fallen to more traditional ranges and had receded below their prewar marks. Only petroleum, which until 1919 was not important enough to warrant a separate census category, exported more than 10 percent of its output, and vehicles, machinery, rubber, nonferrous metals, and forest products (largely manufactures of wood) exported more than 5 percent of their production.

This trend toward declining export dependence and, in turn, liberalness, was partially offset by rising foreign direct investment by American industry, which took hold in the late nineteenth century and accelerated rapidly after World War I. In 1929, the leading foreign investors (foreign direct investment divided by book value of fixed capital, by sector) were in machinery and equipment (23.3 percent), mining and petroleum (17.7), motor vehicles (14.9), and rubber products (13.8).[20] Although the categories differ slightly, the similarity between this list and that of the export-dependent industries in Table 2.2 is striking. The most important foreign investors were also the most export-dependent industries. As a result, it is possible to infer that increased foreign direct investment did not create new interests in trade liberalization, but most likely served to reinforce the liberal tendencies of the already export-dependent sectors. Thus the essential political cleavage between sectors was not affected, but the commitment to a liberal trade policy was probably strengthened for sectors that both invested in and exported to foreign markets.

From these trends in the industrial structure of the United States, it is possible to infer that the underlying need and demand for trade protection by American manufacturers gradually eased over the period examined here. Export dependence rose until 1919, and its later decline was partially offset by increased foreign direct investment. As more industries exported and later invested abroad, they reflected the new underlying competitive strength of the American economy and developed important cross-cutting cleavages in trade policy.

[20]See Jeff Frieden, "Sectoral Conflict and U.S. Foreign Economic Policy, 1914–1940," *International Organization* 42 (Winter 1988).

The dominant political pressures on Congress nonetheless remained protectionist. The statistics on export-dependence just cited do not capture collective action problems. Both Joan Hoff Wilson and William H. Becker, in their widely cited studies of the role of business in American politics during this period, confirm the already well-accepted observation that protectionist producers organize more readily than free-trade producers or consumers. Both Wilson and Becker find that smaller and less internationally competitive industries were more politically active on the tariff than were the larger, more internationally competitive sectors, which tended to become involved in tariff making only when their interests were directly threatened.[21] Although the underlying demand for protection within the United States may have eased slightly over the period, the protectionists still sang louder than others in the chorus serenading Congress.

Before World War I, the interests of American finance were closely linked to those of industry and, by implication, were largely protectionist. Finance began to expand its international lending decades before, but these foreign activities remained relatively small compared to domestic operations. During and after World War I, however, American finance greatly expanded its role in the international economy and developed interests separate from those of American industry as a whole. As a net creditor after the war, the United States played a major role in international financial markets. American banks now possessed an interest in Europe's ability to pay, which necessitated lower tariffs in the United States and a reversal in America's traditional balance-of-trade surplus. In advocating a more liberal trade strategy, American finance allied itself not with industry as a whole but only with the largest and most internationally oriented segments of the industrial community.[22]

As American industry and finance became more internationalist over time, agriculture drifted toward protectionism.[23] Southern farmers, the world's premier growers of cotton and tobacco, feared few competitors and generally supported free trade throughout the late nineteenth and early twentieth centuries. As high-cost producers of wool, Northeastern and Midwestern sheep growers benefited from protection and sup-

[21]Becker, *Dynamics of Business-Government Relations*; and Wilson, *American Business and Foreign Policy.*

[22]The changing interests of finance are best described by Jeffry A. Frieden, "Studies in International Finance: Private Interest and Public Policy in the International Political Economy" (Ph.D. diss., Columbia University, 1984), pp. 29–110; see also Wilson, *American Business and Foreign Policy*, pp. 16 and 110.

[23]One of the best overviews of farm interests and policy is Murray R. Benedict, *Farm Policies of the United States, 1790–1950* (New York: American Book–Stratford Press, 1953).

79

ported the policy (see Chapter 3). The interests of most farmers, however, were more complex and mixed.

In the early phases of the period studied here, farmers sold most of their products in the home market and were largely indifferent or slightly favorable to protection, believing—perhaps not without merit— that high tariffs provided a spur to domestic economic growth. After 1902, however, the ranks of farmers began to split as the "Iowa idea" gained widespread attention. Because farmers sold their marginal products in the unprotected international market, which thereby determined prices in the domestic market as well, and bought their goods in the protected home market, the Iowa idea convinced many farmers that they were actually suffering rather than benefiting from high tariff policies—leading some Republican legislators from the Midwest to vote against the party's Payne-Aldrich Act of 1909.

By 1921, farmers had reversed their position and become generally supportive of protection. After World War I, agricultural prices fell and stocks rose dramatically. The new position of the United States as a net creditor and the confusion over war debts and reparations limited the ability of Europeans to import American agricultural goods. And as European farmers returned to production, facilitated by renewed protection, prices fell (see Chapter 5). As Murray R. Benedict notes, "By the spring of 1921, American agriculture found itself in a more unfavorable position than it had experienced at any time in the memory of men then living, or possibly at any time since the nation's beginnings."[24] Yet conditions grew worse. This prolonged crisis altered the historic position of American agriculture in the nation's trade balances. A major contributor to the national trade surplus before 1919, farm imports exceeded farm exports on a regular basis after the mid-1920s.[25]

Protection now offered a real advantage to agriculture, and farmers supported it wholeheartedly, demanding and receiving increased protection for their products in 1921, 1922, and 1930. As the logrolling found by E. E. Schattschneider in the making of the Smoot-Hawley Tariff of 1930 demonstrates, farmers were increasingly willing to offer their support to manufacturers in return for increased tariffs on farm commodities.[26]

Nearly all Americans were both producers and consumers in the period 1887–1939, although few identified themselves with the latter.

[24]Ibid., p. 172.

[25]See David A. Lake, "Export, Die, or Subsidize: The International Political Economy of American Agriculture, 1875–1940," *Comparative Studies in Society and History* (forthcoming).

[26]E. E. Schattschneider, *Politics, Pressures, and the Tariff* (New York: Prentice-Hall, 1935).

Protectionists consistently emphasized the benefits of higher profits and wages for producers. Tariff reformers noted that the tariff led to higher prices and, despite higher wages, lower real incomes. Even though the second position is paramount today, the protectionists were clearly winning the rhetorical war before World War II.

When Louis D. Brandeis appeared before the House Ways and Means Committee in 1897 as a "representative of the consumers," he was jeered by the audience. Yet the emergent middle class, led by Brandeis and other progressive reformers, soon mobilized—albeit weakly—consumer interests into the tariff-making process. As Walter Lippmann wrote in 1914, "We hear a great deal about the class-consciousness of labor. . . . My own observation is that in America today consumers'-consciousness is growing very much faster." This consumer consciousness was driven by the rapidly expanding "new middle class," composed of technicians and salaried professionals, clerical workers, salespeople, and public service personnel. Whereas the population as a whole increased by 230 percent between 1870 and 1910, this new middle class grew by almost 800 percent, from 756,000 to 5,609,000 people.[27]

Despite their consumer consciousness and in part because of their rapidly growing numbers, these new white-collar workers were difficult to mobilize, and they exerted little direct impact on the producer-dominated and relatively closed congressional tariff-making process. The one exception occurred in 1913, when Woodrow Wilson made a strong appeal to the public in general and his progressive supporters in particular to offset the influence of the tariff lobby (see Chapter 5).

It is virtually impossible to aggregate the political influence of these four conceptual groups within society and reach a definitive statement on the balance between the pressures supporting free trade or protection exerted on the tariff-making process and manifested in Congress, the principal representative agency of the state. Nonetheless, several tentative conclusions may be suggested. Industry and finance gradually became more internationalized and liberal over time, although protectionists continued to be politically dominant in the former. Although its interests were mixed beforehand, agriculture clearly moved in a protectionist direction after 1919. Consumers emerged as a political force after the turn of the century and supported a policy of freer trade, but their influence in the halls of Congress was relatively minor. In sum, protectionist pressures, at the very least, were mixed and most likely did not expand in importance during the period 1887 to 1939. Although societal interests may have become more liberal over time, protectionist

[27]Richard Hofstadter, *The Age of Reform: From Bryan to F.D.R.* (New York: Vintage, 1955), pp. 172, 218; Lippmann quoted p. 171.

interests continued to exert a disproportionate influence because of the inherent difficulties of mobilizing latent free-trade-oriented manufacturers and consumers. Thus, although the predictions of the interest-group model are not particularly clear, there seems to be little reason to expect significant shifts in trade strategy during this period. Specific anomalies for an explanation of trade strategy based on interest groups are discussed in Part II.

Societal factors are most important in this analysis as a counterweight to the national trade interest derived from the international economic structure. As discussed in Chapter 1, the United States remained an opportunist throughout the period examined here. The national trade interest is consequently reflected in the preference ordering P/FT > FT/ FT > P/P > FT/P. The preference ordering of American society during this same period appears to have been P/FT > P/P > FT/FT > FT/P. The first preference, P/FT, satisfied both protectionists and export-oriented sectors. Assuming that protectionists dominated Congress, P/P would then be preferred over FT/FT. The last preference, of course, was FT/P, because both protectionists and export-oriented sectors would be dissatisfied. Although the absolute differences between the national trade interest and society's trade interest may have varied over the period, the central conflict between society and the representative element of the state, on one hand, and the foreign policy executive, on the other, clearly revolved around the second and third options. In the first and second phases of American trade strategy (discussed in Chapters 3 and 4, respectively), when the United States could free ride on Britain's hegemonic leadership and obtain its first choice of P/FT, little conflict existed between society and the foreign policy executive. Both the national trade interest and societal demands could be easily reconciled. Only when Britain declined and the United States could no longer free ride would conflict between the foreign policy and representative elements of the state become acute.

The State and State Structure

In the United States, Congress is the principal representative element of the state. During the period studied here, three constituent agencies were formed: the Departments of Agriculture, Commerce, and Labor. Despite their role as representatives of specific functional interests, these agencies played relatively minor roles in the debates over trade policy.[28] Congress was central. In this body geographic constituents are

[28]The Department of Agriculture was formed as the Agricultural Division of the Patent Office in 1839, established as a separate agency with bureau status in 1862, and elevated to a regular department with cabinet rank in 1889. The department was the first single-interest service agency in the government. Until the expansion of agricultural support

represented by individual legislators, and functional interests, with a degree of overlap, are represented by substantive committees. Within Congress, trade policy is formulated primarily by the House Ways and Means Committee and the Senate Finance Committee. The foreign policy executive is principally composed of the president, in his role as commander in chief of the armed forces and head of government, and the State Department.[29]

The American state is relatively decentralized but not anarchic. Perhaps more than any other, the American state was designed to be fragmented. Fearful of centralized political power, the founding fathers purposely dispersed authority within the governing apparatus. They also created numerous checks and balances by giving many if not all parts of the state a role in each and every policy decision. This system has led, as Samuel Huntington notes, to a "fusion of functions and division of power."[30] The decentralized structure of the American state is highlighted by international comparisons. As Peter J. Katzenstein cogently summarizes,

> The structure of French governmental institutions is highly centralized and their functions are differentiated. In the United States that structure is

---

programs in the 1930s, the Department of Agriculture focused primarily on education, seeking to improve agricultural methods and disseminate this knowledge to farmers.

The Department of Commerce and Labor was created in 1903. Its early mandate was to support smaller businesses, which needed extra assistance compared to larger firms in their quest for foreign markets. The initial mandate of the Commerce Department was reconceptualized under the leadership of William C. Redfield, appointed as secretary of commerce by Woodrow Wilson in 1913. Redfield was the first secretary actively to court support from big business for the department. Ostensibly seeking to bridge the gap between small and large business, Redfield concentrated his efforts on the latter. The department avoided the tariff issue because of its divisiveness. No clear stand could be taken on this issue without alienating some important group of business constituents. After the war, the power and role of the Commerce Department expanded, in large part because of the personal influence and prestige of Herbert Hoover, the new secretary. As secretary, Hoover sought to exert greater control over international economic relations, thereby challenging the traditional supremacy of the State Department in foreign policy. Despite strong support from the business community, Hoover was ultimately unsuccessful. The role of the Commerce Department in the tariff-making process during the 1920s was strongly colored by the moderately protectionist views of the secretary (see Chapter 6).

The Department of Labor was separated from Commerce in 1913. Although organized labor was generally but not unanimously free-trade-oriented in the 1920s and 1930s, the Labor Department took a protectionist stand. In 1927, James L. Davis, the second secretary of labor and a former union official, maintained that workers' interests were best promoted by protection. The agency's stand was invoked by protectionists to support their cause, but the Department of Labor itself was not a key actor in the tariff-making process, perhaps because of its split with organized labor on this issue.

[29]The secretary of war, later renamed defense, might also be included in the foreign policy executive, although in the period examined here he was seldom involved in trade policy.

[30]Samuel Huntington, *Political Order in Changing Societies* (New Haven: Yale University Press, 1968), p. 110.

decentralized and fused. The French conception of authority as absolute and the concentration of power in the state contrasts with the American view of authority as circumscribed and the conception of power ameliorated by a system of checks and balances. General de Gaulle represented the French state as a President-in-tails, pursuing the art of statecraft in magisterial aloofness from everyday politics. Richard Neustadt's description of Truman typifies him as a President-in-shorts ready for continual bargaining and persuasion and always in search of a deal. France has been faulted for the "overinstitutionalization" of its political institutions, America for its "underinstitutionalization."[31]

The decentralized structure of the state clearly constrains the policy-making process. As David B. Truman notes, the "diffusion of leadership and disintegration of policy are not hallucinations."[32] In seeking to create a political system responsive to the varied needs of society, the designers of the Constitution ensured an ongoing struggle among the elements of the state, that policy would ultimately result from the striking of pragmatic bargains, and that overall coherency in policy would be low.

In the Constitution, Congress was given specific authority to raise revenue and set tariff rates. Depositing that authority with Congress ensured that trade policy would be responsive to the needs of society, or at least the needs of politically mobilized groups within society. The tariff is an infinitely divisible and symmetrical political good. Congress can easily divide categories of goods and "tailor-make" rates for individual producers. During the period 1887–1934, societal conflict on the tariff was resolved through logrolling or the creation of encompassing coalitions.[33] As Senator Knute Nelson of Minnesota sarcastically noted during the Payne-Aldrich debate in 1909, the tariff was based on the principle of "You tickle me and I tickle you. You give us what we on the Pacific Coast want for our lead ore and for our citrus fruit, and we will tickle you people of New England and give you what you want on your cotton goods."[34] Even with the passage of the Reciprocal Trade Agreements Act in 1934, an event often interpreted as signaling an enhancement of the executive's role in the formulation of trade policy, Congress still maintained ultimate control by ceding authority to the president for

[31]Peter J. Katzenstein, "International Relations and Domestic Structures: Foreign Economic Policies of Advanced Industrial States," *International Organization* 30 (Winter 1976): 15–16.
[32]David B. Truman, *The Governmental Process: Political Interests and Public Opinion*, 2d ed. (New York: Knopf, 1971), p. 529.
[33]See Lowi, "American Business," for the best theoretical grounding of this classic argument.
[34]Quoted in Richard Cleveland Baker, *The Tariff under Roosevelt and Taft* (Hastings, Neb.: Democrat Printing, 1941), pp. 89–90.

only limited periods of time. In the era studied here, Congress reigned supreme and served the interests of the many producers who clamored for aid.

For the same reason that Congress was dominant in issues regarding trade, the president and the State Department were relatively isolated from the policy-making process. This is not to argue that the foreign policy executive lacked influence. The distribution of authority did, however, create a specific pattern of intrastate and state-society relations which endured over the entire period.

The principal political task for the foreign policy executive was to penetrate and gain access to the otherwise closed and jealously guarded congressional tariff-making process. The president, of course, possesses veto power over any tariff bill passed by Congress. But because of the months of work and careful bargaining that Congress normally devoted to omnibus tariff legislation and the identification of the tariff as a "party issue," the president was often reluctant to exercise his veto power; in the period studied, the president explicitly threatened such action only in 1894, 1909, and 1930, and these threats were not taken seriously. More often, the president would intervene informally through the definition of the party platform and consultations with congressional leaders to shape the final legislation. Nevertheless, the informal power and personal influence of the president ultimately rested in the legislature's need to obtain executive approval of the tariff bill. The State Department, and more precisely, the secretary of state—often the individual most clearly cognizant of the constraints and opportunities of the international economic structure—could also shape legislation through consultation and the exercise of personal influence. Though lacking the veto power of the president, the secretary often exercised considerable influence because the post was normally awarded to an "elder statesman" of the party.

The foreign policy executive possesses two strategies for increasing its leverage over tariff policy. Despite its relative isolation from the tariff-making process, the foreign policy executive can mobilize societal groups with complementary interests into the policy-making process. Numerous domestic coalitions potentially exist. During the period examined here, American society was far from united on questions of protection or free trade and activism or passivism. And as Kenneth Arrow's paradox and coalition theory indicate, even under weak and plausible assumptions, majorities and coalitions are likely to be unstable.[35] The structure of interests facing the government is not rigid or

[35]Kenneth Arrow, *Social Choice and Individual Values*, 2d ed. (New Haven: Yale University Press, 1963); on coalition theory see Robert Abrams, *Foundations of Political Analysis* (New York: Columbia University Press, 1980), pp. 41–101 and 235–79.

predetermined. Instead, it resembles a clay which the relatively autonomous elements of the state can—within limits—mold and shape in ways they desire. To the extent that society is open to manipulation, the role of the foreign policy executive is magnified in importance. Somewhat paradoxically, one implication of a decentralized state structure is that it creates many actors and points of entry into the government.

By appealing to particular groups whose interests overlapped with its own, the foreign policy executive during the period examined here was able to circumvent the usual protectionist lobbies and place new offsetting pressures on Congress. As discussed in more detail below, Secretary of State James G. Blaine adopted this strategy in 1890 when he rallied midwestern farmers, who had not previously been active on the tariff issue, behind his proposal for bilateral reciprocity agreements with Latin America. President Woodrow Wilson followed a similar course in 1913, when he denounced the tariff lobby and thereby activated his progressive supporters. By mobilizing various groups, the foreign policy executive was able to turn the decentralized structure of the state into a source of strength.

The foreign policy executive's second strategy is to use its unique position at the intersection of the domestic and international political systems to generate several entries into the otherwise closed congressional tariff-making process. The foreign policy executive can redefine domestic political issues as foreign policy issues, thereby gaining a legitimate policy-making role it otherwise would not have and strengthening its influence relative to its own society. Accordingly, President Grover Cleveland initiated the process of redefining the tariff in 1887, when he emphasized the export advantages that would derive from his duty-free raw materials program. From then on, nearly every president emphasized the foreign policy implications of the tariff. The foreign policy executive can also use its authority to enter into legitimate transnational coalitions and thereby change the options facing Congress. The final recommendations of the International American Conference of 1890 proposed—partly at Secretary of State Blaine's urging—that bilateral reciprocity agreements be used to expand trade within the hemisphere. By agreeing to the recommendations of the conference as an official representative of the United States, Blaine effectively increased his bargaining leverage relative to the protectionists in Congress. If the legislature now failed to adopt reciprocity, it would risk disappointing the same Latin American countries the United States had so recently attempted to court. Secretary of State Cordell Hull attempted a similar but ultimately unsuccessful strategy in 1933, when he set off for the London Economic Conference with hopes of obtaining the consent of other countries to the opening of negotiations for global tariff reductions.

86

A focus on the structure of the state reveals which elements of the state will be the primary locus of decision making in a particular issue area and the domestic political strategies available to the relatively isolated foreign policy executive. Although the structure of the state does not determine outcomes, it does create a pattern of politics which endures over time. The legislature's constitutionally delegated authority over trade policy forced the foreign policy executive to influence Congress indirectly by mobilizing social groups. In doing so, it transformed its isolation into an important source of influence. The foreign policy executive was also able to use its role as the sole authoritative maker of foreign policy to redefine the political debate and alter congressional options.

CONCLUSION

To the extent that Realists and neo-Realists have looked inside the black box of domestic politics, they have seen only a rational and unitary state acting in the often vaguely defined national interest. In this chapter, I started from this familiar ground but took a different path. By disaggregating the state, domestic politics once again becomes important.

The foreign policy executive is the critical link in the process by which the constraints and opportunities of the international economic structure are transformed into trade strategy. Concerned with national power and welfare, the foreign policy executive seeks to adopt strategies consistent with the national trade interest. In doing so, the foreign policy executive acts as a conduit, channeling the constraints and opportunities of the international economic structure into the domestic political process.

Yet despite the efforts of the foreign policy executive, the nation-state may choose not to follow its national trade interests. Competing demands exist. Society pursues its material interests through the representative elements of the state. Because of the relative nature of power and problems of collective action, the politically mobilized societal interests must differ from the national trade interest. Out of the resulting bargaining process, trade policy emerges, but not necessarily in a form consistent with the desires of the foreign policy executive.

Despite the disproportionate authority granted to Congress, American trade strategy in the period 1887–1939 did reflect the constraints and opportunities of the international economic structure. In the early phases of the period, societal interests and the national trade interest, though not identical, were not incompatible. Each set of interests could be satisfied at little or no cost to the other. Later, confronting a national trade interest which increasingly pointed toward the need for freer trade, the foreign policy executive was able to force through a fundamental reform of the tariff immediately before World War I. Finally, as the national trade interest continued to grow out of step with societal interests, the foreign policy executive was able to gain primary control over the tariff in the 1920s and 1930s. This historical progression of policy and the policy-making process highlights the success of the domestic political strategies adopted by the foreign policy executive and suggests the importance and high political salience of the constraints and opportunities of the international economic structure.

PART II

AMERICAN
TRADE STRATEGY

CHAPTER THREE

Free Riding on
Free Trade, 1887–1897

During the decade between 1887 and 1897, the United States transformed its tariff from a passive instrument of pure protection into a more active tool which could protect the home market and aid in the expansion of American exports. The two national political parties were bitterly divided on the tariff during this period.[1] The Democrats called for duty-free raw materials, while the Republicans campaigned on protectionism and, after 1890, trade expansion through bilateral reciprocity agreements. Despite their differences in rhetoric, however, the two parties pursued common goals and trade strategies in the early 1890s. Both sought to maintain the "American system" of moderately high protection. Both also sought to expand American exports, particularly to Latin America, by lowering tariffs within the United States on a selected and limited number of raw materials. The question that confronted Americans at this time was not free trade versus protection but how best to expand American exports while incurring the smallest disruption to the American system. Despite their intense rivalry, Republicans and Democrats offered surprisingly similar answers.

The opportunity to pursue both protection and export expansion was created by the position of the United States as an opportunist within an international economic structure of British hegemony. America's increasing relative productivity generated both the ability and the incentive to expand exports, and Britain's openness and leadership within the

[1]Tom E. Terrill, *The Tariff, Politics, and American Foreign Policy, 1874–1901* (Westport, Conn.: Greenwood, 1973), examines the intense rivalry between the Democratic and Republican parties and their stands on the tariff during this period. Terrill argues that the tariff was so contentious because it was the only issue on which the two major parties could disagree without alienating their important ethnic and religious constituencies.

91

international economy left the United States free to adopt protection at home. As an opportunist within a structure of British hegemony, the United States had the ability to free ride. It could, in other words, obtain its preferred outcome of protection at home and free trade abroad (P/FT) with little or no direct cost to itself. The United States consciously accepted this opportunity.

THE INTERNATIONAL ECONOMIC STRUCTURE, 1887–1897

During the period from 1887 to 1897, the United Kingdom was the largest nation within the international economy, controlling twice the trade of its nearest rivals. It was also the most productive country, although its lead over the United States was gradually declining (see Table 1.1). Despite the recent growth of protectionism in Europe and elsewhere, Great Britain remained committed to free trade and a liberal international economic regime.[2] Correspondingly, tariffs were low, as they had been since 1846, and Britain continued to support open-door or nondiscriminatory policies at home, abroad, and in its colonies.[3] Not until 1896, at the close of this first phase, would a significant movement for tariff protection emerge in the United Kingdom.[4]

Despite its advocacy of liberalism abroad, the United Kingdom appears to have made little if any real effort to reverse the slide toward protection begun in Europe during the Great Depression of 1873–97 and in the United States after the Civil War.[5] Rather than seeking to encourage more liberal trade policies in its principal competitors, Brit-

[2] For an overview of British trade policy in this era, see F. W. Hirst, *From Adam Smith to Philip Snowden: A History of Free Trade in Europe* (New York: Adelphi, 1925); S. B. Saul, *Studies in British Overseas Trade, 1870–1914* (Liverpool: Liverpool University Press, 1960); Albert H. Imlah, *Economic Elements in the Pax Britannica: Studies in British Foreign Trade in the Nineteenth Century* (Cambridge: Harvard University Press, 1958); and Peter A. Gourevitch, "International Trade, Domestic Coalitions, and Liberty: Comparative Responses to the Crisis of 1873–1896," *Journal of Interdisciplinary History* 8 (Autumn 1977): 281–313.

[3] Tariff levels varied over the British colonies. At this time, however, all possessed "open-door" or nondiscriminatory tariff structures. Thus Britain received no special tariff favors from her colonies.

[4] This tariff reform movement was led by Colonial Secretary Joseph Chamberlain, who proposed and championed an imperial preference scheme (see Chapters 4 and 5).

[5] Britain settled instead for its second choice of free trade at home and protection abroad (FT/P in the southwest cell of Figure 1.2). For Britain, the costs of inducing or coercing the United States and other European powers into pursuing greater free trade appears to have exceeded the benefits likely to be obtained from such action. For the limited efforts taken by Britain, see Timothy J. McKeown, "Hegemonic Stability Theory and 19th Century Tariff Levels in Europe," *International Organization* 37 (Winter 1983): 73–91; and Arthur A. Stein, "The Hegemon's Dilemma: Great Britain, the United States and the International Economic Order," *International Organization* 38 (Winter 1984): 355–86.

92

ain increasingly turned toward the developing markets of Asia, Latin America, and Africa, where its political and economic superiority was more secure.[6]

That the continued openness of the British market left the country vulnerable to the policies of its competitors was recognized by Lord Salisbury in a speech at Hastings on May 22, 1892: "We live in an age of a war of tariffs. Every nation is trying . . . [to] get the greatest possible protection for its own industries, and at the same time the greatest possible access to the markets of its neighbors. . . . In this great battle Great Britain has deliberately stripped herself of the armor and the weapons by which the battle has to be fought. . . . by saying that we will levy no duties on anybody." In concluding, Lord Salisbury sounded a theme that was to become prevalent in forthcoming decades: free trade "may be noble, but it is not business."[7] In the early 1890s, however, business had not yet usurped nobility in Britain's commercial relations.

For the United States, the international economic structure of British hegemony created an era of nearly unparalleled opportunity. As a result of Britain's commitment to free trade, the United States was able to pursue and obtain its preferred trade strategy (P/FT), or first choice in the preference orderings identified in Chapter 1.[8] By absorbing approximately half of all American exports at this time, the openness of the British market satisfied, in large part, the desire of the United States for free trade abroad.[9] The United Kingdom's passivity, as Salisbury recognized, also enabled the United States to exploit British policy. The United States was able to build a tariff wall around its domestic market to protect its increasing returns industries from competitive imports without fear of British retaliation. Somewhat paradoxically, even though the

[6]See E. J. Hobsbawm, *Industry and Empire: The Making of Modern English Society*, Vol. 2, *1750 to the Present* (New York: Pantheon, 1968), pp. 110–26.

[7]Reprinted in James P. Boyd, *Men and Issues of '92* (n.p.: Publishers Union, 1892), pp. 191–92.

[8]France and Germany enjoyed similar opportunities. As spoilers, both countries had strong preferences for protection at home and free trade abroad (first choice = P/FT). Although according to the theory developed above, free trade would have been compromised to obtain protection at home, Britain's free-trade policies alleviated any such necessity. As long as England and her colonies remained open, France and Germany could freely export those products in which they specialized. Likewise, under Britain's passive trade strategy, France and Germany could erect high tariff barriers at home without fear of retaliation. For a good description of German and French trade policies in the late nineteenth century, see Percy Ashley, *Modern Tariff History: Germany—United States—France* (New York: Dutton, 1920).

[9]Between 1887 and 1890, the United Kingdom accepted on average 51.7 percent of all American exports. This average fell only slightly to 48.1 percent between 1891 and 1897 (U.S. Bureau of the Census, *Historical Statistics of the United States: Colonial Times to 1970, Part II* [Washington, D.C.: U.S. Government Printing Office, 1972], pp. 903–6).

United States was only a middle-sized power within the international economy, Britain's unilateral commitment to nonretaliation also enabled America to exploit whatever market power it possessed through an optimal tariff. Finally, and for similar reasons, the United States was also free to target British markets in the developing regions, and particularly in the independent nation-states of Latin America. As an opportunist, in short, the United States was able to free ride on British free trade.

Possessing an extensive and dynamic domestic market as well as a full complement of natural resources, the United States was one of the few countries in the late nineteenth century which could have chosen to pursue an autarkic trade strategy. Indeed, foreign trade averaged only 14 percent of America's Gross National Product during this phase, as compared to 45 percent for the United Kingdom, 50 percent for France, and 30 percent for Germany.[10] Conversely, the United States also had the second most productive economy and was potentially competitive in a relatively broad array of agricultural and manufactured goods.[11] It might also have been able to withstand the rigors of international competition associated with policies of free trade. Yet, despite this extensive range of viable policies, the trade strategies actually under discussion in the United States were considerably narrower and strongly influenced by the position of the country within the international economic structure.

In the absence of a strong national desire for export expansion, the moderate protectionists—those who argued that exports were important only at the margin and that first priority had to be given to the security of the home market—dominated American trade strategy making after the Civil War.[12] Although proposals for export expansion had circulated in Washington and the country at large—and indeed, great

[10]These data are from Simon Kuznets as presented in Kenneth Waltz, *Theory of International Politics* (Reading, Mass.: Addison-Wesley, 1979), p. 212. Years of comparison vary slightly by country.

[11] For a general discussion of America's export strength, see Matthew Simon and David E. Novack, "Some Dimensions of the American Commercial Invasion of Europe, 1871–1914: An Introductory Essay," *Journal of Economic History* 24 (December 1964): 591–605; and Novack and Simon, "Commercial Responses to the American Export Invasion, 1871–1914: An Essay in Attitudinal History," *Explorations in Entreprenurial History*, 2d ser. 3 (Winter 1966): 121–47.

[12]The two best histories of American tariff policy are Frank W. Taussig, *The Tariff History of the United States*, 8th ed. (New York: Putnam, 1931); and Edward Stanwood, *American Tariff Controversies in the Nineteenth Century* (Boston: Houghton Mifflin, 1903). Both Terrill, *Tariff*, and Walter LaFeber, *The New Empire: An Interpretation of American Expansion, 1860–1898* (Ithaca: Cornell University Press, 1963), do an excellent job of placing the tariff debates into the larger context of American foreign policy.

progress had been made in port, canal, and railroad development[13]— the tariff remained a passive instrument of pure protection. As America's relative labor productivity and international competitiveness increased, however, the opportunity costs of not pursuing export expansion rose, eventually leading to a shift in the center of political debate. By the late 1880s, the foreign policy executive—with little pressure from society—recognized the potential benefits of export expansion and sought to reorient the tariff accordingly. The United States could have continued to pursue a rigidly protectionist trade strategy, the option generally favored in the country. Yet to do so would have foregone the benefits of export expansion. Likewise, a strategy of free trade, which would have led the market gradually to increase American exports, was also possible. Had such a course been adopted, however, the United States would have forsaken the benefits of protecting its increasing returns industries and exploiting its optimal tariff. Fortunately for the United States, greater free trade was not necessary as long as Britain remained committed to economic openness and a nonretaliatory trade strategy.

Like Britain, the United States singled out Latin America as an area of fruitful export expansion, at least in part because of the region's relatively high level of economic development and well-established patterns of trade. Also important for the United States was the region's geographic proximity, which provided an economic advantage as well as fitting into a larger political strategy of American regional dominance.[14]

Most American products entered Latin American markets on relatively equal terms with those of Britain and other European producers. In several cases, particularly in railroad equipment and construction and shipbuilding, equality of opportunity was insufficient to displace the special trading relationships between British producers and their Latin American consumers. The United States sought more favorable or preferential access to these markets. In other instances, particularly agriculture, Europeans had not developed the market or established trade because they lacked a comparative advantage. In these areas, the United States had to cultivate its own export markets without European assistance. The road toward United States export expansion in Latin America, in short, had already been paved, mostly by Great Britain. The

---

[13]Terrill, *Tariff*, p. 18; and William Appleman Williams, *The Roots of the Modern American Empire: A Study of the Growth and Shaping of Social Consciousness in a Marketplace Society* (New York: Random House, 1969), p. 106.

[14]See Terrill, *Tariff*; LaFeber, *New Empire*; and Williams, *Roots of the Modern American Empire*.

United States merely needed to extend and reshape it to fit its own requirements.

During the early 1890s, the important markets the United States already possessed in Europe were taken for granted and no new policies were perceived as necessary to maintain the nation's existing access. Indeed, perhaps because of Britain's commitment to openness, the United States believed that it could safely ignore threats of tariff retaliation directed against its own protectionist policies by the continental European powers. In 1894, the Wilson-Gorman Act reimposed a duty on raw sugar, thereby abrogating the reciprocity treaties negotiated under the McKinley Act of 1890, and provided for countervailing duties against countries that subsidized their sugar exports. Both of these provisions had serious implications for German sugar exports to the United States, which depended on the preferential access gained through reciprocity and the extensive export bounties granted by the German government. On July 16, 1894, after the final form of the new tariff bill had begun to emerge in Congress, Germany issued a strongly worded warning to the United States: "The Imperial Government is . . . at present unable to say whether it will be possible for it, in view of the increasing agitation on account of the proposed measure, to restrain the interested parties from demanding retaliatory action, which the Imperial Government, owing to the friendliness and fairness that characterize its intercourse with the United States, desires to avoid."[15] Despite the importance of Germany as a market for American exports, the government was unmoved by this protest. American decision makers in both Congress and the executive appeared to believe that either the threat of retaliation was not serious, although the Germans later carried it out, or that if Germany did retaliate, the effect upon American trade would be relatively mild. Later in the decade, as the United States faced a new round of protectionism in Europe—much of which was directly or indirectly aimed at American exports (see Chapter 4)—this American arrogance would change dramatically. Only in an international economy dominated by British openness could the United States afford to ignore threats of retaliation.

Thus, as a result of the international economic structure of British

[15]U.S. Congress, Committee on Ways and Means, *Reciprocity and Commercial Treaties*, 54th Cong., 1st sess., Report 2263 (Washington, D.C.: U.S. Government Printing Office, 1896), p. 22. There was some doubt during the legislative debate that such a threat had indeed been made. A letter published in the *Congressional Record* on June 29, 1894 (p. 6997), from Walter Q. Gresham, then secretary of state, stated that he was aware of no representation by Germany. Several attached newspaper articles from Germany, however, asserted or at least did not deny that a threat had been issued. Despite the confusion, the threat was clearly made as the letter quoted attests.

hegemony and the trade strategies of other countries, the United States had few incentives to reduce its own tariffs. Britain would not retaliate. Continental Europe, it was believed, could be safely ignored. And export expansion to Latin America required only selective concessions on items of interest to the countries of that region, primarily raw materials. The tension between simultaneous export expansion and import protection could be easily overcome through a differentiated tariff which maintained the existing structure of protection while encouraging exports through selective reductions in duties.

The incentive to free ride on Britain's hegemonic leadership was clearly recognized by contemporary American scholars and policy makers. William Graham Summer, Yale University's leading political economist, wrote: "The best thing which could happen, from our point of view, is that England should 'grab' all the land on the globe which is not owned by some first-class power. She would govern it all well, on the most enlightened and liberal principles, and we could all go to it for pleasure or gain as our interests might dictate. She would then have all the trouble, care and responsibility, and we should all share the advantages."[16] Likewise, Richard Olney, apparently frustrated by the problems it caused for America's relations with Europe during his tenure as secretary of state (1895–97) under President Grover Cleveland, was acutely aware that the United States was free riding on Great Britain:

> Do we want the same rights and facilities of trade . . . accorded to the people of any other country? We loudly hark Great Britain on to the task of achieving that result, but come to the rescue ourselves without a gun, nor a man, nor a ship with nothing but our "moral support." . . . So far as our foreign relations are concerned, the result is that we impress [other countries], however unjustly, as a nation of sympathizers and swaggerers— without purpose or power to turn our words into deeds and not above the sharp practice of accepting advantages for which we refuse to pay our share of the price.[17]

As an opportunist within an international economic structure of British hegemony, the United States faced an era of nearly unprecedented opportunity. The international economic structure created strong incentives for the United States to pursue both protection and export expansion. The resulting political task that confronted foreign policy leaders in this phase was not compromising protection in favor of export

---

[16]Quoted in Lloyd Gardner, ed., *A Different Frontier: Selected Readings in the Foundation of American Economic Expansion* (Chicago: Quadrangle, 1966), p. 81.
[17]Ibid., pp. 93–94; Olney was discussing the case of China in particular, but his remarks are relevant for American policy in general.

expansion, but merely "internationalizing" the tariff, or transforming it into an active instrument of both protection and expansion.

TRADE STRATEGY

Despite their sharply divided rhetoric, both the Republican and Democratic parties, led by individuals from within the foreign policy executive, concurred on the objectives of American trade strategy between 1887 and 1897. Exports were to be expanded abroad and the protectionist system maintained at home. These goals were to be accomplished by reducing the tariff on a selected number of raw materials. The Democrats called for duty-free raw materials but removed only the tariff on raw wool. This policy would, the party argued, expand American exports—primarily agricultural products, steel, and railroad materials— to the wool-producing regions of the world, although de facto it was limited to Latin America's southern cone. The Republicans advocated bilateral reciprocity treaties between the United States and the several Latin American countries, in which the former would admit sugar, coffee, tea, and raw hides free of duty while the latter would grant in return preferential duties on a specified list of American agricultural and manufactured items. By focusing on Latin America, trade expansionists sought to redirect the trade of that region—previously dominated by Great Britain—away from Europe and toward the United States. Foreign policy leaders, in other words, attempted to preserve America's protectionist system but to change the policies and actions of the Latin American countries. This combination of international activism and domestic protection is the distinguishing characteristic of American trade strategy in this first phase.

Although many proposals for tariff reform had circulated before 1887, none had the impact of Democratic President Grover C. Cleveland's call for duty-free raw materials. Cleveland devoted his 1887 Annual Message to Congress entirely to the tariff question to emphasize the importance of his proposed reforms. Recognizing that the protectionist system could and should be maintained, Cleveland asked for only a moderate reform of the raw materials schedules to cheapen the costs of manufacture, lower prices, and—most important for the argument advanced here—increase exports. Duty-free raw materials, Cleveland concluded, "would appear to give [domestic manufacturers] a better chance in foreign markets with the manufacturers of other countries, who cheapen their wares by free material. Thus our people might have the opportunity of extending their sales beyond the limits of home consumption."[18]

Cleveland's proposal was soon introduced in Congress by Roger Q. Mills, chairman of the House Ways and Means Committee. The Mills bill, as it was known, was passed by the Democratic House but defeated in the Republican-dominated Senate. In the upper house, the Republicans submitted a traditionally protectionist bill, which eventually formed the basis for the McKinley Tariff of 1890.[19]

Cleveland's proposal stimulated the "Great Debate" in the presidential election of 1888.[20] Despite the importance of the issue and the clearly defined positions of both parties on the tariff, the election failed to yield a mandate for either platform: Cleveland received a plurality of one hundred thousand popular votes, and Benjamin Harrison, his Republican challenger, obtained a majority of votes in the electoral college.

The defeat of Cleveland's first reelection bid and of the Mills bill might be interpreted as demonstrating the importance of party and electoral politics. It is more significant, however, that the Republicans adopted a similar program for export expansion in 1890, only three years after Cleveland's original proposal.

The McKinley Tariff

In the Great Debate of 1888, the Republicans emphasized their continued commitment to protectionism. To fulfill pledges made during the campaign, the Republicans submitted a tariff bill to Congress in 1890 designed "to be a measure of protection from its enacting clause to its closing paragraph." The explicitly protectionist nature of the bill was praised by William McKinley (R.-Ohio), chairman of the House Ways and Means Committee: "We do not conceal the purpose of this bill—we want our own countrymen and all mankind to know it. It is to increase production here, diversify our productive enterprises, enlarge the field, and increase the demand for American workmen."[21]

In drafting the McKinley Act—like all tariff bills, named after its

[18]"Third Annual Message," in James D. Richardson, comp., *A Compilation of the Messages and Papers of the Presidents*, 10 vols. (New York: Bureau of National Literature, 1911), 7: 5174.
[19]Taussig, *Tariff History*, provides an excellent concise review of the legislative history of the ill-fated Mills bill, pp. 252–56.
[20]The 1888 presidential election and its relationship to the tariff is discussed in Terrill, *Tariff*, pp. 132–40.
[21]First quote from Speech by Burrows, *Congressional Record*, 51st Cong., 1st sess., 1890, p. 4318; McKinley quote in ibid., p. 4253.

principal author—the Ways and Means Committee sought to impose duties on any article that could be produced in the United States and to admit free of duty those goods which Americans could not produce at all or in sufficient quantities to meet domestic demand.[22] As a result, tariff levels were actually increased from those of the last tariff act passed in 1883 (see Table 3.1). The McKinley Act raised the tariff on dutiable imports from an average of 45.1 to 48.4 percent. Items on the free list (goods that entered without paying any duty at all) were expanded from 33.6 to 50.8 percent, thereby lowering the rate of duty on all imports from 29.9 to 23.7 percent.

The Republicans attempted to defuse the issue of duty-free raw materials championed by the Democrats by reforming the "draw-back" provision. Previously, 90 percent of all customs paid on any good consumed in the manufacture of an item for export were reimbursed to the manufacturer upon the completion of a complex set of administrative requirements. The McKinley Act raised this draw-back from 90 to 99 percent of the duty. The Republicans argued that the draw-back provision was more effective than the Democratic proposal for duty-free raw materials because it applied to all materials consumed in the production of the final exported product and not just a limited number of officially defined raw materials. In practice, however, the administrative requirements were so cumbersome that few manufacturers took advantage of the provision.[23]

The McKinley Act is perhaps best known for its reciprocity provision. Reciprocity, as embodied in the 1890 tariff, was not a replacement for protection. "What I [desire]," Secretary of State James G. Blaine and reciprocity's foremost advocate explicitly stated, "is a system of reciprocity not in conflict with a protective tariff, but supplementary thereto." Or, as Blaine's senatorial ally Eugene Hale (R.-Me.) defined it, reciprocity "is an extended protection, an external protection for American labor."[24]

As finally enacted, the reciprocity provision kept sugar, molasses, coffee, tea, and raw hides on the free list unless the president found that the exporting country, in view of the free introduction of these goods, imposed duties on American products that were reciprocally unjust and

[22]U.S. Senate, Committee on Finance, *Customs Tariffs: Senate and House Reports, 1888, 1890, 1894, and 1897*, 60th Cong., 2d sess., 1909, Sen. Doc. 547 (Washington, D.C.: U.S. Government Printing Office, 1909), p. 244.
[23]See McKinley's defense of the draw-back provision, *Congressional Record*, 51st Cong., 1st sess., 1890, p. 4247.
[24]Blaine quoted in J. Laurence Laughlin and H. Parker Willis, *Reciprocity* (New York: Baker and Taylor, 1903), p. 186; Hale quote in *Congressional Record*, 51st Cong., 1st sess., 1890, p. 9511.

Table 3.1. Levels of duty by tariff act, Phase I*

Year of tariff act	Level of duty on all imports	Level of duty on dutiable imports	Percentage of all imports on free list
1883	29.9	45.1	33.6
1890	23.7	48.4	50.8
1894	20.5	41.2	50.0

*Average rates of duty and average percentage of imports on free list computed for all complete years tariff act in effect.

SOURCE: *Statistical Abstract of the United States* (Washington, D.C.: U.S. Government Printing Office, selected years).

unreasonable. With the exception of tea, all of these products were imported from Latin America.[25] The bill also specified rates of duty to be imposed on the several commodities if the president determined that a nation failed to make appropriate concessions. In the most generous grant of tariff-making authority given by Congress to the executive until 1934, no congressional approval was required for any of the presidential actions called for in this provision.

The first reciprocity agreement was signed with Brazil on January 31, 1891. Agreements were also reached with Spain for Cuba and Puerto Rico; with the United Kingdom for Barbados, Jamaica, Leeward Islands, Trinidad, Windward Islands, and British Guiana; and with Salvador, Nicaragua, Honduras, and Guatemala. Each agreement contained tariff concessions by the foreign country on live animals; grains, particularly oats, barley, rye, and corn; meat products; bridge-building materials; cottonseed and related products; railway cars, wagons, and other materials; and timber and iron for shipbuilding. As in the Democratic plan articulated in the duty-free raw materials platform, the Republicans exchanged lower duties on raw materials for expanded exports of agricultural and infrastructure materials.[26]

The essential objective in these agreements was to gain an advantage in the Latin American markets at the expense of European producers and to admit free into the United States sugar, molasses, coffee, tea, and raw hides—goods that were not produced at all or in sufficient quan-

[25]Approximately 15 percent of raw hides imported into the United States came from England. But like wool, Britain exported little of its domestic hide production. Most of the hides exported from Britain originated in the colonies, Russia, Holland (probably reexports), Germany, and the United States. As written, the reciprocity provision might also have applied to Great Britain because of its role in the hide trade. But because Britain had few tariffs and treated all nations equally, the reciprocity provision was not expected and did not apply to trade relations between the two countries.

[26]Laughlin and Willis, *Reciprocity*, p. 211.

tities within the United States. As J. Laurence Laughlin and H. Parker Willis wrote in 1903, reciprocity in the McKinley Act was a form of coercion, "since we offered not a differential advantage to the countries concerned, but . . . only a differential disadvantage."[27] Of all the countries examined by President Harrison and Blaine and determined to discriminate unjustly against the United States, only Colombia, Haiti, and Venezuela refused to grant the United States tariff concessions in their markets. As a result, these nation-states were subjected to the retaliatory duties specified in the act.

The United States also negotiated reciprocity agreements with the German Empire and Austria-Hungary, allowing beet sugar produced in these countries to enter duty-free in exchange for tariff concessions the two nation-states had recently accorded each other. The United States did not gain any new trading advantages in these agreements but merely maintained the market access it had formerly enjoyed. Although fore-shadowing the trade strategy adopted in 1897 (discussed in Chapter 4), these two European reciprocity agreements were merely by-products of the McKinley Act: extending reciprocity to European beet and sugar producers was not considered in the legislative debates. Indeed, Senator George G. Vest (D.-Mo.) noted during the debate on reciprocity that Europe was specifically excluded because the manufactures of that region would come into direct competition with American manufacturers.[28]

The Wilson-Gorman Tariff

In 1892, Cleveland turned the tables on Harrison, beating the incumbent in the presidential election and returning to office for a second term. Strongly advocating the duty-free raw materials platform during the campaign, Cleveland and his supporters soon introduced the proposal in Congress for the second time.

As originally submitted to the House, the Wilson-Gorman Act of 1894 added several important raw materials to the duty-free list, including wool, coal, iron ore, and lumber. Hides and raw sugar, placed on the free list in 1890, remained untaxed in the House version of the bill. Easily passing the House, the bill encountered greater opposition in the traditionally more protectionist Senate, where the Democrats possessed only a slim majority. When the bill finally emerged from the upper

---

[27]Ibid., p. 112.
[28]*Congressional Record*, 51st Cong., 1st sess., 1890, p. 7803.

chamber, after the addition of 634 amendments, only wool and lumber remained on the duty-free list.[29]

Of these various raw materials, wool was the most important. Duty-free coal and iron ore would have benefited only a handful of manufacturers in New England and the Pacific Northwest, where proximity and the comparative ease of ocean transport offered foreign producers a small cost advantage. Likewise, free lumber was of concern to only a limited number of mills concentrated along the Canadian border. Sugar and hides were quite important, but the political battle over these products had already been fought under the Republicans, although oddly enough the verdict on free sugar was reversed under the Democrats in the Senate.

The woolen schedule, on the other hand, was critical;[30] given its importance to the American textile industry and its pivotal position in the protectionist coalition, had the Democrats failed to obtain this important proposal their efforts would have been judged a complete failure even if the others had passed. As William L. Wilson, chairman of the House Ways and Means Committee and principal author of the bill, stated in his opening speech, "I myself believe that if every other item in this bill were stricken out, if in the wisdom of this committee every other proposed change were abandoned, yet if we could carry through a bill putting wool on the free list, and reducing the duties on woolen goods, we should make a great, beneficent, revolutionary step in the work of tariff reform that would justify all the efforts we have put forth."[31]

The United States was a high-cost producer of raw wool. Even under high protection, American wool growers could not meet the domestic demand, and a significant quantity of raw wool continued to be imported. By raising domestic wool prices, however, the tariff made it economical for many small farmers in the Midwest and Northeast to keep sheep to supplement their cash incomes, although it increased costs for the manufacturer. The duty on raw wool was the only item in the tariff which yielded a real benefit to the agricultural sector and helped mitigate farm opposition to the tariff as a whole. The acquiescence, indeed support, of the woolen manufacturers for the duty on raw wool was obtained through the "mixed" tariff system. The manufacturer received both a specific duty, nominally equivalent to the tariff on raw

[29]See Taussig, *Tariff History*, pp. 284–319; and Stanwood, *American Tariff Controversies*, pp. 296–358.

[30]For a history of the wool tariff, see Mark A. Smith, *The Tariff on Wool* (New York: Macmillan, 1926), pp. 97–169.

[31]*Congressional Record*, 53d Cong., 2d sess., 1894, Appendix, p. 194.

wool but normally including an extra measure of protection, and an *ad valorem* duty to protect the manufacturing process. The Tariff Act of 1890, for instance, provided for a specific duty of 33 cents per pound (roughly equivalent to the tariff on raw wool) and an *ad valorem* duty of 40 percent on wool cloth not worth more than 30 cents per pound. Under this system of mixed duties, both the wool grower and the manufacturer could be benefited without apparent cost to the other.[32] The Wilson-Gorman Act removed both the duty on raw wool and the compensating specific duty.

The duty-free status of raw wool was expected to have strong positive effects upon America's export trade. As William C. R. Breckinridge (D.-Ky.) declared about the raw materials platform as a whole, "When we give to these men untaxed raw material, we are giving them what is necessary to conquer the world." Not only would exports of manufactured woolen goods increase because of lower prices, but because the party believed that international markets possessed an inherent tendency to balance trade bilaterally between countries, Democrats anticipated that other exports to those countries from which the United States purchased raw wool would also increase. This assumption of bilateral balancing flowed throughout the Democratic party platform on tariff reform but can be seen most clearly in an exchange between Senator William B. Allison (R.-Iowa) and Roger Q. Mills, author of the 1888 tariff bill, a Cleveland intimate, and now senator from Texas:

Mr. Allison. But I understood the Senator to say that if we bought bronchos from Mexico we would send them flour in payment?

Mr. Mills. Yes.

Mr. Allison. I supposed that trade was conducted in a little different way; that we exported a certain amount to a certain country, and if we did not import an equivalent amount they sent to us coin or its equivalent.

Mr. Mills. They send to us the value, it may be coin, which is simply the instrument of exchange, but at some time either during that year or the next year—or perhaps they may have paid for it in the preceding year—they will pay [in tangible goods] something just in proportion to the amount we send to them. There can be no getting away from that.[33]

[32]Manufacturers presented considerable resistance to the repeal of the duty on raw wool. In spite of the confusion in the highly intricate wool schedule, the manufacturers felt they understood the old system (Taussig, *Tariff History*, p. 295; and Stanwood, *American Tariff Controversies*, p. 337).

[33]Breckinridge quote in *Congressional Record*, 53d Cong., 2d sess., 1894, p. 712; Allison-Mills debate in ibid., p. 5861. See also statements by Mills, p. 4025, and Palmer, p. 4068. Richard C. Edwards, "Economic Sophistication in Nineteenth Century Congressional Tariff Debates," *Journal of Economic History* 30 (December 1970): 802–38, provides an insightful discussion of the economic theories underlying the Democratic and Republican platforms.

This assumption of bilateral balancing is critical to understanding the Democratic program of export expansion. Without such an assumption, the duty-free raw materials program could be interpreted as a modestly liberal trade strategy. By increasing American imports, exports as a whole would have been stimulated through the market mechanism. In a liberal trade strategy, it is immaterial which commodity imports are increased; it is the aggregate change that is important. Under the assumption of bilateral balancing, however, the duty-free raw materials program becomes more mercantilist. It was adopted not as a tool to expand exports indiscriminately but to expand exports to particular regions and countries. Under the Democrats' assumption of bilateral balancing, the goods selected for inclusion in the program—in this case, raw wool—are of central importance. The United States primarily imported raw wool from the United Kingdom, Australia, New Zealand, Russia, South America, China, and Turkey. Nearly all of the wool imported by the United States from the United Kingdom, however, originated in one of Britain's major suppliers: Australia, New Zealand, East Indies, South Africa, Russia, Turkey, South America, and France.[34] The benefits of free wool were expected to be derived largely from increased trade with South America, the United States's "natural" market to the south. America's capacity for expanding exports to the other wool-producing regions was limited by high transportation costs and the colonial ties of others. Even more important, there was a natural complementarity in trade between North and South America which was not believed to exist elsewhere.[35] The southern cone, the most prosperous area of Latin America,[36] did not produce sufficient quantities of grains or infrastructural materials (railroad and shipbuilding equipment and

[34]In 1891, for instance, Britain exported 400.9 million pounds of raw wool. Of this amount, only 16.7 million pounds was produced domestically, the rest consisting of reexports (B. R. Mitchell with Phyllis Deane, *Abstract of British Historical Statistics* [Cambridge: Cambridge University Press, 1962], p. 194).

[35]The hindrances to American exports created by the lack of a merchant marine—which often necessitated shipping American goods through London—and colonial ties, as well as the complementarity of the North and South American markets were themes that ran subtly through the tariff debates of this era. These beliefs were not limited to Democrats but were fully shared by their Republican brethren. Because of this consensus, however, these important propositions were seldom discussed. They are inferred here from the congressional debates. For others who share this view that the trade expansionists focused primarily on Latin America, see Terrill, *Tariff*, LaFeber, *New Empire*, and Williams, *Roots of the Modern American Empire*.

[36]In 1895, Argentine per capita income was approximately equal to those of Germany, Holland, and Belgium, and higher than those of Austria, Italy, Switzerland, and Sweden (Carlos F. Diaz Alejandro, *Essays on the Economic History of the Argentine Republic* [New Haven: Yale University Press, 1970], pp. 1–66).

materials) to meet the domestic demand, and these were the areas in which policy makers hoped to expand exports most dramatically.

Under the Wilson-Gorman Act, imports of raw wool from Latin America increased more rapidly than from any other region. Imports rose by 18 percent from Australia and New Zealand, 21 percent from China, and 13 percent from Turkey, but fell by 59 percent from Russia. Raw wool imports from Uruguay and Argentina increased by 60 and 90 percent respectively. As the Democrats expected, American exports to South America also increased dramatically. Under the Wilson-Gorman Act exports as a whole fell by approximately 15 percent, largely because of the third slump of the Great Depression between 1893 and 1897.[37] Exports to Europe fell by 21 percent and those to Latin America as a whole declined by 4 percent, but exports to South America actually increased by 9 percent. Thus, despite what would now be recognized as the erroneous assumption of bilateral balancing, the Democratic policy of duty-free raw materials succeeded in its goal of expanding exports to Latin America.

Despite the free-trade rhetoric often associated with the duty-free raw materials platform, it must be emphasized that the Wilson-Gorman Act was not an assault on protection. The limited intent of the legislation, even before the Senate substantially raised the level of protection in the bill, was clearly set forth by Wilson in the Ways and Means Committee Report:

> The bill on which the committee has expended much patient and anxious labor is not offered as a complete response to the mandate of the American people [for free trade]. It no more professes to be purged of all protection than to be free of error in its complex and manifold details. However we may deny the existence of any legislative pledge or the right of any Congress to make such a pledge for the continuance of duties that carry with them more or less acknowledged protection, we are forced to consider that great interests do exist whose existence and prosperity it is no part of our reform either to imperil or to curtail.[38]

Moreover, the average rate of tariff on dutiable imports was reduced from 48.4 percent in the McKinley Act of 1890 to 41.2 percent. Likewise, the average rate of duty on all imports was reduced from 23.7 to 20.5 percent. The magnitude of the free list remained essentially the

---

[37]See Charles Hoffman, *The Depression of the Nineties: An Economic History* (Westport, Conn.: Greenwood, 1970), esp. chap. 5.
[38]U. S. Senate, Committee on Finance, *Customs Tariffs*, p. 282.

same (see Table 3.1). Rather than being a liberal internationalist tariff or an attack on protectionism, the Democratic program of duty-free raw materials was designed to maintain the essential structure of American tariff protection.

Although nearly identical in intent and strategy, the Democratic and Republican trade expansion programs differed in one important respect: the duty-free raw materials program relied more upon international market forces (or rather, a particular view of these forces referred to as bilateral balancing), whereas reciprocity allowed the state to intervene directly in the process of exchange. Nonetheless, both sought to limit the actual increases of imports into the United States through continued protection. Both approaches also sought to expand the exports of the United States within a relatively narrow range of commodities by removing the duties on specific raw materials. Finally, Latin America, which had previously been a British trading preserve, was singled out by Republicans and Democrats as the principal outlet for the products of America's increasingly productive economy.

This strategy was at least partly successful. During the 1880s, United States exports to Latin America averaged $67.96 million. From 1890 to 1897, these exports expanded to an average of $89.38 million per year, for an increase of 31.5 percent. During the same period, exports to Europe—still the United States's most important market—increased only 15.8 percent and total American exports increased by 19.0 percent. Through this export drive, the United States slowly chipped away at Britain's commercial preeminence in the region.[39] Britain remained the most important trading partner for many countries in Latin America, but the United States was rapidly gaining.

This relatively successful American trade strategy was made possible by the international economic structure of British hegemony. The United Kingdom's commitment to free trade and its self-abnegating strategy of nonretaliation created the opportunity for the United States to protect its domestic economy, exert its albeit limited market power, and expand its exports to Latin America—all at Britain's expense. The United States carefully exploited this opportunity.

---

[39]The trade data for this period are unfortunately incomplete. Data are available for selected South American nations, where Britain appears to have been most firmly entrenched. Between 1883 and 1897 the ratio of American to British exports increased from .14 to .23 in Argentina, .21 to .48 in Brazil, .12 to .25 in Peru, and decreased from .20 to .18 in Chile. Data for 1883 from Boyd, *Men and Issues of '92*, p. 298. Recalculated by author for ratios. Data from 1897 from U.S. Congress, House of Representatives, *Commercial Relations of the United States with Foreign Countries during the Years 1896 and 1897*, Vols. 1 and 2, 55th Cong., 2d sess., House Doc. 483 (Washington, D.C.: U.S. Government Printing Office, 1898).

THE DOMESTIC POLICY PROCESS

In spite of their partisan differences and continued protectionist pressure in Congress, foreign policy leaders in both parties concurred that the tariff had to be "internationalized," or reconceptualized as an instrument of both protection and export expansion. They rapidly accomplished this task. Within three years, between Cleveland's initial proposal and the passage of the McKinley Act, the transformation was nearly complete; the tariff would never again be simply a means of protection. That both parties adopted the same trade strategy despite their partisan differences is strong support for a systemic explanation of trade strategy.

Both reciprocity and duty-free raw materials were put forth and championed by individuals in positions of authority within the foreign policy executive. The politically mobilized groups within society as manifested in Congress were highly protectionist. There were almost no countervailing societal pressures on trade restrictions. As noted in Chapter 2, the largest and most internationally oriented industries became involved in tariff politics only when their immediate interests were directly threatened. The smaller internationally oriented industries, which benefited from a specialized market niche, generally turned to the government for assistance in export promotion, becoming an important constituency in favor of reciprocity and, to a lesser extent, duty-free raw materials.[40] Yet these desires for export expansion were not manifested in Congress, in which protectionist logrolling was not only tolerated but advocated as a just principle. Not a single brick could be removed from the tariff wall, protectionist congressmen argued, for fear of bringing the entire interdependent structure down. Nor did the smaller internationally oriented producers exert significant pressure upon the government for reciprocity and duty-free raw materials; in both cases, action by the foreign policy leaders preceded popular pressure. As will be seen, in at least 1890 foreign policy leaders actually created the popular pressure necessary to bend a recalcitrant Congress to their will.

Blaine, Reciprocity, and the McKinley Tariff

James G. Blaine, a moderate protectionist, had long been interested in expanding trade to Latin America. As secretary of state in the administration of President James A. Garfield, Blaine issued invitations for an

---

[40]The interests of American business groups are discussed in William H. Becker, *The Dynamics of Business-Government Relations: Industry and Exports, 1893–1921* (Chicago: University of Chicago Press, 1982), pp. 1–47.

International American Conference to discuss trade and hemispheric affairs.[41] These invitations were later withdrawn when, after the death of Garfield, President Chester A. Arthur replaced Blaine with Frederick T. Frelinghuysen. In his unsuccessful 1884 campaign for president against Cleveland, Blaine emphasized relations with Latin America, writing in his letter accepting the nomination that "we seek the conquests of peace; we desire to extend our own commerce, and in an especial degree with our friends and neighbors on this continent."[42] In 1889, after defeating Cleveland for the presidency, Harrison asked Blaine to preside over the State Department again not only because of his position as an "elder statesman" within the Republican party but also because of their similar views on foreign affairs, particularly regarding commerce with Latin America.[43] Indeed, during the 1888 campaign, Harrison echoed Blaine's well-known ideas on expansion, declaring that "we do not mean to be content with our market. We should seek to promote closer and more friendly commercial relations with the Central and South American States."[44]

Despite Arthur's withdrawal of the invitations to the International American Conference, support for the plan did not disappear. Cleveland reissued the invitations before the 1888 election, perhaps to demonstrate further his commitment to export expansion. After Harrison's election, the task of organizing the conference once again fell to Blaine. In the conference, Blaine had two principal objectives: the adoption of a hemispheric arbitration treaty, which was accepted, although only seven states signed the document, and the erection of an inter-American customs union, which was rejected by the Conference in favor of bilateral reciprocity treaties between interested countries of the region. Failing in his grander proposal, Blaine then focused his attention on the concept of reciprocity.[45] With the support of the conference for reciprocity, Blaine increased the costs of congressional rejection of his export expansion plans. If the legislature now failed to adopt reciprocity, it would dampen the widely applauded feelings of inter-American solidarity spawned by the meeting.

[41]Discussed in detail by LaFeber, *New Empire*, p. 47, and Terrill, *Tariff*, pp. 45–48.

[42]Reprinted in James G. Blaine, *Political Discussions: Legislative, Diplomatic, and Popular* (Norwich, Conn.: Henry Bull, 1887), pp. 428–29.

[43]Most telling in this regard is a letter from Harrison to Blaine dated January 17, 1889, reprinted in Albert T. Volwiler, *The Correspondence between Benjamin Harrison and James G. Blaine, 1882–1893* (Philadelphia: American Philosophical Society, 1940), pp. 44–45.

[44]Quoted in Terrill, *Tariff*, p. 134.

[45]For a discussion of the International American Conference and its results, see Alice Felt Tyler, *The Foreign Policy of James G. Blaine* (Minneapolis: University of Minnesota Press, 1927), pp. 165–90.

While the International American Conference was in session, the House of Representatives began debate on a protectionist and internationally passive draft of the McKinley bill. Congress proposed to take the duty off raw sugar and coffee, "necessities" of life which the United States did not produce in sufficient quantities to meet the home demand, impose duties on raw hides for the first time in twenty-five years, and raise the tariff on raw wool. The latter two actions, Blaine feared, would needlessly antagonize the Latin American nations, with whom he was then actively negotiating, and the former would take away his only bargaining chip because over 87 percent of the products of Latin America already entered the United States duty-free.[46] Blaine succeeded in maintaining hides on the free list and in moderating the increased duty on raw wool, but he failed to convince Congress of the importance of using sugar, coffee, and other products as instruments of reciprocity. The House passed the McKinley bill on May 21 without provision for reciprocity. Blaine then turned his attention to the Senate, presenting an emotional plea for reciprocity before the Finance Committee. According to the newspaper correspondent W. F. Curtis, who covered the hearing,

> Mr. Blaine, in the impetuous manner that is characteristic of him, declared that if sugar were placed on the free list the greatest results sought for and expected from the International Conference would be sacrificed. He declared that it would be the most inexcusable piece of folly the Republican Party was ever guilty of . . . [and that] he would give two years of his life for two hours on the floor of the Senate when the sugar schedule was under consideration. . . . [As a closing shot, Blaine threatened] Pass this bill, and in 1892 there will not be a man in all the party so beggared as to accept your nomination for the Presidency.[47]

An apocryphal but often repeated story follows in which Blaine, to emphasize his point during the hearing, smashed his silk top hat with his fist. Despite his efforts, and the possible loss of his hat, the Senate Finance Committee reported the bill to the full Senate with free sugar and without provision for reciprocity.

The congressional leadership resisted reciprocity for three reasons. First, Blaine could not guarantee that under his plan sugar would enter free of duty. Raw sugar was the single largest revenue item in the tariff,

[46]See Terrill, *Tariff*, pp. 162–63, Tyler, *Foreign Policy of Blaine*, pp. 184–87, and David Saville Muzzey, *James G. Blaine: A Political Idol of Other Days* (New York: Dodd, Mead, 1935), pp. 437–51.
[47]Quoted in Muzzey, *Blaine*, pp. 444–45.

providing 23 percent of all tariff revenue and 13 percent of all federal government revenue in 1888. The growing federal budget surplus was the Achilles heel of protectionists; tariff reformers, including Cleveland, had used the issue to good effect. By placing sugar on the free list, protectionists hoped to reduce the surplus and remove an important issue from partisan debate.[48] Fearful of leaving domestic sugar growers unprotected, however, Congress also provided a direct subsidy of approximately $7 million per year to these producers, both to solidify their political support and to reduce the budget surplus.

The congressional leadership also failed to see the importance of foreign markets. McKinley stated this position most directly. "We do not depreciate the value of our foreign trade; we are proud of it," he argued. "It is of great value and must be sacredly guarded, but what peculiar sanctity hangs about it which does not attach to our domestic trade? . . . If our trade and commerce are increasing and profitable within our own borders, what advantage can come from passing it by, confessedly the best market, that we may reach the poorest by distant seas?"[49]

Finally, the congressional leadership appears to have believed that even if exports required stimulation, the tariff was not the proper instrument. As McKinley stated in his opening speech on the bill, "I am not going to discuss reciprocity . . . I leave that to the illustrious man who presides over the State Department under this Administration and to my distinguished friend, the Chairman of the Committee on Foreign Affairs of this House [Mr. Hitt]. This is a domestic bill; it is not a foreign bill."[50]

On June 4, Blaine sent the final report of the International American Conference containing the recommendation on reciprocity to Harrison, along with a letter in which he detailed the hindrances to trade with South America and demonstrated that European trade in the region was increasing but the trade of the United States was decreasing. The United States, he argued, would be the greatest gainer from reciprocity. President Harrison submitted the report and Blaine's letter to Congress on June 19, under a cover letter in which he threw his full support behind reciprocity:

> If sugar is placed upon the free list, practically every important article exported from [the Latin American] States will be given untaxed access to our markets, except wool. The real difficulty in the way of negotiating profitable reciprocity treaties is that we have given freely so much that

[48] Ibid., p. 442.
[49] *Congressional Record*, 51st Cong., 1st sess., 1890, pp. 4253–54.
[50] Ibid., p. 4250.

would have had value in the mutual concessions which such treaties imply. I can not doubt, however, that the present advantages which the products of these near and friendly States enjoy in our markets, though they are not by law exclusive, will, with other considerations, favorably dispose them to adopt such measures, by treaty or otherwise, as will tend to equalize and greatly enlarge our mutual exchanges.[51]

Upon receiving the president's message, Senator Hale introduced a sweeping reciprocity amendment "hastily" drafted by the secretary of state. The amendment authorized the president to admit free of duty all and any goods from any country in the hemisphere as long as that country admitted free of duty a specified list of American agricultural and manufactured items. The Hale amendment was intended only as an opening gambit and a basis for debate, although it appears to have reflected Blaine's maximum desires.[52] Taken literally, the amendment would have seriously altered the system of American protection, granting the president nearly unrestricted authority to set tariff rates, placing wool—the foundation of the protectionist coalition—on the free list, and opening the possibility of reciprocity with Canada, the only country in the region which could seriously compete with the United States in agriculture and certain manufacturing industries.

Blaine then stepped up his efforts to publicize reciprocity, taking his case directly to the public through letters and public speeches. In a widely reprinted letter written to Senator William P. Frye (R.-Me.), Blaine stated, "I do not doubt that in many respects the tariff bill pending in the Senate is a just measure and that most of its provisions are in accordance with the wise policy of protection; but there is not a section or a line in the entire bill that will open a market for another bushel of wheat or another barrel of pork."[53] Blaine's efforts now began to meet with considerable success. At least one member of the House Ways and Means Committee from a western state and a bitter opponent of reciprocity complained that "Blaine's plan has run like a prairie fire all over my district."[54]

Meanwhile, President Harrison, through quiet, behind-the-scenes diplomacy, searched for compromise language that would allow for both free sugar and reciprocity. On July 25, Senator Nelson Aldrich (R.-R.I.), on behalf of the Senate Finance Committee, introduced an amendment,

[51]Reprinted in Richardson, comp., *Messages and Papers*, 7:5509.
[52]On Blaine and the Hale Amendment, see Muzzey, *Blaine*, pp. 448–49.
[53]*Congressional Record*, 51st Cong., 1st sess., 1890, pp. 4253–54.
[54]Quoted in Muzzey, *Blaine*, p. 447, and Gail Hamilton, *Biography of James G. Blaine* (Norwich, Conn.: Henry Bull, 1895), p. 687. This quote has been widely reprinted. The original source, the speaker, and the context are unknown.

apparently drafted within the White House, which fulfilled this task.[55] It was adopted with few revisions on September 10. The House continued to resist the concept of reciprocity, however, and acceded to the Senate amendment only after several conference committee meetings and seven days of Republican caucuses.[56]

Although Blaine did not receive everything he wanted, the final legislation did meet his most importance objectives. Sugar, coffee, tea, and even hides were made available for use in the negotiation of reciprocity treaties with no congressional limitations on the executive. Blaine succeeded, in part, because of his determination and willingness to risk alienating important members of the congressional leadership.[57] Also important were the transnational coalition created in the International American Conference and Blaine's attempt to circumvent the usual protectionist lobbies in Congress by appealing directly to the public and particularly to farmers for support. Finally, and perhaps most important, reciprocity was eventually successful because the concept, once the correct legislative language was found, was not in conflict with protection, as Blaine himself noted. Blaine could thus readily compromise on the breadth of products covered by reciprocity (that is, the difference between the Hale and final committee amendments) to secure reciprocity for sugar and coffee. Under reciprocity, both protectionists and trade expansionists could be easily satisfied.

Cleveland and the Wilson-Gorman Tariff

Cleveland had not clearly spelled out a plan for tariff reform in the 1884 election campaign, and no strong actions were taken during the first years of his administration, but he nonetheless staffed his first cabinet with committed tariff reformers.[58] Cleveland was often criticized for delaying the 1887 tariff message. Yet "if he had announced this policy earlier," Cleveland believed, "the country would not have been prepared for it."[59] Despite the years of preparation and many clues to the direction he eventually intended to take, Cleveland's call for duty-free raw materials startled Congress and the nation. Developed by a small group of Cleveland's closest advisers at the president's summer

[55]On Harrison's role in drafting the reciprocity amendment, see Harrison to Blaine, July 23, 1890, in Volwiler, *Correspondence between Harrison and Blaine*, pp. 111–12.

[56]For a more detailed examination of the passage of the reciprocity amendment, see Terrill, *Tariff*, pp. 159–83.

[57]Charles Edward Russell, *Blaine of Maine: His Life and Times* (New York: Cosmopolitan, 1931), p. 420.

[58]Terrill, *Tariff*, pp. 109–11.

[59]George F. Parker, *Recollections of Grover Cleveland* (New York: Century, 1909), p. 104.

retreat, Oak View, the tariff message was recognized as a bold stroke of presidential leadership by supporters and detractors alike.[60]

Cleveland was also committed to expanding exports to Latin America. It was Cleveland who issued the second invitations for the International American Conference at which Blaine presided. During his second administration, Cleveland first appointed Walter Q. Gresham (1893–95) and later Richard C. Olney (1895–97) as secretary of state. Both men were committed expansionists, who—with the president's backing—led the nation into an extremely active political role in Latin America, intervening in the Brazilian Revolution of 1894, the dispute over the Mosquito Coast in Nicaragua, and the Venezuelan Boundary Crisis of 1895–96 in efforts to limit and reduce British influence in the hemisphere and expand American commercial and political ties in the region.[61]

The Democratic duty-free raw materials platform shared the same objectives but was less successful legislatively than was the Republican policy of reciprocity. The 1894 tariff was drafted by William L. Wilson, then chairman of the House Ways and Means Committee and a Cleveland intimate who had participated in the 1887 Oak View conference. As passed by the House, the Wilson bill contained the full list of duty-free raw materials requested by the president. The bill encountered considerable resistance in the Senate, which historically was more inclined toward higher duties than the lower house.[62] More important for the fate of the Wilson bill, the Democrats possessed only a slim majority in the Senate, which had already been weakened by the bitter conflict over the repeal of the Sherman Silver Purchase Act in 1893. The Wilson bill, as passed by the House, removed the subsidy to domestic sugar producers but left raw sugar on the free list to avoid abrogating the reciprocity agreements signed under the McKinley Act. This proposal was strongly resisted by the two senators from Louisiana, whose votes were necessary for the passage of the bill. Their opposition, as well as that of others who desired similar treatment for the industries in their

[60]See Terrill, *Tariff*, pp. 109–40. Cleveland's presidential papers contain many congratulatory letters from a wide cross-section of the American public in the weeks following his December 1887 message. He apparently saved few notes of criticism.

[61]These three episodes in American expansion are described by LaFeber, *New Empire*, pp. 210–29 and 242–83.

[62]The Senate is typically more protectionist than the House, even though economic interests tend to be more concentrated in the latter. Three explanations are generally given for this trend: the Senate is a more individualistic institution with weaker committee chairs, debate is unlimited, and an unlimited number of amendments are permitted on the Senate floor. See Robert E. Baldwin, *The Political Economy of U.S. Import Policy* (Cambridge: MIT Press, 1985), pp. 15–17; and Robert A. Pastor, *Congress and the Politics of U.S. Foreign Economic Policy, 1929–1976* (Berkeley: University of California Press, 1980), pp. 162–63.

states, initiated the usual logrolling politics. [63] Under the leadership of Arthur Gorman, who Wilson believed was beholden to the trusts either through bribery or financial interest,[64] the Senate passed a considerably narrowed duty-free raw materials measure by a 39 to 34 margin.

The House-Senate conference committee then deadlocked on the measure. The House held to its broader duty-free raw materials bill, and the Senate—hemmed in by continued fears of defections from its slim majority—insisted upon its more circumscribed version. Cleveland, hoping to break this impasse in favor of the House bill, took the unprecedented step of intervening in the proceedings of the conference committee. On July 2, Cleveland sent a letter to Wilson which was read into the *Congressional Record*. In the passage most offensive to Senate Democrats, Cleveland stated:

> Every true Democrat and every sincere tariff reformer knows that this bill in its present form . . . falls far short of the consummation for which we have long labored, for which we have suffered defeat without discouragement, which, in its anticipation, gave us a rallying cry in our day of triumph, and which, in its promise of accomplishment, is so interwoven with Democratic pledges and Democratic success, that our abandonment of the cause or the principles upon which it rests means party perfidy and party dishonor.[65]

By equating the House version of the bill with the "true" Democratic position on the tariff, Cleveland alienated the Senate. Had Cleveland made another bold appeal to public support, as he had done in 1887 and as Blaine successfully did in 1890, or had the president openly criticized the various lobbies seeking to influence Congress, which would have been consistent with his "clean" government stance and was so successfully used by Woodrow Wilson in 1913 (see Chapter 5), Cleveland might have succeeded in expanding support for the House bill. But by publicly criticizing the Senate, Cleveland merely strengthened the resolve of the upper house and made any compromise appear as humilia-

[63]"The truth is," Senator Shelby M. Cullom (R.-Ill.) later declared, "we were all—Democrats as well as Republicans—trying to get in amendments in the interest of protecting the industries of our respective states." See Robert McElroy, *Grover Cleveland: The Man and the Statesman*, 2 vols. (New York: Harper and Brothers, 1923), 2:111.

[64]Wilson wrote that "my services on the Conference Committee on the Tariff Bill [1894] gave me enough glimpses of [Gorman's] conduct in that contest to assure me that he was the bribed attorney of the Sugar Trust and of other trusts or jobbers, who wished their interests taken care of in the tariff revision" (Festus P. Summers, ed., *The Cabinet Diary of William L. Wilson, 1896–1897* [Chapel Hill: University of North Carolina Press, 1957], p. 60).

[65]Allan Nevins, ed., *Letters of Grover Cleveland, 1850–1908* (Boston: Houghton Mifflin, 1933), p. 355.

tion. To pass any bill at all, the House was eventually forced to acquiesce to all of the 634 Senate amendments.[66] Torn between wanting to veto the bill and desiring to keep free wool and other reforms, Cleveland eventually allowed the bill to become law without his signature.

The failure to obtain the complete duty-free raw materials program has often been attributed to the political ineptitude of the president. Specifically, Cleveland is often cited with three tactical mistakes: not calling for a special session of Congress immediately after his inauguration in 1893 to revise the tariff and, rather, expending his limited political capital on the repeal of the Sherman Silver Purchase Act; not taking a forceful leadership role early in the 1894 tariff debates; and mishandling the bill during its final weeks in Congress.[67] All of these factors played a role. Just as important, however, was the nature of the duty-free raw materials platform.

Unlike reciprocity, under which both protectionists and export expansionists could be easily satisfied, duty-free raw materials were perceived as challenging the dominant mode of tariff making: the logrolling coalition of mutual noninterference in which the wool producers and wool manufacturers were key players. To institute the duty-free raw materials program, choices had to be made. Most groups could continue to receive protection, but a few industries had to be denied and placed outside the logrolling coalition.

In spite of its legislative difficulties, the Wilson-Gorman Act was not a failure as its detractors often imply.[68] Frustrated by the lack of total legislative success, tariff reformers have often failed to recognize that the bill met its most important objective—free wool—and articulated and implemented a positive program of export expansion. The bill should be judged for these successes. And it is here that the Wilson-Gorman Act most closely mirrors its Republican counterpart.

[66]In nearly every tariff bill in American history, the conference committee has, in a very real sense, written the final version. Often, what emerged from the conference room bore little resemblance to the two bills that went in. By accepting all of the Senate amendments, the House circumvented this normal process of consensus building. It also resulted in numerous "jokers" becoming law even though they were not intended to. Senator John Sherman (R.-Ohio) remarked that "there are many cases in the bill where enactment was not intended by the Senate. For instance, innumerable amendments were put on by the Senators on both sides of the chamber . . . to give the Committee of Conference a chance to think of the matter, and they are all adopted, whatever may be their language or the incongruity with other parts of the bill" (quoted in Henry Jones Ford, *The Cleveland Era: A Chronicle of the New Order in Politics* [New Haven: Yale University Press, 1919], p. 199).

[67]For example, see Terrill, *Tariff*, pp. 191–94; and Horace Samuel Merrill, *Bourbon Leader: Grover Cleveland and the Democratic Party* (Boston: Little, Brown, 1957), pp. 187–89.

[68]Merrill declares that the Wilson-Gorman Act was a "distinct victory for the high protectionists" (*Bourbon Leader*, p. 189). See also Harold U. Faulkner, *Politics, Reform and Expansion, 1890–1900* (New York: Harper & Row, 1959), p. 161.

The internationalization of the tariff was initiated and most forcefully urged by individuals within the foreign policy executive. Although the national trade interest and desires of the dominant social groups were not difficult to reconcile, the existing protectionist coalition nonetheless resisted the redefinition of the tariff. The success of foreign policy leaders in transforming the national trade interest into trade strategy derived from the executive's redefinition of the tariff as a foreign policy issue, thereby legitimating the president's involvement in tariff making; the creation of a transnational coalition in the International American Conference, which raised the stakes of a congressional rejection of reciprocity; and the mobilization of previously neutral groups, particularly the farmers, into the process of tariff making, circumventing the usual protectionist coalition.

CONCLUSION

Despite their political antagonisms and the specific differences between their respective tariff bills, both Republican and Democratic foreign policy leaders pursued the same trade strategy during the period 1887–97. Both Republicans and Democrats sought to maintain protection for the home market. And both parties sought to expand exports by removing duties on selected raw materials primarily imported from Latin America. Previously a passive instrument of protection, the tariff was internationalized or reconceptualized as a more active tool of both protection and export expansion.

This protectionist but more active trade strategy was grounded in the incentives created by the United States's position as an opportunist within an international economic structure of British hegemony. The United States was able to fulfill its desires for protection at home and export expansion abroad only because the United Kingdom continued to pursue a liberal and passive trade strategy. As long as Britain remained committed to free trade and abstained from protection, the United States could protect its increasing returns industries, exploit its market power through an optimal tariff, and expand its trade with traditional English markets in Latin America while continuing to ship nearly half of its exports to the United Kingdom. As Britain's interests evolved in later phases, American trade strategy would shift in response. But in the period between 1887 and 1897, the United States faced an era of opportunity in which its preferred policies could be easily obtained. The United States responded to this opportunity by free riding on free trade.

The interpretation of American trade strategy and political process developed in this chapter raises questions for more traditional, domestically oriented explanations. Many studies have focused on competition between the political parties as a source of tariff policy.[69] In this view, the Republicans were the party of protection and the Democrats the party of free trade. Variations in tariff policy, then, are explained by changes in party power. The argument presented here, however, highlights the commonalities in trade strategy, which cannot, in turn, be explained by party competition.

Other studies have emphasized the importance of interest-group politics.[70] Yet, as Table 2.1 demonstrates, few industries in the United States were dependent upon exports in 1889. More important, in both the reconceptualization of the tariff from a tool of pure protection into an instrument of protection and export expansion and in the specific policies designed to meet the declared and similar goals of the two administrations, foreign policy leaders originated and most forcefully advocated the new policies. In the case of reciprocity in 1890, foreign policy leaders prevailed only by actively building public support and pressuring a reluctant Congress. In 1894, important beneficiaries of the duty-free raw materials program—particularly the woolen manufacturers—actively opposed it. Thus trade strategy in the early 1890s cannot be seen merely as a reflection of competition between social interests, whether class or group based. Although interest-group pressures and party competition no doubt played a role, the internationalization of the tariff after 1887 can be better understood as a response by foreign policy leaders to the opportunities of the international economic structure.

---

[69]For example, see Terrill, *Tariff*; Taussig, *Tariff History*; and Stanwood, *American Tariff Controversies*.

[70]See Becker, *Dynamics of Business-Government Relations*; E. E. Schattschneider, *Politics, Pressures and the Tariff* (New York: Prentice-Hall, 1935); and Theodore Lowi, "American Business, Public Policy, Case-Studies, and Political Theory," *World Politics* 16 (December 1964): 677–715.

CHAPTER FOUR

British Decline and
American Opportunism, 1897–1912

In the years 1897–1912, the United States maintained high tariff protection at home and expanded its strategy of bilateral bargaining, first adopted in the McKinley Act of 1890, to new regions of the globe. In the Dingley Act of 1897, the United States offered reciprocal reductions in duties to the countries of continental Europe and threatened penalty duties against Latin American nation-states unless they granted concessions on items of special interest to the United States. Reflecting new confidence in its ability to compete in international markets, the United States adopted an open door or nondiscriminatory trade strategy in the Payne-Aldrich Act of 1909, which granted lower duties to all countries that did not unduly discriminate against American goods. In both tariff acts, the United States eschewed liberal free-trade principles and actively sought to exploit the trade strategies of other countries to obtain its preferred outcome of protection at home and free trade abroad.

American trade strategy was influenced during this period by the international economic structure of declining British hegemony and, more specifically, by its own increasing relative labor productivity. Although declining rapidly, Great Britain remained a hegemonic leader and continued to pursue a passive, nonretaliatory trade strategy throughout this second phase. The United States could at least in part still free ride on Britain and maintain the policies of high protection and export expansion which had, for similar reasons, proven so successful between 1887 and 1897.

In perhaps the most important manifestation of Britain's decline, the United States surpassed the United Kingdom in relative labor productivity in approximately 1897. This important change within the international economic structure broadened America's export horizons and correspondingly stimulated its desire for greater access to foreign markets. Enjoying the virtuous cycle discussed in Chapter 1, American manufacturers became increasingly competitive in international markets and began to seek their fortunes not only in the export markets of Latin America but also in Asia and, more important, continental Europe. At the same time, and perhaps because of the American "export invasion," many European countries increased their tariff barriers and began to discriminate against products from the United States. Threatened with losing these valuable outlets for the results of its ever more productive economy, the United States embraced an active trade strategy of bilateral tariff bargaining, turning first to reciprocity and later to maximum-minimum tariff schedules to breach the European tariff walls being erected against it.

In brief, American trade strategy between 1897 and 1912 was driven by the continued opportunity of free riding on Britain's hegemonic leadership and the desire to reap the benefits of its steadily increasing relative labor productivity in the face of the closure of foreign markets. The United States sought to achieve both aims through a greater reliance on bilateralism reinforced by the coercive power of high tariffs.

THE INTERNATIONAL ECONOMIC STRUCTURE, 1897–1912

Though still a hegemonic leader, the United Kingdom declined rapidly within the international economic structure during the period 1897–1912. Between 1890 and 1900, largely coinciding with the first phase discussed in Chapter 3, Britain's proportion of world trade declined only from 18.5 to 17.5 percent. From the turn of the century until 1913, one year after the close of this second phase, the United Kingdom's share of world trade plummeted from 17.5 to 14.1 percent. More important, the United States surpassed the United Kingdom in relative productivity in approximately 1897, creating an important change within the international economic structure.

During this period of decline, protectionism resurfaced as an important political force in British politics for the first time since 1846.[1] Initiated in 1896 and led by Colonial Secretary Joseph Chamberlain, Britain's imperial preference movement had emerged as a small but

---

[1] For a discussion of the early tariff reform movement in Great Britain, see Alan Sykes, *Tariff Reform in British Politics, 1903–1913* (Oxford: Clarendon, 1979); and Hon. George Peel, *The Tariff Reformers* (London: Methuen, 1913). British policy is discussed in more detail in Chapter 5, below.

potent political force by 1903. In 1906 the movement had grown strong enough to split the Conservative party, costing the Tories the election that year. With the Liberal victory and the disarray in the Conservative ranks, the advocates of imperial preference clearly remained a minority despite their growing strength. Britain's commitment to free trade appeared secure, albeit slightly weaker than before, and the United States continued to premise its trade policy on this commitment.

As in the first phase discussed in Chapter 3, the continued openness of the British market created the opportunity for the United States, as a single opportunist, to free ride within the international economy. Although it could not do so with quite the impunity as before, the United States could nonetheless maintain protection at home, thereby securing the benefits of its optimal tariff and subsidizing its increasing returns industries, and expand exports to Latin America, Asia, and other British trading preserves with little or no fear of retaliation from the hegemonic leader.

The most serious constraint on the United States during this period was its new position as the most productive nation-state within the international economy and, partially related to this situation, the growth of protectionism and discrimination in continental Europe. Enjoying both high and rapidly expanding relative labor productivity, the United States entered into a virtuous cycle of expanded exports and growth, greater economies of scale and trade surpluses, expanded exports and growth, and so on. As its exports became increasingly competitive in world markets, America's interests in export expansion grew as well.

In addition, the United States's rising relative labor productivity stimulated a shift in the composition of exports away from agriculture and other primary products and toward more capital-intensive manufactures. As a result, Anglo-American trade, traditionally based on the complementarity between the resource-rich United States and industrial Britain, though still important, became less central. The British market alone could no longer satisfy American needs, a conclusion reflected in trade patterns. In 1888 the United States shipped 52 percent of its exports to the United Kingdom. By 1897 Britain's share of American exports had fallen to 46 percent, and by 1912, at the end of this second phase, to a mere 26 percent.[2]

As its relative labor productivity increased, America's export horizons expanded far beyond Britain and Latin America to include Asia and

[2]U.S. Department of Commerce, Bureau of the Census, *Historical Statistics of the United States, Colonial Times to 1970* (Washington, D.C.: U.S. Government Printing Office, 1975), Ser. U317–334, pp. 903–4.

continental Europe. Of the two, Europe—and particularly Germany and France—was more troubling to American policy makers. Abandoning free trade in 1879, Germany subsequently negotiated bilateral tariff treaties with Austria-Hungary in 1891, Italy, Belgium, and Switzerland in 1892, Russia in 1894, Japan in 1896, and Spain in 1899. Each so-called "Caprivi treaty," named for Bismarck's successor as chancellor, lowered duties on a wide variety of products and generalized these concessions to all nation-states with which Germany possessed unconditional most-favored-nation (MFN) treaties.[3] Because the United States adhered to only the conditional MFN principle, these concessions were not automatically extended to American products.[4]

France followed Germany in the direction of discriminatory trade practices and increased protection in the Meline Tariff of 1892. Significantly raising tariff levels in France, the act also instituted minimum and maximum schedules, the latter to be applied to all countries that discriminated against or placed high duties upon French products. Most European countries secured the preferred rates of the French minimum schedule; only Portugal joined the United States on the higher, maximum schedule. In addition, the minimum schedule was eventually extended in whole or in part to Colombia, San Domingo, Ecuador, Mexico, Paraguay, Uruguay, Venezuela, Egypt, and Japan—all countries with which the United States desired increased commercial relations. Canada and Argentina, whose agricultural products competed with American exports in the French market, also received the minimum schedule.[5]

As these bilateral agreements were negotiated and implemented by Germany and France in the mid-1890s, American exporters began to face significant discrimination against their goods in continental markets.[6] Indeed, this was their intended effect. With its rapidly rising

---

[3]For a discussion of the origins and effects of these Caprivi treaties see Percy Ashley, *Modern Tariff History: Germany—United States—France* (New York: Dutton, 1920), pp. 60–90; see also U.S. Tariff Commission, *Reciprocity and Commercial Treaties* (Washington, D.C.: U.S. Government Printing Office, 1919), p. 204.

[4]In the unconditional form of the MFN, principal concessions granted to one country are automatically extended to all other countries with MFN status. Under the conditional form, however, concessions are extended only when third countries grant equal or equivalent concessions to what the second country originally made to obtain the benefit. For a concise history and discussion of America's nearly unique interpretation of the MFN principle, see Wallace McClure, "A New American Commercial Policy: As Evidenced by Section 317 of the Tariff Act of 1922," *Columbia Studies in History, Economics, and Public Law* 114 (1924): 118–30 and 160–87.

[5]Ashley, *Modern Tariff History*, pp. 331–46.

[6]See, for instance, the argument of Albert J. Hopkins (R.-Ill.), *Congressional Record*, 55th Cong., 1st sess., 1897, p. 136.

relative labor productivity, the United States captured market after market during the 1890s and engendered the enmity of jealous European producers. As the United States surpassed Britain, Europe grew increasingly apprehensive of the American "export invasion of Europe," an infelicitous term used by many Americans with predictable effects abroad. Reacting to this invasion, Count Agenor Goluchowski, minister of foreign affairs in Austria-Hungary, called for a concerted commercial policy in Europe to meet the challenge from the United States:

> The destructive competition with transoceanic countries [i.e., the United States] . . . requires prompt and thorough counteracting measures if vital interests of the peoples of Europe are not to be gravely compromised. They must fight shoulder to shoulder against the common danger, and must arm themselves for the struggle with all the means at their disposal. . . . The European nations must close their ranks in order successfully to defend their existence.[7]

As a German publicist wrote in 1902, "No question regarding commercial matters was more often discussed in the old world, especially after . . . 1898 [that is, the Spanish-American War], than that of American competition," which resembled a "spectre" or "invasion."[8]

Reconciling the competing constraints and opportunities of the international economic structure—and specifically, the desires to free ride on Great Britain, expand exports to Latin America and other developing regions, and maintain access to continental markets in the face of European closure—was the central political problem for America's trade strategists during this period. One possible option, suggested by several American free traders and strongly advocated by the Europeans, would have been for the United States to lower its tariff and adopt the unconditional MFN principle, thereby automatically sharing in the lower duties negotiated among the European powers. Both lower tariffs and unconditional MFN were necessary for this first option to succeed. The United States would have had to reverse its past adherence to the conditional MFN principle and renegotiate its existing trade agreements if it were to share in the benefits of unconditional MFN. In any renegotiations, however, considerable pressure would have been placed on the United States to reduce its overall tariff rates. France, for instance, explicitly linked the issues in its tariff legislation, which specified that its maximum

---

[7]Quoted in Charles S. Campbell, Jr., *Special Business Interests and the Open Door Policy* (Hamden, Conn.: Archon, 1968), p. 6.

[8]Ibid., p. 5.

schedule applied to countries that either discriminated against or imposed high duties on French products. Through this linkage, the desire of the United States to protect its domestic economy and impose whatever optimal tariffs it possessed came into direct conflict with the goal of expanding exports to the Continent and elsewhere. In this first possible strategy, pursuing one objective hindered the other.

A second option, which resolved this conflict and promised success on both fronts, was a bilateral bargaining tariff backed by high duties. Not only would the desire for domestic protection be satisfied, but selective reductions in these high duties or threats of even higher retaliatory duties could be used as effective levers to pry concessions out of other countries on items of interest to the United States. High but negotiable tariffs, in other words, maximized the United States's international bargaining power but still allowed it to maintain protection.

A strategy of bilateral bargaining would clearly engender international conflict. And lower tariffs combined with unconditional MFN might have been more effective at reducing trade barriers in the system as a whole, as achieved under British hegemony in the mid-nineteenth and American hegemony in the mid-twentieth centuries. At this time, however, the United States ignored such systemwide concerns, desiring instead to exploit the strategies of others so as to obtain its preferred outcome of protection at home and free trade abroad. Promising success, this second strategy was strongly advocated by state officials within the foreign policy executive.

TRADE STRATEGY

The years 1897–1912 were a period of rapid change in the foreign relations of the United States. Politically, the United States emerged as a middle-sized global power, claiming victory in the Spanish-American War, participating in the joint use of military force by the major European powers in China during the Boxer Rebellion, constructing a deepwater navy, "taking" the Panama Canal, and attending its first meeting of the great European powers in the Algeciras Conference of 1906. America's trade interests expanded as well. The Philippines, America's newly won colony, opened up Asia to Yankee traders. And the United States also began its export invasion of Europe.

As in the first phase discussed in Chapter 3, the United States maintained high protection and pursued an active, bilateral trade strategy. In the Dingley Act of 1897, the United States returned to reciprocity as an instrument of export expansion. Twelve years later, the United States adopted the slightly more liberal Payne-Aldrich Act with its activist maximum-minimum tariff schedules.

What distinguishes this second phase from the first, however, is the shift in the geographic focus of American activism. Between 1887 and 1897, American trade strategy was designed to expand exports to Latin America, largely at Britain's expense. After 1897, the United States maintained this earlier interest but increasingly focused its attention on preserving and expanding its more important markets in Europe, and particularly in France and Germany.

The Dingley Tariff

In its substantive provisions, the Dingley Act of 1897 bears important similarities to the McKinley Act of 1890, embracing both protection and reciprocity. This is hardly surprising given the opprobrium directed at the Wilson-Gorman Tariff, a result of its association with the third slump of the Great Depression of 1873–96, and the election of William McKinley, author of the 1890 bill and the champion of protection, as president in 1896. Yet, though it clung to the successful policies of the first phase, the Dingley Act also reflected the new concern of the United States with expansion into European markets.

Soon after McKinley's election, the Republican members of the House Ways and Means Committee, under the direction of Nelson Dingley of Maine, began preparing a new tariff bill. Congress met in special session, called by the president immediately after his inauguration, to revise the tariff. The Dingley bill was passed by the House in record time but stalled in the Senate, where the Finance Committee, under the chairmanship of Nelson Aldrich, submitted a bill with rates substantially below those in the previous McKinley Tariff. The Senate rebelled against these lower rates, however, and subsequently rewrote the bill on the floor of the chamber.

The Dingley Act, as agreed upon by the conference committee and signed into law on July 24, 1897, raised the tariff on dutiable imports from 41.2 percent in the Wilson-Gorman Act to 47.6 percent, only 0.8 percent below the rate of the McKinley Tariff (see Tables 3.1 and 4.1). The free list was reduced to 45.1 percent, below the level of both the 1890 and 1894 acts. Finally, the Dingley Act raised the level of duty on all imports from 20.5 to 26.2 percent, 2.5 percent higher than the McKinley Tariff. Although certain Republican leaders, including Aldrich, publicly questioned for the first time the need for such high duties, the party's substantive commitment to protectionism nonetheless remained intact.

Table 4.1. Levels of duty by tariff act, Phase II*

Year of tariff act	Level of duty on all imports	Level of duty on dutiable imports	Percentage of all imports on free list
1894	20.5	41.2	50.0
1897	26.2	47.6	45.1
1909	20.0	41.0	51.3

*Average rates of duty and average percentage of imports on free list computed for all complete years tariff act in effect.
SOURCE: *Statistical Abstract of the United States* (Washington, D.C.: U.S. Government Printing Office, selected years).

In the Dingley Act, reciprocity was also broadened, deepened, and fashioned into a potentially powerful instrument of trade policy. Reciprocity, perceived as the only popular element of the ill-received McKinley Act of 1890, was certain to be a part of the new tariff.[9] Furthermore, the president, who strongly opposed the concept when it was presented by Blaine earlier in the decade, had now emerged as its strongest supporter. The final bill contained two sections on reciprocity, each passed by a different house of Congress and combined by the conference committee. In shaping their respective provisions, both houses concurred that reciprocity should be extended so as to help preserve and expand America's access to markets in Europe; the only question was how this goal could best be accomplished.

Section three of the bill, the reciprocity provision which originated in the House, authorized the president to suspend the duty on argols (crude tartar as deposited in wine casks), brandies, champagne, still wines, paintings, and statuary if the exporting country entered into an equivalent and reciprocal commercial treaty. This inducement was aimed at the continental European powers, and France in particular. Section three further authorized the president to impose penalty duties on coffee, tea, tonka beans, and vanilla beans if the exporting country failed to grant reciprocal and equivalent concessions to the United States in view of the free introduction of these products. Except for tea, which was a principal export of China and Japan, the other products were exported solely by the Latin American countries. The duty on sugar, the free admission of which had been central to the reciprocity provision of 1890, could no longer be manipulated in an active trade strategy; under the system of bounties granted between 1890 and 1894 and the tariff of

[9]See, in particular, Albert J. Hopkins's speech on reciprocity, *Congressional Record*, 55th Cong., 1st sess., 1897, p. 133.

1894, sugar growing had emerged as a politically important tariff-dependent industry in the United States.[10]

Except for the negotiating authority on brandies, champagne, still wines, coffee, and tea, the bargaining leverage given to the president by this section was weak. This was, indeed, the principal criticism of section three. As Representative Winfield S. Kerr (R.-Ohio) argued in introducing a more extensive but unsuccessful reciprocity amendment, "The defect in this bill is that it does not offer enough to get what we want and must have."[11]

This criticism was repeated in the Senate. In noting why the Senate Finance Committee struck out the lower house's reciprocity section, Aldrich stated that "it seemed to [us] that the provisions of the House bill in this regard would not prove effective." The committee, he went on, would try to draft a more efficacious provision.[12] Senator William B. Allison, chairing the Finance Committee because of Aldrich's prolonged illness, finally introduced a reciprocity provision on June 10, nearly two months after the Senate debate had begun. Section four, as it would eventually be numbered, empowered the president to enter into commercial treaties of no more than five years' duration with any country if negotiated within two years after the passage of the bill. The president, moreover, was authorized to lower duties by 20 percent on any good or eliminate the tariff entirely on any item that was the natural product of a foreign country and not of the United States. Tempering this sweeping authority, section four stipulated that any reciprocity treaty negotiated under this provision would require not only the constitutionally mandated Senate ratification but the approval of Congress as well.

To strengthen section four, the Senate raised the rates of duty contained in the Dingley Act as "bargaining chips" to be used in future negotiations. Although there is considerable debate over how extensive this process was, John Ball Osborne, joint secretary to the Reciprocity Commission appointed by McKinley to implement the reciprocity provision of the act, later stated, "When the rates of duty enumerated in the [act] . . . were being formulated, it was clearly understood . . . that each and every rate was subject to reduction to the extent of one-fifth under the operation of the reciprocity section. The rates were consequently made one-fifth higher than would otherwise have been justified." Although Aldrich and other protectionists denied that all rates were increased for this reason, they did agree that duties on certain articles,

[10]Tom E. Terrill, *The Tariff, Politics and American Foreign Policy, 1874–1901* (Westport, Conn.: Greenwood, 1973), p. 200.
[11]*Congressional Record*, 55th Cong., 1st sess., 1897, p. 254.
[12]Ibid.

particularly sugar, were made higher than they would have been without the reciprocity provision.[13]

Although its substantive provisions did not explicitly single out the continental powers, section four was clearly intended to penetrate the growing tariff walls and discriminatory trade practices of France and Germany. Senator William E. Chandler (R.-N.H.), a party leader, argued that "I am in favor of improving and strengthening our commercial relations by specific arrangement with other nations, not only with the nations of the Western Hemisphere, but with the nations of Europe." Likewise, Senator Allison turned his attention to Europe: "Europe is today full of maximum and minimum treaties affecting trade relations favorable to those countries with each other." This reciprocity provision, he stated, "is in the same line and for the same purpose."[14] American tariff policy was never made in an international vacuum; policy makers and even legislators were always cognizant of events and policies in other countries. As noted in Chapter 3, for example, the Democrats were certainly aware of German trade policy; yet in 1894 they chose to ignore the strongly worded threat of retaliation if the United States abrogated the reciprocity treaty or imposed countervailing duties on German sugar exports. What is distinctive about the Dingley Act is that for the first time since at least the Civil War the policies of the continental European powers were not only noted but actually incorporated into the legislation. In the Dingley Act, the United States attempted for the first time to fashion a concrete response to trade developments in Europe and expand its access to continental markets.

Despite the promise and intent of the reciprocity provisions in the Dingley Act, American negotiators were more constrained by congressional restrictions on executive authority than in 1890. The second part of section three, which authorized the president to impose penalty duties on coffee, tea, tonka beans, and vanilla beans if the exporting country imposed duties on American products that were reciprocally unequal and unreasonable, was used only once to secure favorable trading arrangements for the United States in Latin America. After five years of negotiations, Brazil finally agreed on April 16, 1904, to reduce its tariff by 20 percent on wheat flour, manufactures of rubber, watches and clocks, inks and colors, and condensed milk when exported from its northern neighbor. The United States, in turn, agreed not to penalize Brazilian coffee exports. These concessions by Brazil were withdrawn the following year in the wake of considerable domestic protest, only to

[13]U.S. Tariff Commission, *Reciprocity and Commercial Treaties*, pp. 202–3.
[14]*Congressional Record*, 55th Cong., 1st sess., 1897, p. 2236–37.

be granted once again in 1906 along with additional concessions on typewriters, refrigerators, pianos, scales, and windmills. Without the bargaining leverage provided by free sugar, no other agreements with the Latin American trading partners of the United States could be profitably negotiated.[15]

Under the first part of section three, John A. Kasson, appointed special reciprocity commissioner by President McKinley, negotiated four European reciprocity or "argol" agreements, as they came to be known. In an agreement signed with France on May 28, 1898, the United States granted to that country all the concessions authorized by the act, except that on champagne, and secured in return the French minimum rates on sausages and lard and a guarantee that previous concessions granted to the United States would be maintained. Kasson also secured for the United States the right to withdraw the concessions on still wines should France impose new duties on American products which the president judged to be unreasonable. As a result, France dropped proposed increases on cottonseed oil and petroleum products.[16] In an agreement reached on July 13, 1900, Germany granted to the United States the minimum rates recently conceded to the other continental European powers in return for concessions by the United States identical to those granted France. The United States also negotiated reciprocity agreements of lesser importance with Portugal in 1899 and Italy in 1900. These section three agreements largely accomplished their minimum objective: they penetrated the rising walls of tariff protection and discriminatory trade practices in Europe which applied to the United States. As the case of France makes clear, however, they did not eliminate these discriminations.

In the early years of the twentieth century, the continental European powers continued their drift toward increased protection and discrimination. The immediate cause of this drift was Germany's attempt to arm itself for the renegotiation of its bilateral tariff treaties due to expire in 1903. In the tariff bill passed in December 1902, Germany both raised its overall level of duties and increased the number of categories in the tariff.[17] Under the new legislation, the maximum schedule was to be the general tariff; any concessions granted were to be the minimum sched-

[15]U.S. Tariff Commission, *Reciprocity and Commercial Treaties*, pp. 285–86, 215.
[16]Ibid., pp. 205–6.
[17]See Ashley, *Modern Tariff History*, pp. 85–90 and 109–16. By increasing the number of categories in the tariff, Germany introduced greater specialization into its schedules so as to enable reductions to be made on some articles without reducing others. Tariff reductions, as a result, could be limited to specific countries in many cases, thus maintaining the form of the unconditional MFN principle but undermining its intent.

ule and would be generalized only to those nation-states with which Germany possessed an unconditional MFN treaty. Germany's trading partners also prepared for the new round of negotiations by raising their tariff levels. Negotiations commenced in June 1904 and ended in January 1905. The new tariff went into effect on March 1, 1906.

In reaction to these developments in Europe, the United States negotiated a second series of argol agreements between 1906 and 1909. In these agreements, the United States extended its earlier concessions on argols, brandies, still wines, paintings, and statuary and agreed to apply the lower duty provided for on champagne in return for nearly all of the minimum schedules in Germany and Spain and selected concessions in France, Portugal, Great Britain (with reference to her colonies), Italy, and the Netherlands.[18] At the end of this round of negotiations, all of the negotiating authority provided for in section three was depleted. Any further negotiations under this provision would have required an additional grant of congressional authority.

Although hailed as an important departure in American tariff policy, section four of the Dingley Act—empowering the president to negotiate tariff reductions of up to 20 percent on any product in exchange for comparable concessions—was ultimately unsuccessful. Of the seven treaties negotiated under its auspices, not one was ever considered by the full Senate or House. The treaty with France was the first to be negotiated, substantively the most important, and perceived as the "test case" for the others. Negotiations were initiated by a French proposal that the United States grant their country the full reduction of 20 percent authorized in the bill on the entire range of its goods imported into the United States in return for the application of France's minimum tariff on all American goods. Special Reciprocity Commissioner Kasson seriously considered this proposal, but it was rejected. In the final treaty signed on July 24, 1899, France extended to the United States the minimum rates on all but 19 of the 654 articles enumerated in its tariff. Of the 19 items, only boots and shoes and machine tools were of importance.[19] All of these concessions had already been granted to France's most-favored nations. The United States, in return, agreed to reduce duties on 126 articles by 5 to 20 percent. Most important, Kasson refused to consider reductions in the woolen schedule, which was of prime importance to France. None of the reductions granted to France had been given to any other country at that time. Soon after the conclusion of negotiations with France, Kasson also signed reciprocity treaties with

[18]U.S. Tariff Commission, *Reciprocity and Commercial Treaties*, p. 224.
[19]Ibid., pp. 216–17.

the United Kingdom for Barbados, British Guiana, Turks and Caicos islands, Jamaica, Trinidad, and Bermuda; with Denmark for St. Croix; and with Nicaragua, Ecuador, the Dominican Republic, and Argentina.

The treaty with France, and specifically Kasson's failure to secure the entire minimum schedule, elicited considerable controversy within the United States, particularly among the boot and shoe manufacturers of Massachusetts. Kasson defended his actions, arguing that his critics did "not take into account that [the treaty] required the consent of France. If the United States could have included them, it would have been done . . . I endeavored to the best of my ability to get [boots and shoes] in, but they absolutely refused to allow them, as obstinately as we, on our part, refused concessions on woolen goods and some other articles they wanted."[20] Although the several treaties were strongly supported by the president, a majority in Congress, and many producer groups, the specifically disaffected groups who felt either damaged or ignored by the French treaty combined with others who feared any real or apparent change in America's commitment to protection to prevent the passage of the treaty. Despite strenuous efforts by McKinley to dislodge the French treaty and others from the Senate Finance Committee, he had not succeeded at the time of his death. Lacking McKinley's base of support within the party, Theodore Roosevelt was forced to rely on Aldrich and other conservative senators who opposed the section four reciprocity treaties. Without the president's active support, the treaties died a quiet death. Disheartened, Kasson resigned on March 9, 1901. No additional treaties were negotiated.[21]

The Payne-Aldrich Tariff

With average rates of duty slightly below those of the Wilson-Gorman Act of 1894, the Payne-Aldrich Act of 1909 was the most liberal tariff passed since the Civil War. Like the Dingley Act, the Payne-Aldrich Tariff was directed at breaching and eliminating the discriminatory tariff walls of continental Europe. It recognized the inadequacies of reciprocity, however, and instituted more active maximum-minimum tariff schedules and embraced the liberal rule of nondiscrimination—or the "open door"—in international trade. Despite these reforms and its slightly more liberal design, however, the bill remained solidly protectionist.

[20]Quoted in ibid., p. 217. See also Edward Younger, *John A. Kasson: Politics and Diplomacy from Lincoln to McKinley* (Iowa City: State Historical Society of Iowa, 1955), pp. 364–79.
[21]U.S. Tariff Commission, *Reciprocity and Commercial Treaties*, pp. 209–14.

The Dingley Act, generally associated with a period of rising prosperity, remained in force longer than any other tariff in American history. Because of the aftereffects of three tariff revisions in eight years, no policy maker voiced much enthusiasm for undertaking another costly reform. Yet, as the first decade of the twentieth century progressed, America's industrial structure continued to evolve and the rates of the Dingley Act became increasingly anachronistic. The short but severe depression or "Roosevelt Panic" of 1907 also severed the link between high protection and prosperity. By the end of his second term, Roosevelt concluded that the time for tariff reform was ripe. Believing the goodwill that typically followed a presidential election necessary for successful revision, however, Roosevelt refused to take up this contentious issue. Rather, he encouraged his hand-picked successor, William Howard Taft, to lead the fight.

In the 1908 presidential campaign, both parties supported tariff reform. The Democratic platform stated, "We favor immediate revision of the tariff by the reduction of import duties." The Republican platform, on the other hand, put forth a new and somewhat ambiguous approach to protection. "In all tariff legislation," it declared, "the true principle of protection is best maintained by the imposition of such duties as will equal the difference between the cost of production at home and abroad, together with a reasonable profit for American industries."[22] Though possessing the virtue of apparent moderation (that is, promising no more than equal costs of production and a reasonable profit), carried to its logical conclusion this true principle of protection would eliminate the basis for all international trade.[23] Nonetheless, this platform plank indicated to many, including Taft, that the tariff would actually be lowered if it were implemented, suggesting that current rates of duty were often perceived as more than sufficient to equalize the differences in the costs of production and yielding more than a reasonable profit.

In his Inaugural Address, Taft called for a special session of Congress to implement the Republican tariff reform program. After reiterating the true principle of protection, Taft asked for a general reduction in the tariff: "It is thought that there has been such a change in conditions since the enactment of the Dingley Act, drafted on a similarly protective principle, that the measure of the tariff above stated will permit the

[22]Quoted in Asher Isaacs, *International Trade, Tariff and Commercial Politics* (Chicago: Irwin, 1948), pp. 212, 211.
[23]Frank W. Taussig, *The Tariff History of the United States*, 8th ed. (New York: Putnam, 1931), p. 363.

reduction of rates in certain schedules and will require the advancement of few, if any."[24]

On March 17, two days after the special session of Congress began, Sereno E. Payne (R.-N.Y.) chairman of the House Ways and Means Committee and a moderate protectionist, introduced a modest downward revision of the tariff. The House quickly passed the bill with few changes. The more protectionist Senate, as it had done several times before, rewrote important sections of the bill by adding a total of 847 amendments—nearly all of which raised the level of protection found in the House bill.

Despite the numerous changes introduced by the Senate, the Payne-Aldrich Act did succeed in lowering the level of protection, but not by as much as originally expected or hoped. The tariff level on dutiable imports was reduced from 47.6 to 41.0 percent (see Table 4.1). Likewise, the free list was expanded from 45.1 to 51.3 percent and the rate of duty on all imports was lowered from 26.2 to 20.0 percent. These were the lowest duties since the Civil War, but they were only marginally lower than those found in the Wilson-Gorman Act of 1894.

Complementing these lower rates, the Republican platform also favored the open door, or the principle of nondiscrimination in international trade (with the exception of colonial reciprocity). Instead of adopting the unconditional MFN principle, however, the Payne-Aldrich Act relied on continued bilateralism through maximum-minimum tariff schedules. There was no doubt from the beginning of the debate that the Payne-Aldrich Act would contain such a provision. Incorporated into the bill by both the House and Senate committees, the maximum-minimum schedules were, as Aldrich noted, widely believed to be the most important part of the 1909 act. Indeed, Payne devoted much of his opening speech in the House to this provision. Even the Democratic minority members of the Ways and Means Committee supported the concept of maximum-minimum schedules, although they argued that the minimum schedule proposed by the Republicans should be the maximum schedule of the bill.[25]

With the exhaustion of the bargaining authority delegated to the president in section three of the Dingley Act and the failure of the section four treaties to gain congressional approval, the maximum-minimum schedules were proposed as a more effective lever to open

[24]James D. Richardson, comp., *A Compilation of the Messages and Papers of the Presidents*, 10 vols. (New York: Bureau of National Literature, 1911), 10: 7749.
[25]Minority Report, reprinted in *Congressional Record*, 61st Cong., 1st sess., 1909, pp. 60–61.

foreign and particularly European markets to American goods while maintaining the essential structure of protection at home. The final version of the bill stated that the maximum schedule, set 25 percent *ad valorem* higher than the minimum schedule, was to be the general tariff and take effect on March 31, 1910, unless the president with the aid of the Tariff Board created by the bill were to certify that the exporting country did not unduly discriminate against American goods. The provision was designed to remove Congress—which had proven to be an impediment in the past—from the decision-making process; tie the hands of the president, thereby forcing him to implement the desired action; and ease the diplomatic controversy which might erupt by providing an inducement for not discriminating against American products rather than a penalty for such discrimination.[26]

In a rhetorical question, Aldrich clearly set forth the objectives of the provision:

> What are the conditions which have led up to this legislation, and what is attempted to be reached by it? Germany and France, and other countries, acting entirely within the legitimate sphere of their own jurisdictions, have enacted maximum and minimum tariffs . . . [which] discriminate unfairly against the United States. . . . We merely propose to put it in the power of our administration to say to a foreign government, "You must either permit the products of the United States to enter your country upon reasonable terms, without unjust discriminations and without preferential duties, or you will pay, when you send your products to the United States, the higher rate of duty."[27]

The reciprocity provision of the Dingley Act, as applied to Europe, did not seek special advantages for American producers, but the United States did not dismiss the option of pursuing such advantages in the future or in Latin America at that time. In the maximum-minimum provision of the Payne-Aldrich Act, however, the United States overturned its earlier conception of reciprocity and embraced the liberal principle of nondiscrimination in trade, to which it had given only sporadic support in the past.[28] In arguing for the maximum-minimum

[26]See Aldrich, in *Congressional Record*, 61st Cong., 1st sess., 1909, p. 285.
[27]Ibid., p. 4090.
[28]Before 1890, American trade policy was largely consistent with the open door. It was not, however, an explicit goal of this policy and it was violated in the reciprocity treaties between the United States and Canada (1854) and Hawaii (1875). The first explicit endorsement of the open-door principle by the United States occurred at the Berlin Conference on the Congo held in 1884. See Younger, *Kasson*, p. 332; and Charles S. Campbell, *The Transformation of American Foreign Relations, 1865–1900* (New York: Harper & Row, 1976).

provision, Representative Edgar Crumpacker (R.-Ind.), a member of the Ways and Means Committee, stated:

> Our foreign commercial and industrial policy ought to be that of the open door. We only ask equal consideration at the hands of foreign countries, and that we should insist upon. I have little respect for reciprocity in its narrow sense—in the sense that it is a system of international dickers under which one line of products may secure special advantages in foreign markets in consideration of a grant of special advantages to a particular line of products in return. . . . The broad reciprocity of treating all competitors and all producers alike is the principle that this country ought to encourage as the permanent commercial policy of the civilized world.[29]

By accepting the open-door principle, the United States displayed its newly found confidence in its ability to compete in international markets. Because of its position as the most productive nation-state within the international economy, the United States no longer needed to rely on the special favors or unilateral advantages that reciprocity often yielded in order to expand exports abroad. In this second phase, the United States gradually recognized that all it needed to reign supreme in export competition was a "fair field and no favor."[30]

President Taft signed the Payne-Aldrich Act into law on August 5, 1909, and immediately charged the State Department and Tariff Board with investigating tariff laws abroad and their effects upon American exports. He also commenced negotiations with foreign countries. In exchange for the application of the minimum schedule, Germany agreed to grant the United States its full minimum schedule. Portugal and Austria-Hungary made similar agreements. In return for the minimum schedule, France tripled the number of American products receiving its minimum tariff. Altogether, the United States successfully negotiated twenty-three agreements. By April 1, 1910, President Taft was able to certify that the United States faced no "undue" discriminations from any country and that the goods of every country would receive the benefits of the minimum schedule.

[29]*Congressional Record*, 61st Cong., 1st sess., 1909, p. 285.

[30]The one exception to this trend was Taft's effort to obtain a reciprocity treaty with Canada. This was one of the central goals of the second half of his administration. An agreement was reached with Canada in January 1911. Significant concessions were made on both sides. After considerable effort, it was approved by the Senate on July 26, 1911, only to be rejected by Canada because of several indiscreet comments by Americans who believed the treaty was the first step toward annexing their northern neighbor. After expending his limited political capital, Taft was then undermined from abroad. See U.S. Tariff Commission, *Reciprocity and Commercial Treaties*, pp. 368–81; and U.S. Tariff Commission, *Reciprocity with Canada: A Study of the Arrangement of 1911* (Washington, D.C.: U.S. Government Printing Office, 1920).

The maximum-minimum schedules of the Payne-Aldrich Act were generally regarded as a success. By securing all of Germany's minimum tariff and a great extension of American goods on France's minimum schedule, the Taft administration breached the continental European tariff walls. Yet, as the case of France again demonstrates, Taft did not succeed in removing all discriminatory trade barriers abroad.

America's ability to negotiate over foreign trade discriminations was limited by the continued strength of the protectionists at home. Whereas in the Dingley Act the protectionists directly thwarted the executive's use of reciprocity to expand American exports by excluding sugar from section three and blocking the ratification of the section four treaties, in 1909 the ability of the president to negotiate abroad was indirectly limited by the still high duties in the Payne-Aldrich Act. Taft and others, despite the downward trend of the 1909 bill, felt that the revision barely met Republican pledges of tariff reform and that the use of the maximum tariff, thereby increasing the rate of protection by 25 percent, would engender considerable domestic dissatisfaction.[31] As a result, Taft made clear his disinclination to use the full bargaining leverage created by the provision in his 1909 Annual Message to Congress. Seeking to quell the anxieties of opponents who feared further increases in the tariff through the maximum-minimum provision, Taft stated:

> The discretion granted to the Executive by the terms "unduly discriminatory" is wide. In order that the maximum duty shall be charged against the imports from a country, it is necessary that he shall find on the part of that country not only discriminations in its laws or the practice under them against . . . the United States, but that the discriminations found shall be undue; that is, without good and fair reason. I conceive that this power was reposed in the President with the hope that the maximum duties might never be applied in any case.[32]

Signaling the domestic constraints on his administration, Taft undermined his ability to negotiate effectively with other countries. Nevertheless, the Payne-Aldrich Act achieved greater success in dismantling discriminatory European trade restrictions than its immediate predecessor.

THE DOMESTIC POLICY PROCESS

McKinley, Reciprocity, and the Dingley Tariff

The principal debate over American trade strategy in 1897 and the years immediately following was not between Republicans and Demo-

---

[31] Taussig, *Tariff History*, p. 405.
[32] Richardson, comp., *Messages and Papers*, 10: 7806.

crats. The former controlled both houses of Congress and the presidency. Rather, it was between the president, who was more concerned with the changing interests of the United States within the international economic structure, and the Senate conservatives, who primarily emphasized party unity and constituent support—backing the president's program only so far as it promoted this goal.

Between 1890, when he chaired the House Ways and Means Committee, and 1897, when he accepted the presidency, McKinley was transformed from an ardent protectionist who questioned the need for foreign markets into the nation's strongest advocate of export expansion and reciprocity. Although reciprocity was one of the few popular provisions of the 1890 tariff, this conversion does not appear to have occurred simply for reasons of political expediency; the Senate conservatives with whom the president had been closely associated did not undergo a similar evolution in their thought, and McKinley now spoke so strongly on the issue that it is hard to question his sincerity. Rather, the president's new position on export expansion appears to have resulted from two considerations. First, the greater international power and prestige enjoyed by the United States—especially after the Spanish-American War—encouraged McKinley and others to take a more active role in foreign affairs. Second, McKinley's new position as president and leader of the foreign policy executive opened him to different institutional interests and constraints than he had confronted as a representative from Ohio.[33]

Like Cleveland and Blaine, McKinley became the spokesman for America's national trade interest. Having made his congressional reputation as an expert on the tariff, McKinley was closely associated with the success or failure of this policy and deeply knowledgeable about its inner workings and details. McKinley's role in foreign affairs was enhanced by the weakness and ill health of his secretary of state, John Sherman, a former Republican senator from Ohio who was appointed to the cabinet only to create a place in the Senate for Marcus Hanna, the president's political associate and friend.[34] Although Sherman had chaired the Senate Foreign Relations Committee for many years, personal rancor over the ensuing appointment scandal and a failing memory rendered him an ineffective secretary of state who played at best a marginal role in the administration.

McKinley cajoled legislators, consulted informally with key members of the legislature, kept abreast of developments within Congress, and intimated to the press that he did not favor any radical increase over the

[33]Margaret Leech, *In The Days of McKinley* (New York: Harper, 1959), pp. 141–42.
[34]Ibid., p. 99.

Wilson-Gorman rates. Yet he did not become directly involved in the congressional debates over the tariff as had his two predecessors. Rather, McKinley adopted a relatively low political profile while the tariff bill was under discussion.[35] The president's reticence may have derived from his confidence in congressional tariff-making procedures, which he had so recently led, or memories of irritation at Blaine's attempts to influence the 1890 act.

McKinley was also confident he could rewrite the bill once it was passed by Congress. Assured that reciprocity would be adopted in the final bill, McKinley intended to use this provision to lower duties and reshape the final measure to his liking.[36] Accordingly, once the bill was passed, McKinley took a more active role in formulating trade strategy. He appointed Kasson, a respected diplomat, as special reciprocity commissioner and encouraged him vigorously to pursue the new legislative provisions contained in sections three and four. Once the section four treaties were negotiated, McKinley submitted them to Congress with his strong support.

The treaties, however, languished in committee under the opposition of Senate conservatives, and particularly Aldrich, who controlled the powerful Finance Committee. For Aldrich, and other conservative legislators reciprocity was merely a political expedient to be used in the larger pursuit of party harmony and constituent politics. In the making of both the 1890 and 1897 tariff bills, the Senate leadership was threatened by defections from western "Silver" Republicans, whose votes were needed to pass any bill. Aldrich appears to have thrown his support behind Blaine's reciprocity proposal in 1890 not because he was persuaded by the arguments but as a means of satisfying western interests, which were strongly in favor of reciprocity as a means of expanding the region's agricultural exports. Aldrich used reciprocity in a similar but more complex manner in 1897. As a means of keeping potentially renegade western Republicans securely within the party fold, the 1896 Republican platform had declared in favor of bimetalism, and McKinley had promised to begin negotiations with the European powers, of which Great Britain was the most important, over international monetary reform. Soon after the election and in a move welcomed by conservative Republicans, France offered to exchange its support on bimetalism for favorable treatment in the forthcoming tariff deliberations. When France noted that it was far from satisfied with the House version of the

[35]On McKinley's role in the passage of the Dingley bill, see Lewis L. Gould, *The Presidency of William McKinley* (Lawrence: Regents Press of Kansas, 1980), pp. 43–44.
[36]Ibid.

Dingley bill, Aldrich responded with significantly lower duties in the draft bill submitted by the Senate Finance Committee. After losing control of the bill on the floor of the upper chamber, partly to the Silver Republicans, who preferred "free coinage" to any agreement on bimetalism, Aldrich and his allies moved to reciprocity as embodied in section four as a means of mollifying France. Even with French support, which was by now only halfhearted, the United States was unable to persuade Great Britain on bimetalism, and negotiations were terminated. Soon after the passage of the Dingley Act, the Senate conservatives' most important motivation for supporting reciprocity had evaporated.[37]

Although Aldrich continued to voice his support for the concept of reciprocity, he declared his firm opposition to all of the section four treaties, and particulary the treaty with France, stating that the so-called "Kasson treaties" were "jug-handled affairs in which very little was obtained by the United States for what was given away."[38] Several reasons have been advanced for the opposition of Aldrich and others to the treaties. After the failure of the bimetalism negotiations, Aldrich and his allies broke with the Silver Republicans and may have withdrawn their support on issues such as reciprocity, which were of concern to the westerners. Many in the United States, including Aldrich and the conservatives, were disillusioned with France because of its only modest support on bimetalism and its actions during the Spanish-American War. Most important, legislators were under strong pressure to oppose the treaties from societal groups whose interests would be damaged by one or more of the proposed agreements. Although a majority of producer groups favored reciprocity, the wool, tobacco, and sugar growers feared competition from the Caribbean island colonies covered by the treaties. In addition, many New England textile manufacturers feared competition from France, and the boot and shoe manufacturers were disappointed that their goods were excluded from the treaty. With the latter two groups making up Aldrich's base of support in Rhode Island, the negatively affected manufacturers and agricultural interests were able to form an effective veto group over the treaties.[39]

Congressional opposition to the section four treaties directly threat-

[37]On the link between silver, France, and the Dingley Act see H. Wayne Morgan, *William McKinley and His America* (Syracuse: Syracuse University Press, 1963), pp. 278–79; and Gould, *Presidency of McKinley*, pp. 40–41.
[38]Nathaniel W. Stephenson, *Nelson W. Aldrich: A Leader in American Politics* (New York: Charles Scribner's Sons, 1930), p. 178.
[39]On the politics of reciprocity, see Younger, *Kasson*, pp. 364–79; and U.S. Tariff Commission, *Reciprocity and Commercial Treaties*.

ened McKinley's "greatest ambition," which according to Margaret Leech, was to "round out his career by gaining American supremacy in world markets" and develop "commerce as an agency of international accord."[40] Following Blaine's example of 1890, McKinley launched a nationwide speaking tour designed to break the treaties out of committee by building public awareness of America's growing need for export markets and public support for reciprocity. The tour and McKinley's speeches culminated at the Pan-American Exposition in Buffalo. McKinley's final speech is worth quoting at length because it demonstrates the evolution in his thought since 1890, his awareness of the changed interests of the United States within the international economy, and his attempt to rally public opinion behind reciprocity.

> Our industrial enterprises which have grown to such great proportions affect the homes and occupations of the people and welfare of the country. Our capacity to produce has developed so enormously and our products have so multiplied that the problem of more markets requires our urgent and immediate attention. . . .
>
> A system which provides a mutual exchange of commodities is manifestly essential to the continued healthful growth of our export trade. We must not repose in fancied security that we can forever sell everything and buy little or nothing. If such a thing were possible, it would not be best for us or for those with whom we deal. We should take from our customers such of their products as we can use without harm to our industries and labor. Reciprocity is the natural outgrowth of our wonderful industrial development under the domestic policy now firmly established. What we produce beyond our domestic consumption must have a vent abroad. The excess must be relieved through a foreign outlet and we should sell everywhere we can, and buy wherever the buying will enlarge our sales and productions, and thereby make a greater demand for home labor.
>
> The period of exclusiveness is past. The expansion of our trade and commerce is the pressing problem. Commercial wars are unprofitable. A policy of good will and friendly trade relations will prevent reprisals. Reciprocity treaties are in harmony with the spirit of the times; measures of retaliation are not. If, perchance, some of our tariffs are no longer needed, for revenue or to encourage and protect our industries at home, why should they not be employed to extend and promote our markets abroad?[41]

This was, however, McKinley's last public speech. How effective it would have been in dislodging the treaties from committee is unclear; as the

[40]Leech, *In the Days of McKinley*, pp. 141–42.
[41]"President McKinley's Last Public Utterance to the People, Buffalo, New York, September 5, 1901," in Richardson, comp., *Messages and Papers*, 9: 6620–21.

president's second term began in 1901, the Senate conservatives clearly appeared on the defensive. Yet the course of American politics immediately underwent an important and unexpected shift. McKinley was shot the day after his reciprocity speech and died one week later, leaving the government in the hands of Theodore Roosevelt.

Despite his election as vice-president, Roosevelt was an "outsider" without a strong base of support in the national Republican party. An early free trader, Roosevelt had modified his heretical views on the tariff while governor of New York so as to gain wider acceptance within the Republican organization.[42] Nonetheless, his views remained suspect. Already troubled by McKinley's efforts in favor of reciprocity at Buffalo, the Senate conservatives were deeply worried that Roosevelt would hold true to his public promise to carry out his predecessor's policies. Recognizing his need for congressional supporters, however, Roosevelt quickly approached Aldrich and his senatorial allies. Within a few weeks, a "Gentlemen's Agreement" was made between the new president and the elder party statesmen, Aldrich, Allison, John Spooner of Wisconsin, and O. H. Platt of Connecticut, trading political support for the quiet death of reciprocity. In his first Annual Message to Congress, Roosevelt accordingly brought the pending reciprocity treaties to the legislature's attention but did not ask for their passage. Despite the efforts of Secretary of State John Hay encouraging the president to support the treaties strongly, Roosevelt refused to raise the issue of the tariff—preferring to bequeath this question to his successor.

The success of McKinley's strategy for export expansion was clearly hampered by the need for subsequent approval of the section four reciprocity agreements by Congress, where a small but powerful minority could block the program. McKinley may have erred by not pushing harder for greater bargaining leverage in section three and executive discretion in section four while the Dingley bill was still being written by Congress. Yet, as H. Wayne Morgan writes on this point, "Had McKinley pressed for more, he would likely have ended with less, for the majority of Congress were far behind him on reciprocity."[43]

Roosevelt, Taft, and the Payne-Aldrich Act

The 1909 Tariff Act was passed in the absence of real executive leadership. Taft was reluctant to pursue and assume the presidency and,

[42]See Richard Cleveland Baker, *The Tariff under Roosevelt and Taft* (Hastings, Neb.: Democrat Printing, 1941), pp. 12–76; and James Ford Rhodes, *The McKinley and Roosevelt Administrations, 1897–1909* (New York: Macmillan, 1922), p. 220.
[43]Morgan, *McKinley*, p. 280.

indeed, somewhat repulsed by the bargaining at the center of American politics. Naturally inclined to avoid conflict, Taft was a timid and politically inept president. He knew neither how to mobilize public opinion nor to manage relations with Congress, although when passionately driven he managed to do both passably well.[44] But under normal conditions, Taft had a special knack for doing good badly. As Woodrow Wilson, Taft's successor, stated in November 1910, "If I were to sum up all the criticisms that have been made of the gentleman who is now President of the United States, I could express them all in this: The American people are disappointed because he has not led them. . . . They clearly long for someone to put the pressure of the opinion of all the people of the United States upon Congress."[45]

Although it cannot be ruled out, there is little evidence that Taft or his secretary of state, Philander C. Knox, who is widely recognized as having "lacked qualities of statesmanship,"[46] either understood or was sensitive to the constraints and opportunities of the international economic structure. The president was supportive of lower duties and the maximum-minimum schedules, but the trade strategy revealed in the Payne-Aldrich Act did not originate in his administration. Rather, Taft's trade strategy was set by Roosevelt and most forcefully advocated by members of the former president's inner circle. Although Roosevelt himself refused to act on the tariff issue, he constructed the framework that would guide his less energetic successor.

After the turn of the century, the momentum behind tariff reform gradually increased because of pressure from the larger internationally oriented firms, some of which were already beginning to invest abroad, and exporters, who were generally unhappy with the high Dingley rates and the failure of the section four reciprocity treaties. Roosevelt equivocated on the tariff, suggesting in 1903 that revision might be possible if he were reelected but only if there was "some reasonable hope of bringing the party up to that position." Indeed, as expected given the position of the United States within the international economic structure and Britain's continuing hegemony, no strong desire existed to lower the tariff, even among Roosevelt and his closest advisers. Writing to Senator Henry Cabot Lodge from Africa while the Payne-Aldrich bill was under

---

[44]For Taft as a person and president, see Judith Icke Anderson, *William Howard Taft: An Intimate History* (New York: Norton, 1981), pp. 21–36. Taft's more passionate approach to policy was demonstrated by his role in the passage of the Philippine Schedule of the Dingley Act and the Canadian reciprocity agreement.
[45]Paolo E. Coletta, *The Presidency of William Howard Taft* (Lawrence: University Press of Kansas, 1973), p. 56.
[46]Ibid., p. 183.

consideration, Roosevelt cogently summarized his position on the tariff: "Of course you are bound to have dissatisfaction with any Tariff Bill simply because, as far as I can see, there is no real ground for dissatisfaction, of a serious kind, with the present tariff; so that what we have to meet is not an actual need, but a mental condition among our people who believe there ought to be a change."[47]

Pandering to this "mental condition," the 1908 Republican platform nonetheless declared in favor of tariff reform, and Taft—lacking a deep commitment to the issue but possessing a strong sense of obligation—set himself to the task. While the bill was being prepared for the special session of Congress, Taft was persuaded by Speaker Joseph Cannon not to intervene in the House and Senate proceedings until the measure reached the conference committee. Later criticized for his quiescence, Taft was supported in this course at the time by Payne, Aldrich, and Roosevelt. Paolo E. Coletta concludes that, although he consulted often with Cannon and Aldrich, like McKinley "Taft felt that the branches of government were coordinated and that he should not intrude upon the workings of the law-making department." Though agreeing not to interfere directly, Taft was fully ready to use his constitutionally designated veto power if necessary. In an interview with Robert LaFollette (R.-Wisc.), leader of the Senate insurgents who opposed the Payne-Aldrich bill, Taft threatened, "You and your associates in the Senate go ahead, criticize the bill, amend it, cut down the duties—go after it hard. I will keep track of your amendments. I will read every word of the speeches you make, and when they lay that bill down before me, unless it complies with the platform, I will veto it."[48] Despite this strongly worded warning, few expected Taft to follow through on his threat and veto a completed bill. The logrolling proceeded as usual.

When the bill reached the conference committee, the congressional leadership—as promised—asked for Taft's suggestions. Originally expecting to have considerable influence at this stage, Taft was surprised to find himself facing a conference committee which Cannon had packed with protectionists. Nonetheless, Taft forcefully demanded the limited changes he could effect—particularly lower duties on lumber and gloves. After considerable resistance, the conference committee eventually conceded. Taft declared victory and signed the bill. But the victory, however sweet, was truly small.

The Payne-Aldrich Act was ill-received in the nation at large; many

---

[47]*Selections from the Correspondence of Theodore Roosevelt and Henry Cabot Lodge*, 2 vols. (New York: Charles Scribner's Sons, 1925), 2:7, 335.

[48]Coletta, *Presidency of Taft*, pp. 61, 63.

voters believed that the Republicans had failed to carry through their campaign promises. Rather than following the examples of Harrison, Blaine, and Cleveland by speaking out on the bill before it was passed, Taft undertook a nationwide speaking tour soon after its completion to build public support for the measure. Demonstrating again his remarkable lack of tact and timing, Taft declared in Winona, Wisconsin, the heartland of the LaFollette-led insurgency, that "this [Payne-Aldrich Act] is the best tariff bill that the Republican party has ever passed."[49] In the uproar that followed this statement, Taft later recognized that the "comparative would have been a better description than the superlative."[50] Nonetheless, Taft continued to defend the bill and went down to defeat on this issue and others in 1912.

The maximum-minimum schedules of the Payne-Aldrich Tariff were a popular and important departure in American trade strategy. Although similar measures had been in use in Europe for over two decades, the precise origin of support for maximum-minimum schedules in the United States remains unknown. By the middle of the first decade of the twentieth century, however, two important and related sources of support clearly existed. The first group of supporters were the political and economic expansionists closely associated with President Roosevelt's inner circle or "tennis cabinet." Within this circle, Lodge—a member of the Senate Finance Committee in 1909—was strongly advocating maximum-minimum schedules to the president as early as June 1905.[51] The second supporter was Elihu Root, then secretary of state and later—during the deliberations on the Payne-Aldrich bill—senator from New York. Upon completing a tour of South America in the fall of 1906, Root came out in support of maximum-minimum schedules in an address before the Trans-Mississippi Commercial Congress: "A single straight-out tariff was all very well in the world of single straight-out tariffs; but we have passed on, during the course of years, into a world for the most part of maximum and minimum tariffs, and with our single-rate tariff we are left with very little opportunity to reciprocate good treatment from other countries in their tariffs and very little opportunity to defend ourselves against bad treatment."[52]

Although the vigor of Roosevelt's support for the concept is unclear, the president was keenly aware that the momentum behind the maximum-minimum proposal came from within the executive branch. Writ-

[49]Ibid., p. 73.

[50]Donald F. Anderson, *William Howard Taft: A Conservative's Conception of the Presidency* (Ithaca: Cornell University Press, 1973), p. 208.

[51]*Correspondence of Roosevelt and Lodge*, 2:129.

[52]Philip C. Jessop, *Elihu Root*, 2 vols. (New York: Dodd, Mead, 1938), 2:215.

ing to Lodge in August 1906, Roosevelt noted that Representative James Sherman (R.-N.Y.) objected to the maximum-minimum concept and that Cannon had been silent on the issue. As for the general population, Roosevelt wrote, "I do not believe that the voters as a whole know anything about the maximum and minimum. I do not think they have been educated up to it."[53]

With support from Roosevelt and Root, the 1908 Republican National Convention, chaired by Lodge, included the proposal for maximum-minimum schedules in the call for tariff reform. As in the question of lower duties, Taft does not appear to have possessed strong views on the matter, but he supported the proposal as a continuation of the Roosevelt program to which he was pledged.

In the formulation of the Payne-Aldrich Tariff, the most important debate in Congress concerning the maximum-minimum schedules occurred not over the wisdom of the objectives behind the policy but over the most effective means of implementing it. The House version of the bill provided for a minimum schedule to be the general or common tariff and a maximum schedule, approximately 20 percent higher, to be levied against the goods of those countries found to discriminate against American exports. Concerned with diplomatic expediency and drawing upon his experience as secretary of state, Senator Root proposed the language finally adopted by the conference committee, which granted inducements for nondiscrimination rather than penalties for discrimination.

In the formulation of American trade strategy as revealed in the Payne-Aldrich Act, Taft and even more so Secretary of State Knox were "bit players" carrying through proposals decided upon in the Roosevelt administration. Had Taft exerted greater leverage over Congress early in the Payne-Aldrich debates, perhaps through the shrewd use of patronage, the tariff might have been lower. Still free riding on Great Britain and expecting bilateral negotiations to succeed, however, no one—Roosevelt and Root included—perceived a strong need to lower America's high tariff barriers at this time.

Britain's declining hegemony and America's new position as the most productive nation-state within the international economic structure were more evident in the maximum-minimum proposal, in which American leaders attempted to fashion a more effective instrument to scale the tariff walls of Europe. Although Taft did not play a major role in passing this legislation, the momentum behind the policy was clearly but not exclusively focused within the foreign policy executive of the Roosevelt administration.

[53]*Correspondence of Roosevelt and Lodge*, 2:227.

CONCLUSION

American trade strategy between 1897 and 1912 offers mixed support for interest-group and political-party explanations. Between 1889, one year before the McKinley Act, and 1899, two years after the Dingley Act, the proportion of American manufacturers either moderately or highly dependent upon exports more than doubled, expanding from 28.1 to 57.6 percent of all industry by value (see Table 2.1). Yet the average rates of duty in 1890 and 1897 were essentially the same, and the second bill may actually have been higher.

The internationalization of American industry continued over the first decade of the twentieth century, with the proportion of moderate and highly export-dependent manufacturers increasing to 63.6 percent of American industry in 1909. Although this evolution is in the correct direction to explain the greater liberalness of the Payne-Aldrich Act, such a slow and marginal shift seems insufficient to explain the differences between the 1897 and 1909 tariffs. Recognizing that nearly two-thirds of American industry was exporting at least some of its production, however, does explain why Taft was constrained from threatening to impose even higher duties upon imports in the maximum-minimum schedules.

To the extent that the McKinley, Dingley, and Payne-Aldrich acts all share a commitment to high protection, their Republican sponsorship appears important. Yet differences do exist between these acts, particularly regarding the varying provisions on export expansion and the comparative liberalness of the Payne-Aldrich Tariff, which cannot be explained by appeals to their common lineage. Most political-party explanations recognize, of course, that party platforms are written to reflect changing political environments, but nearly all treat this environment in an ad hoc manner, ultimately begging the question and rendering the explanation unsatisfactory.

Despite the shift in instruments from reciprocity to maximum-minimum schedules, American trade strategy in this second phase reflected a single underlying purpose: to preserve and expand exports, particularly to continental Europe, while causing the smallest disruption possible to the American system of protection. This amalgam of protection and export expansion bears an affinity to the first phase of American trade strategy discussed in Chapter 3. The passive, nonretaliatory trade strategy of Great Britain enabled the United States to continue its policy of domestic protection and export expansion first pursued between 1887 and 1897. Yet the more important constraint facing American trade strategists during this second phase was the expanding trade horizons of the United States coupled with the growing protectionism and discrimination of the continental European states. Seeking to ensure access for its exporters while taking advantage of Britain's passivity, the United States responded to the Europeans through bilateral bargaining reinforced by the coercive power of high tariffs, using first reciprocity and later, as its confidence in its ability to compete internationally grew and the negotiating authority granted to the executive in the Dingley Act expired, maximum-minimum schedules. Rather than unilaterally lowering its own duties and adopting the unconditional MFN principle, the United States sought to use its high tariffs as a bilateral battering ram against the tariff walls of Europe. Adopted without regard for the stability and openness of the international economy as a whole, this strategy of high tariffs and bilateral bargaining was relatively successful in obtaining minimum tariff schedules in Germany and, to a lesser extent, France.

This strategy was made possible by the position of the United States as a single opportunist within an international economic structure of declining British hegemony and motivated by its own high and rapidly expanding relative labor productivity. The latter created the incentive to expand exports, and the former the opportunity to do so without significant alterations in the existing policy of protection.

The principal conflicts and debates over American trade strategy in this period occurred between Congress, which channeled manifest societal demands into the policy process, and the foreign policy executive. In 1897, McKinley, formerly an ardent protectionist, emerged as the most important advocate of reciprocity and export expansion. Although Taft's role in the formulation of trade strategy and particularly the maximum-minimum schedules was less apparent and decisive, he nonetheless implemented a strategy developed primarily within Roosevelt's foreign policy executive. In both cases, the executive championed policies designed to respond to the constraints and opportunities of the international economic structure but was hindered by legislative protectionism. Sugar was excluded from section three of the Dingley Act, and the section four treaties were never ratified by Congress. And the utility of the maximum-minimum schedules was limited by the still high duties of the Payne-Aldrich Act. Had McKinley and Taft demanded more in the legislative process, or had the former not been assassinated in 1901, the outcome might have been different. Yet, despite legislative constraints, in both instances the United States did succeed in at least partially breaching the tariff walls of Europe—its most important systemically derived objective.

CHAPTER FIVE

The Politics of Opportunistic Accommodation, 1912–1930

The United States departed dramatically from its historic policy of high tariff protection in the Underwood Act of 1913. Containing the lowest rates of duty of any tariff act between the Civil War and the late 1950s, and far lower than those of the Payne-Aldrich Act of 1909, the Underwood Act also explicitly endorsed the principle of reciprocal tariff reductions. Nine years later, in an international economy still unsettled by the war, the United States raised its duties moderately in the Fordney-McCumber Act of 1922. It compensated for this decline in liberalism by adopting a more active trade strategy and the unconditional most-favored-nation principle. Contrary to the received wisdom on American tariff policy, and especially to the view of the Fordney-McCumber Act as simply a return to traditional Republican protectionism, this third phase of American trade strategy is characterized, I argue, by tariff restraint at home imposed by a fear of foreign retaliation. For the first time in American history, protection at home was compromised in favor of export expansion.

In the years immediately preceding World War I, the United Kingdom evolved from a hegemonic leader into an opportunist. This change in the international economic structure was primarily manifested in British domestic politics by a growing movement within the Conservative party for protection and imperial preferences. Having captured the party by 1912 and confident of winning the next election, the tariff reformers' relative success signaled that Britain's near century-old commitment to free trade at home and abroad could no longer be taken for granted.

This transformation of the international economic structure from hegemony into bilateral opportunism placed unprecedented constraints on American trade strategy in the years after 1912. Whereas the United States safely free rode on Britain's hegemonic leadership in the past, it now had little choice but to accommodate the new mixed interests of its major trading partner. These new constraints, primarily manifested in domestic political discourse as a fear of foreign retaliation for continued protectionism, prompted the accommodative trade strategy adopted in 1913 and pursued until the late 1920s.

Although the fear of retaliation, rooted in the structure of bilateral opportunism, restrained American tariff levels throughout this phase, the trade strategy of the United States was also affected by the level of international economic instability. As Britain's position gradually evolved within the international economic structure before World War I, the United States responded with the freer trade policy of the Underwood Act. The war, however, created significant political problems that were difficult to resolve. It also sharply disrupted century-old patterns of trade, money, and investment flows. All of these disruptions combined to create widespread international economic instability. As discussed in Chapter 1 and this chapter, instability increases the desires of opportunists for protection and decreases their willingness to cooperate. As expected, both Great Britain and the United States adopted higher but still restrained levels of protection following the war, and Anglo-American cooperation proved difficult.

LEARNING TO TANGO

The International Economic Structure

By 1912 the United Kingdom was no longer a hegemonic leader. Britain's position within the international economic structure had been rapidly declining since approximately 1900. The United States surpassed Great Britain in relative productivity during the late 1890s, and the latter's share of world trade fell from 17.5 percent in 1900 to 14.1 percent in 1913. As Britain's position evolved, the structure of the international economy changed, just before World War I, from hegemony to bilateral opportunism.

Britain experienced a small but growing protectionist movement in the early twentieth century. Led by Colonial Secretary Joseph Chamberlain, the tariff reformers made two demands: imperial preferences, in which Britain would abandon the unconditional MFN principle for reciprocal tariff preferences with its colonies, and a 10 percent duty on manufactured imports. These measures were necessary, Chamberlain argued, because of Britain's faltering trade position, which was largely the result of foreign tariffs designed to repel British goods. Tariff reform, according to Chamberlain, offered a way to prevent Britain from sliding into "decadence, impotence, and anarchy."[1] Britain's economic self-defense, in other words, required a return to protection and an expansion of its special trade relations with the colonies.

Throughout the prewar era, the issue of tariff reform threatened to split the Conservative party, which contained large factions of both free traders and reformers. In 1903, recognizing that he did not enjoy the full support of the party and expecting Prime Minister Arthur Balfour to join the ranks of the reformers with time, Chamberlain resigned from the cabinet so he could propagandize more freely. Balfour simultaneously engineered the resignation of the most outspoken free traders in the cabinet. With party unity as his principal goal and having created room for maneuver, Balfour fashioned a compromise program by announcing his support for protection and preferences while denying that it was "practical politics" to seek such a change in policy in the near future.[2] This compromise satisfied few. The party remained divided, and the Conservatives were voted out of office in 1906. Despite the growing strength of the tariff reformers, when the Payne-Aldrich Act was passed in the United States in 1909 Britain still appeared committed to free trade; even though protection was once again a contested political issue, the Conservatives were in opposition and the party was deeply divided.

While in opposition, Balfour could more easily side with Chamberlain, which he did in part by asserting that the Liberal government needed to "broaden the base of taxation" if its ambitious military and social reform programs were to be adequately funded.[3] Balfour continued to equivocate, searching for language that would signal his support for tariff reform without alienating the free traders. To the surprise of the Conservatives, the Liberals submitted and passed a "free-trade" budget in 1909, which made up the expected deficit through a highly progressive or graduated direct tax on income. The battle then moved to the more conservative House of Lords, which blocked the bill, precipitating a constitutional crisis by the unprecedented interference of the upper house in the passage of a revenue bill. In the elections that followed in January 1910, the Liberals retained control of the government, although the Conservatives increased the number of seats they controlled in the House of Commons. More important, the tariff re-

[1]Alan Sykes, *Tariff Reform in British Politics, 1903–1913* (Oxford: Clarendon, 1979), pp. 56, 218.
[2]Ibid., p. 51.
[3]Hon. George Peel, *The Tariff Reformers* (London: Methuen, 1913), pp. 31–47.

150

formers swept the Conservative Party, perhaps in part because of their financial and political backing of protectionists against standing free-trade members of their own party.[4]

Despite the expanded support for reform and his own increasingly protectionist views, Balfour continued to mediate between the two wings of the party. When a second election was called for December 1910, Balfour again searched for a compromise position on protection, announcing that if the Conservatives were elected any taxes on food imports—the basic building block of imperial preferences—would be submitted directly to the electorate for approval through a referendum. Perceived as simply postponing the day when preferences could be enacted, reformers opposed Balfour's newest strategy. In December the Conservatives were defeated again. Under increasing criticism from tariff reformers for his equivocal leadership, and after having led his party to three defeats in five years, Balfour resigned early in 1912 and was replaced as party leader by Bonar Law.

Although he had supported Balfour on the referendum issue, Law "had always been one of the most enthusiastic supporters of the tariff reform policy,"[5] and under his leadership the influence of the protectionists reached new heights. Throughout 1912, the Conservatives were increasingly confident that the government would fall and that they would be swept into power. Meanwhile, the party rallied around reform; although there was still disagreement between the "free fooders" and "wholehoggers," as the two principal factions came to be known, virtually all members of the Conservative party backed protection in some form. At a nationwide party conference in November of that year, one "reliable authority" declared that there was "an ovation from the 12,000 delegates there assembled which has never . . . been rivaled. On what were they united? On Tariff Reform and effective Imperial Preference."[6] By 1912—even though the Conservatives remained a minority in Parliament—the overthrow of Britain's near century-old policy of free trade appeared closer than ever before.

This rising protectionist sentiment among Britain's political elite was clear evidence that the structure of the international economy had changed and, more directly, that the continued leadership of the former hegemonic power could no longer be taken for granted. Conservatives continued to espouse free trade in principle but argued that the protectionist policies of other countries necessitated that Britain arm itself for

[4]Herbert G. Williams, *Through Tariffs to Prosperity* (London: Philip Allan, 1931), p. 22.
[5]Ibid., p. 23; Sykes writes that Law was "associated with the most extreme elements of the tariff reform movement" (*Tariff Reform*, p. 253).
[6]Peel, *Tariff Reformers*, p. 165, quotation on p. 5; and Sykes *Tariff Reform*, p. 256.

economic conflict and consolidate its imperial trading bloc. In other words, they rejected Britain's traditional dominant strategy of free trade at home, through which countries such as the United States had successfully exploited London's passivity. As a result, Britain's trade preferences increasingly resembled a prisoner's dilemma (see Figure 1.3), in which an unequivocal commitment to free trade would result in the "sucker's payoff" (FT/P)—an outcome preferred even less than universal protection (P/P).

The new position of the United Kingdom within the international economic structure posed a fundamental challenge to American trade policy. The proposed protective tariffs in the United Kingdom directly threatened American exports to its single most important market; although Britain's share of American exports had been steadily declining since the early 1890s, the English market still accounted for 24.2 percent of all American exports in 1913.[7] British protectionism also indirectly threatened American exports to other countries by delegitimating the policy of free trade; even after all the other major economic powers had turned to protectionism, Britain's adherence to the policy of free trade lent credence to the sophisms of Smith, Ricardo, and other economists. The imperial preference policy, seen in Britain as a necessary complement to protection, threatened even greater consequences for the United States by signaling that Britain was abdicating its position of leadership within the international economy and turning inward upon its colonial trading bloc. The reciprocal advantages to be exchanged between the United Kingdom and its colonies threatened not only America's access to the important British market but the ability of the United States to export to the various colonies as well. The net effect of Britain's growing tariff reform movement was to undermine confidence in the nation's commitment to free trade, thereby reducing the attractiveness of continued American free riding. The United States now had to consider the new, mixed trade interests of the United Kingdom in formulating its own trade strategy.

As in any prisoners' dilemma, the United States and the United Kingdom could adopt either mutual free trade (cooperate) or mutual protection (defect), but they could not simultaneously realize their preferred strategies of protection at home and free trade abroad. Thus the United States faced an important choice. It could, on one hand, continue its policy of domestic protection, further alienate Britain, and risk losing its

---

[7]U.S. Department of Commerce, Bureau of the Census, *Historical Statistics of the United States, Colonial Times to 1970* (Washington, D.C.: U.S. Government Printing Office, 1975), ser. U317–334, pp. 930–34.

most important export market. This loss, if it were to occur, would affect a broad range of American exporters. The Conservatives' proposed duty on manufactures would damage East Coast and Midwest industry, and imperial preferences would largely exclude American agricultural products from the British market and manufactures from the several colonial markets. Even though the Conservatives were not in power, this first option threatened high costs for the United States. On the other hand, the United States could reduce its domestic protection, thereby reinforcing the weakened position of British free traders, defusing the protectionists—who since Chamberlain had consistently maintained that foreign trade barriers were the source of the country's trade problems—and facilitating the continued openness of its principal export market. Reducing tariffs in the United States would not be easy, of course, for it required a basic alteration in the entrenched "American system" of protection—an alteration that would bring the politically dominant protectionists and the national trade interest into direct and fundamental conflict for the first time. Yet, if coupled with a more active trade strategy directed at maintaining or expanding free trade abroad, reducing protection promised significant rewards.

The Underwood Act and American Trade Strategy

Tariff reform was nearly inevitable in 1913. As discussed in Chapter 4, the Payne-Aldrich Tariff was unpopular, despite the efforts of President William Howard Taft to build support for the measure. The tariff issue, as before, divided the Democrats and Republicans. It was also one of the first issues which divided Taft and his former supporter, Theodore Roosevelt, ultimately causing the latter to bolt from the Republican party in the 1912 election.[8] Although it certainly aided him in the contest, Wilson did not owe his election to the Republican split. Wilson garnered 45.2 percent of the popular vote and 435 electoral college votes, to 29.7 percent and 88 votes for Roosevelt and 25.1 percent and 8 votes for Taft. If Roosevelt had not been in the race, many of his progressive supporters would likely have voted for Wilson, perhaps yielding him a smaller but nonetheless significant margin of victory. In addition, the Democrats captured both houses of Congress in 1912 for the first time since 1894, despite the absence of significant Progressive or "Bull Moose" party competition at this level. More important, in 1912

[8]On Taft, Roosevelt, and the tariff, see Judith Icke Anderson, *William Howard Taft: An Intimate History* (New York: Norton, 1981), pp. 212–24; and Donald F. Anderson, *William Howard Taft: A Conservative's Conception of the Presidency* (Ithaca: Cornell University Press, 1973), p. 120.

both Wilson and Roosevelt favored tariff reform. Together, they accounted for over 75 percent of the popular vote.

Despite their mutual criticisms of the Payne-Aldrich Act and calls for reform, however, Roosevelt and Wilson adhered to different programs. Reflecting his Republican background, Roosevelt continued to espouse a more paternalistic vision of government and sought to "get the tariff out of politics" through the creation of an independent Tariff Commission, which would scientifically determine import duties.[9] Wilson dismissed the commission concept and was determined to push through Congress a new omnibus tariff bill that would embody the principles of the "New Freedom."

The Underwood Tariff Act of 1913 was based on the principle of a "competitive tariff," as articulated in the Democratic platform of 1912.[10] In contrast to the "true principle of protection" of the Payne-Aldrich Act, which if taken to its logical conclusion would have prohibited all imports, a competitive tariff would allow, indeed encourage, the importation of foreign goods to compete with American producers. The concept of competition was critical: the tariff was not to be abolished or set so low as to damage an industry severely, but it was to be low enough to allow substantial importation.[11] In fact, under the Underwood Act, imports were expected to increase by approximately $123 million, or 7.4 percent of all imports in 1912.[12] It is important that, despite the reduction in the tariff, both Wilson and the Democrats as a whole specifically rejected the doctrine of free trade and desired to retain a modest degree of protection for American industry.

During the years that the Underwood Act was in effect, the average rates of duty were lower than in any period since at least the Civil War and lower than would be obtained until 1958.[13] The tariff on dutiable goods was reduced from 41.0 percent in the Payne-Aldrich Act to 26.8 percent, and the average rate of duty on all imports was lowered from

[9]Henry F. Pringle, *Theodore Roosevelt: A Biography* (New York: Harcourt, Brace, 1931), p. 567.

[10]See Asher Isaacs, *International Trade, Tariff and Commercial Policies* (Chicago: Richard D. Irwin, 1948), p. 215.

[11]U.S. Congress, House of Representatives, Ways and Means Committee, *A Bill to Reduce Tariff Duties, to Provide Revenue for the Government, and for Other Purposes: A Report to Accompany H.R. 3321*, 63d Cong., 1st sess., 1913, pp. xvi–xvii.

[12]The figure of $123 million was often cited in the debates. See in particular the opening speech of F. M. Simmons, chairman of the Senate Finance Committee, *Congressional Record*, 63d Cong., 1st sess., 1913, p. 2552. Total imports for 1912 were $1,653.3 million (*Statistical Abstract of the United States* [Washington, D.C.: U.S. Government Printing Office, 1916], p. 328).

[13]*Statistical Abstract of the United States* (Washington, D.C.: U.S. Government Printing Office, selected years).

Table 5.1. Levels of duty by tariff act, Phase III*

Year of tariff act	Level of duty on all imports	Level of duty on dutiable imports	Percentage of all imports on free list
1909	20.0	41.0	51.3
1913	8.8	26.8	67.5
1922	13.9	38.2	63.5

*Average rates of duty and average percentage of imports on free list computed for all complete years tariff act in effect.

SOURCE: *Statistical Abstract of the United States* (Washington, D.C.: U.S. Government Printing Office, selected years).

20.0 to 8.8 percent (see Table 5.1). Correspondingly, the free list was increased from 51.3 to 67.5 percent of all imports. As the British magazine *The Economist* wrote, the Underwood bill is "the heaviest blow that has been aimed against the Protective system since the British legislation of Sir Robert Peel between 1842 and 1846."[14]

Two mutually reinforcing issues were central to the Underwood tariff debate both within the country at large during the 1912 election campaign and in the government while the bill was under consideration.[15] The congressional debate centered primarily on trusts. By sheltering the domestic market from imports, the protective tariff was thought to encourage the process of industrial concentration. Lower tariffs, which would provide new competition for the trusts within the American market, were intended, at least in part, to halt and, it was hoped, reverse this process. As a progressive candidate, Wilson campaigned hard on the trusts issue.

More important, Wilson emphasized the changing structure of the international economy and the need for the United States to adapt its policies accordingly. Wilson noted that the rapid economic development of the nation-state, through which the United States was outstripping

[14]*Economist* 76 (April 12, 1913): 867.

[15]Considerable debate also occurred over the role of the Democratic caucus in the tariff-making process. At the root of this Republican disgruntlement lay the frustration of its party allies in the business community. Whereas in the past businessmen had faced a friendly Ways and Means Committee, they now confronted a committee committed to rolling back the favors these businessmen previously enjoyed.

Conversely, there was widespread acceptance, if not support, for the levying of a tax on incomes in the Underwood Act. On the relationship between the tariff and the institution of an income tax, see Ben Baack and Edward John Ray, "The Political Economy of the Origin and Development of the Federal Income Tax," *Research in Economic History*, Suppl. 4 (1985), pp. 121–38; and Baack and Ray, "Special Interests and the Adoption of the Income Tax in the United States," *Journal of Economic History* 45 (September 1985): 607–25.

the progress of its European rivals, had altered both the economic structure of the country and America's interests within the global economy. This concern appeared in many of Wilson's speeches on the tariff and was most clearly stated in his first message to Congress:

> It is clear to the whole country that the tariff duties must be altered. They must be changed to meet the radical alteration in the conditions of our economic life which the country has witnessed within the last generation. While the whole force and method of our industrial and commercial life were being changed beyond recognition the tariff schedules have remained what they were before the change began, or have moved in the direction they were given when no large circumstance of our industrial development was what it is to-day. Our task is to square them with the actual facts.[16]

Similarly, early in the 1912 campaign, Wilson argued:

> After the Spanish War was over we joined the company of nations for the first time. . . . Now we are getting very much interested in foreign markets, but the foreign markets are not particularly interested in us. We have not been very polite, we have not encouraged the intercourse with foreign markets that we might have encouraged, and have obstructed the influence of foreign competition. So these circumstances make the tariff question a new question, our internal arrangements and new combinations of business on one side and on the other our external necessities and the need to give scope to our energy which is now pent up and confined within our own borders.[17]

Sounding many of the themes first articulated by President Grover Cleveland in the late 1880s, Wilson also believed that America's economic progress was even more constrained by the policy of protection in 1912 than in the past. In the campaign, Wilson argued that "if prosperity is not to be checked in this country we must broaden our borders and make conquest of the markets of the world. That is the reason why America is so deeply interested in . . . breaking down . . . that dam against which all the tides of our prosperity have banked up, that great dam which runs around all our coasts and which we call the protective tariff."[18]

Finally, Wilson asserted that because of the changing nature of the international economy, the United States could no longer be a reclusive nation. American policies did affect other nation-states, he noted, and

[16]Arthur S. Link, ed., *The Papers of Woodrow Wilson*, 56 vols. (Princeton: Princeton University Press, 1966–   ), 27:270, hereafter cited as *WWP*.
[17]*WWP*, 23:641–42.
[18]*WWP*, 25:38.

they could be expected to retaliate: "All trade is two-sided. You can't sell everything and buy nothing. You can't establish any commercial relationships that aren't two-sided. And if America is to insist upon selling everything and buy nothing, she will find that the rest of the world stands very cold and indifferent to her enterprise."[19]

Although Wilson did not single out growing British protectionism as the catalyst for his efforts at lowering duties or link lower American tariffs to the continuation of British free trade as the theory of international economic structures might lead us to expect, one theme consistently emerges from these speeches which is consonant with the constraints and opportunities of the structure of bilateral opportunism: the United States could no longer take the liberalness of others for granted, and it must lower its tariff to ensure continued openness by other countries. Accordingly, the lower duties of the Underwood Act were designed, in the words of Wilson's congressional supporters, to free "the highways of trade" and take advantage of "our great national opportunities in the markets of the world."[20]

The Democratic rationale for tariff reform in 1913 bears important similarities to the platform of the Cleveland Democrats articulated between 1887 and 1894, but it differs in two essential ways.[21] First, the 1894 revision of the tariff was more restricted in scope. The Democrats sought only duty-free raw materials and obtained only free wool. This was a narrow trade strategy which attempted to increase exports by increasing the purchasing power of a few selected Latin American nation-states. In 1913, on the other hand, while recognizing the continued importance of duty-free raw materials, the Democrats obtained reductions across all tariff schedules and demonstrated the country's ability and confidence to compete in the global market. Second, Wilson recognized that American policy did have an impact upon other nation-states and that it was no longer possible for the United States to assume that the international economy would remain open. In 1894, the Democrats de facto denied the impact of American policies upon others and specifically ignored a threat of retaliation against American exports by Germany.

[19]<i>WWP</i>, 25:341.
[20]<i>Congressional Record</i>, 63d Cong., 1st sess., 1913, pp. 662, 2553.
[21]The failure of the reform effort in 1894 is often attributed to the slim Democratic majority in the Senate, whereby all the senators on that side of the aisle had to be appeased in order to muster sufficient votes to pass the measure. See Tom E. Terrill, <i>The Tariff, Politics, and American Foreign Policy, 1874–1901</i> (Westport, Conn.: Greenwood, 1973), pp. 192–93. The Democratic majority in the Senate was also small in 1913, but the logrolling was restrained. See below, and Sidney Ratner, <i>The Tariff in American History</i> (New York: Van Nostrand, 1972), pp. 44–45.

The Underwood Act also sought to combine its liberalism with the activism of American trade strategy developed in the earlier phases. Section four of the final bill authorized the president to negotiate trade agreements "looking toward freer trade relations and further reciprocal expansion of trade and commerce," without limiting the executive in the magnitude or breadth of the reduction in duty.[22] Although this provision did not delegate any power to the president not already provided for in the Constitution, and its critics at the time argued that it was superfluous for this reason, it was significant in two ways. First, section four specified that both houses of Congress must approve the treaty but that neither could offer any amendments. Other countries might be more willing to enter into negotiations with the president, trade expansionists hoped, if Congress could not subsequently alter any agreement they might reach. Yet by specifically requiring the approval of both houses, Congress must have also realized that, considering its past unwillingness to accept reciprocity treaties, it was creating a high hurdle for any agreement to surmount. Second, by stating that the potential treaties should look toward "freer trade relations," Congress created a presupposition toward lower duties. Although either house could still veto an agreement, the will of Congress was clearly defined in favor of reciprocal reductions of duty and freer trade. In this provision, the United States clearly identified its interests with greater openness in the international economy and expressed a willingness to lower its own tariff further to obtain reductions abroad.

In summary, the Underwood Act marks a significant shift in American trade strategy. Recognizing the changing nature of the international economy, the United States adopted a new and liberal trade strategy, subordinating its desires for protection at home to the dictates of export expansion abroad for the first time. In addition, through section four, although it was likely to be of only limited effectiveness, Congress supported the goal of freer trade within the international economy as a whole and expressed a willingness to work toward this end. In short, the United States accepted the constraints of bilateral opportunism and moved toward freer trade.

How successful this policy would have been remains unclear. In the year between the passage of the Underwood Act and the outbreak of the war, business opposition to the measure was mild. None of the catastrophic results predicted by the protectionists occurred and at least some portions of the business community appeared to recognize that they could continue to produce, indeed prosper, under severely re-

[22]U.S. Congress, House, Ways and Means Committee, *Bill to Reduce Tariff Duties*, p. 89.

duced protection. In April 1914, even the protectionist *Journal of Commerce* noted that the steel industry had suffered no ill effects from the Underwood Act, with iron and steel imports for the first quarter of the year nearly 10 percent below those for the first four months of 1913.[23] Given the evolutionary nature of the international economic structure and American trade strategy since 1887, it is reasonable to expect that, had the war not intervened, American policy would have continued along the same trajectory and the tendency toward freer trade at home would have been strengthened with time.

Whether or not America's new, more liberal trade strategy helped moderate British protectionism is also unclear. Soon after Law rose to lead the Conservative party, the issue of home rule for Ireland re-emerged and displaced tariff reform as the principal cleavage in British politics.[24] Before either issue could be resolved, however, war broke out, transforming the political agenda.

Wilson and the Domestic Policy Process

Woodrow Wilson, who employed several innovative political techniques to force congressional adherence to the Democratic party's pledge of tariff reform, played a critical role in the successful passage of the Underwood Act. In the usual struggle between the foreign policy and representative elements of the state, Wilson was the key actor. Determined to be his own secretary of state, Wilson appointed William Jennings Bryan to the post only under significant pressure from the party to acknowledge the "Great Commoner's" long years of service.[25] In most areas of foreign affairs, Wilson instead relied heavily on Colonel Edward House, the self-described "power behind the throne."[26] Yet House did not take an active interest in the tariff, leaving Wilson to chart the course of his administration's trade strategy almost single-handedly.

Soon after the November election, Chairman Oscar W. Underwood—one of Wilson's principal rivals for the 1912 nomination—and the Democratic members of the House Ways and Means Committee began drafting a new tariff bill. The draft was completed before the inauguration, and Wilson saw it for the first time only after the committee had com-

---

[23]Melvin I. Urofsky, *Big Steel and the Wilson Administration: A Study in Business-Government Relations* (Columbus: Ohio University Press, 1969), p. 50; and Robert H. Wiebe, *Business and Reform: A Study of the Progressive Movement* (Cambridge: Harvard University Press, 1962), p. 142.

[24]Williams, *Through Tariffs to Prosperity*, p. 24.

[25]Wayne C. Williams, *William Jennings Bryan* (New York: Putnam's, 1936), p. 336.

[26]Charles Seymour, arr., *The Intimate Papers of Colonel House*, 2 vols. (Boston: Houghton Mifflin, 1926), 1:243.

pleted its deliberations. In an effort to make the measure more palatable to a wider cross-section of legislators, Underwood had backed away from the sweeping reform promised in the campaign. Wilson insisted that the committee hold firm and demanded in particular that the bill include free food, sugar, leather, and—at Bryan's urging—wool. Although he threatened to veto the bill unless these goods were admitted free of duty, Wilson compromised on sugar, allowing the duty to be gradually eliminated over three years.[27]

When Democratic support wavered under these demands, Wilson soon thwarted it by three innovative moves. In a bold initiative, Wilson appeared before Congress to argue for the Underwood Act, both dramatizing the importance of the issue and building support for the proposed measure. Not since Thomas Jefferson had any president spoken before Congress. Although many critics deemed it inappropriate interference in legislative affairs, Wilson's tactic was well received on the whole and facilitated passage of the bill.[28]

Then, in an attempt to create party discipline, the absence of which Wilson the scholar had decried as the principal weakness of the American political system, the president made support for the Underwood Act a test of party loyalty. Once the measure was approved by the House and Senate Democratic caucuses, Wilson insisted that individual members adhere to all of its provisions, even though they might disagree with individual duties in the bill. Wilson's letter to Senator John Randolph Thornton (D.-La.)—one of only two Democratic senators who eventually voted against the bill—is similar to many others in this regard:

> Undoubtedly, you should have felt yourself perfectly free in the caucus to make every effort to carry out the promises you had made to your own people, but when it comes to the final action, my own judgement is perfectly clear. No party can ever for any length of time control the Government or serve the people which can not command the allegiance of its own minority. I feel that there are times, after every argument has been given full consideration and men of equal public conscience have conferred together, when those who are overruled should accept the principle of party government and act with the colleagues through whom they expect to see the country best and most permanently well served.[29]

By making the tariff a party issue, Wilson alienated several progressive Republicans who might otherwise have supported the measure.[30] None-

---

[27]Arthur S. Link, *Wilson: The New Freedom* (Princeton: Princeton University Press, 1956), p. 180.

[28]Arthur S. Link, *Woodrow Wilson and the Progressive Era, 1910–1917* (New York: Harper, 1954), pp. 35–36.

[29]*WWP*, 28:35.

[30]Link, *Wilson: The New Freedom*, p. 185.

theless, without strict party discipline, the bill might not have passed at all or only in a form unacceptable to Wilson.

Despite Wilson's shrewd manipulation of the public arena and the party, senatorial support for the bill was by no means certain. In light of the large Democratic majority in the House, few lobbyists believed they could overturn the expected outcome. With only a six-vote majority in the Senate, however, the pressure groups hoped the traditionally more conservative and protectionist upper house would accede to their pleas for continued tariffs. When the bill reached the Senate, rumors—most likely stimulated by the lobbyists now descending on Washington—began to circulate on Capitol Hill that Wilson was willing to compromise on his earlier demands. To combat the influence of the lobby, Wilson initiated his third and perhaps most unusual tactic. Appealing to the public and his progressive supporters in particular, the president denounced the tariff lobby:

> I think that the public ought to know the extraordinary exertions being made by the lobby in Washington to gain recognition for certain alterations in the tariff bill. Washington has seldom seen so numerous, so industrious, or so insidious a lobby. . . . It is of serious interest to the country that the people at large should have no lobby and be voiceless in these matters, while great bodies of astute men seek to create an artificial opinion and to overcome the interests of the public for their private profit. It is thoroughly worth the while of the people of this country to take knowledge of this matter. Only public opinion can check and destroy it.[31]

Wilson's remarks were greeted skeptically at first. The *New York Times* noted that it was possible "the President has mistaken for lobbying the ordinary, usual, and perfectly legitimate measures taken by protected interests to present their case to Congress." Expecting to reveal the president's charges as groundless, the Republicans proposed hearings into the activities of the lobby, which were then expanded into an investigation of the financial holdings of senators themselves. Although few patently illegal activities were found, numerous conflicts of interest created by legislators holding stock or other interests in industries or firms seeking protection and considerable expenditures designed to influence public and legislative opinion were revealed.[32] In the end, the president was more than vindicated. And under the light of public scrutiny, the usual logrolling was blocked. Indeed, the bill actually

---

[31]Quoted in Richard Hofstader, ed., *The Progressive Movement, 1900–1915* (Englewood Cliffs, N.J.: Prentice-Hall, 1963), pp. 156–57.
[32]Quoted in Link, *Wilson: The New Freedom,* p. 187, also pp. 189–90.

emerged from the Senate with lower duties than contained in the House version, an unprecedented event.

The differences between the Payne-Aldrich Act of 1909 and the Underwood Act are striking. In both, tariff reform was embraced, but the latter bill was far more ambitious. Interest-group theories do not appear to provide an adequate explanation of these differences. Although data are available only from the decennial census, there is no reason to believe that the structure of American producer groups changed significantly between 1909 and 1913 (see Table 2.1).

The contrasting results of 1909 and 1913 are also attributed by many to party politics: the Republicans were the party of protection and the Democrats the party of reform. Although consistent with the legislative results of 1909 and 1913, partisan competition fails to provide an adequate explanation of American trade strategy in a longer historical perspective. As I argue in Chapter 3, the McKinley Act of 1890 and the Wilson-Gorman Act of 1894, passed by the two opposing political parties, possessed more important similarities than differences. Conversely, the tariff acts of 1890, 1897, and 1909, all passed by Republicans, contained important differences in their provisions for export expansion. And similarly, the tariff rates of the Underwood Act were less than half those found in its Democratic predecessor, the Wilson-Gorman Act. Political-party competition cannot be dismissed as a factor in explaining the divergent policies adopted in 1909 and 1913, but it does appear to provide at best only a partial explanation.

Wilson's success in realizing Democratic pledges of tariff reform also contrasts sharply with Taft's failure to meet his more modest promises in 1909. This difference is often attributed to the two presidents' leadership styles, which no doubt played a role in establishing the final outcome. Taft's political ineptitude is easily documented, and Wilson's advocacy of a strong president acting as leader of his party is displayed in both his academic writings and political practice. Like Blaine, Wilson effectively blocked the dominant protectionist coalition by appealing directly to the public and mobilizing his progressive supporters into the tariff-making process.

The differing leadership skills of the two presidents may have caused the change in American trade strategy between 1909 and 1913 to be more "choppy" or discontinuous than might be expected from a structural perspective, yet mere political acumen cannot explain the outcome without attention to the differing ends to which these skills were directed. Former President Theodore Roosevelt, the force behind the Payne-Aldrich revisions, could still write his friend and adviser Henry

Cabot Lodge in 1909 that "there is no real ground for dissatisfaction, of a serious kind, with the [protectionist Dingley] tariff."[33] In 1913, however, Wilson placed reductions in the tariff at the center of his political reforms. As British trade preferences rapidly evolved in a more protectionist direction between 1909 and 1913, new constraints were placed on American trade strategy. The United States could no longer safely free ride and now had to accommodate Britain's new mixed trade interests. As recognized by Wilson, and predicted by the theory developed in Chapter 1, the United States could best meet these changed circumstances by reducing its own tariff barriers.

THE DISRUPTED DANCE

The International Economic Structure

Britain's trading position was permanently weakened by World War I, particularly as the United States stepped in to fill the void created in Latin America and the dominions when English producers were absorbed by the war economy,[34] yet the international economic structure remained one of bilateral opportunism. At the most fundamental level, the choices facing both the United Kingdom and the United States after the war were essentially the same as in 1913. Each opportunist could either adopt or maintain protection at home, thereby risking retaliation by the other, or accept free trade in hopes of reinforcing a similar policy in its counterpart. As argued in Chapter 1, under conditions of relatively low economic instability and as long as each opportunist expects to interact with the other in the future, free trade is the maximizing and therefore preferred strategy. This prediction is supported by the freer-trade Underwood Act.

The greatest effect of the war, for our purposes here at least, was to destroy the international economic stability which had existed since the early twentieth century. Instability, of course, is partially a political phenomenon and is clearly affected by the policies of the leading countries. Yet the war itself was exogenous to the international eco-

---

[33]*Selections from the Correspondence of Theodore Roosevelt and Henry Cabot Lodge*, 2 vols. (New York: Charles Scribner's Sons, 1925), 2:335.

[34]In 1913, for instance, 63 percent of Indian imports came from Great Britain. By 1918 this had fallen to 54 percent, and by 1920 to 46 percent. During the same period, America's share of the Indian market rose from 3 to 10 percent. The same pattern occurred in Australia. In 1913, 63 percent of Australian imports originated in Britain, but only 48 percent did so in 1918. America's share, on the other hand, increased from 11 to 27 percent (O. Delle Donne, *European Tariff Policies since the World War* [New York: Adelphi, 1928], p. 132, n. 50).

nomic structure (as defined here) and the single most important source of instability. It disrupted the international regimes in trade, money, and investment constructed over the previous century. It also raised a new set of contentious issues: war debts, reparations, German inflation, and—perhaps most important—America's new position as a net creditor and the resulting challenge to British finance.[35] These underlying political sources of instability were reflected in fluctuations in the exchange rate and prices (as measured by the trend-corrected equivalent of the coefficient of variation; see Table 5.2), which, in turn, are the principal determinants of the pattern of international trade. Even under the prewar gold standard, some variation in exchange rates occurred. Between 1919 and 1922 and in the absence of either the gold standard or fixed exchange rates, however, the fluctuations increased by more than a factor of 100. The same pattern is found in basic commodity prices, as reflected in price fluctuations for wheat delivered in Liverpool. Although the increase is smaller, price instability still grew by more than a factor of 10.

The theory developed in Chapter 1 can only predict the general direction of policy change resulting from increased instability within the international economy. Nonetheless, it helps identify two ways in which such instability conspired to raise the level of protection in the United States and the United Kingdom. Stability is a necessary prerequisite for an open international economy. All countries, opportunists included, seek to insulate themselves from international instability. Protection is one commonly used instrument for this purpose. Despite efforts by the United States and the United Kingdom to provide the necessary stability, they failed to regulate the international economy effectively or to pay the price of infrastructure. This failure was partly related to the second effect of instability. International instability, which makes future interactions less likely or predictable, increases the discount rate, or reduces the "shadow of the future," and thereby decreases the incentives for opportunists to cooperate in the adoption of universal free trade. Under conditions of instability, opportunists will tend to value present returns more highly relative to future returns, increasing the temptation to defect or to adopt protection at home. Paradoxically, just as cooperation between the two opportunists becomes more essential in an unstable international economy, it also becomes more difficult.

Great Britain responded to the war and the instability it created by

---

[35]For a discussion of the immediate postwar period, see Carl P. Parrini, *Heir to Empire: United States Economic Diplomacy, 1916–1923* (Pittsburgh: University of Pittsburgh Press, 1969), esp. pp. 40–71.

Table 5.2. International economic instability, Phase III:
Exchange rate and wheat price instability (monthly intervals),
1913 and 1919–1922*

Exchange rate/price	1913	1919–1922
British pound/dollar	.0007736	.0989354
French franc/dollar	.0008864	.3145085
German mark/dollar	.0015088	.3843435
Wheat (good average quality imported red, average spot prices at Liverpool)	.0189721	.1289417

*Instability measured by the standard error of estimate/
mean of the dependent variable for the regression equation:
exchange rate or price = a + b time. This is the trend-
corrected equivalent to the coefficient of variation. See Peter
B. Kennen and Costantine S. Voivodas, "Export Instability
and Growth," *Kyklos* 25 (1972): 791–802.
Source: Exchange rate data from Board of Governors of
the Federal Reserve System, *Banking and Monetary Statistics,
1914–1941* (Washington, D.C.: Board of Governors of the
Federal Reserve System, 1976), pp. 670, 671, and 681; wheat
price data from U.S. Department of Agriculture, *Yearbook of
the Department of Agriculture, 1923* (Washington, D.C.: U.S.
Government Printing Office, 1924), p. 630, and U.S. Department of Agriculture, *Yearbook of Agriculture, 1931* (Washington, D.C.: U.S. Government Printing Office, 1932), p. 602.

abandoning its century-old commitment to free trade and adopting both
protection and a weak form of imperial preference. Britain imposed the
"McKenna duties" in 1915, levied at 33.3 percent *ad valorem* on a variety
of luxury items, including motor cars. These duties were primarily
intended to reduce "unnecessary" foreign imports and economize on
foreign exchange during the war. Yet because no internal excise taxes
were levied on the domestic production of equivalent items, the McKenna duties also served to protect domestic manufacturers. The new duties
were maintained after the war, except for a brief period between August
1924 and May 1925, when Labor controlled the government. In 1921,
the system of protection was extended when approximately sixty-five
hundred strategic products deemed essential for Britain's defense were
made dutiable at 33.3 percent in the Safeguarding of Industry Act. In
conjunction with this return to protection, Britain also adopted an imperial preference system. In 1919, reductions of one-sixth and one-third of
the duty were granted to empire countries on a variety of revenue-
producing commodities and McKenna products respectively. Empire
products were exempted entirely from the Safeguarding of Industry
Act. This system of preferences, however, was of relatively little conse-

quence because few of the goods covered by the McKenna or Safeguarding of Industry duties were produced within the empire. This weakness was partially ameliorated between 1923 and 1927 as additional food and raw material items were added to the list of preferential goods. Yet in 1928, goods entering Britain under the preferential rates still accounted for only 0.1 percent of total imports.[36]

Although the average British tariff on all imports remained relatively low,[37] these new duties were important to the United States as an indication that the United Kingdom had repudiated its commitment to free trade. They also served as a threat of further policy change in the future. Reed Smoot (R.-Utah), the second ranking majority member on the Senate Finance Committee, reflected the widespread uncertainty over future British policy during the 1922 tariff debate. "Does the Senator," he asked rhetorically, "know how many of these safeguarding of industry acts have been passed in England since the armistice was signed?" Revealing his own misunderstanding of these duties, Smoot continued, "Why England has gone so far as to say that all her key industries, so designated by her legislators, shall be protected not by a rate, but by an embargo." Finally, in concluding his remarks on Britain, Smoot declared that "never in the history of the world were conditions so unsettled as they are to-day."[38]

The Fordney-McCumber Act and American Trade Strategy

With the instability created by the war and Britain's return to protection, there was little doubt that the United States would raise its tariff as well. President Wilson vetoed a proposal to raise the tariff on agricultural products on his last day in office, but the measure was promptly passed again and signed into law by President Warren G. Harding as the

[36]On Britain's postwar protectionism, see Williams, *Through Tariffs to Prosperity*; Donne, *European Tariff Policies*, esp. p. 138 for the 1928 figure; National Institute of Economic and Social Research, *Trade Regulations and Commercial Policy of the United Kingdom* (Cambridge: Cambridge University Press, 1943); Deryck Abel, *A History of British Tariffs, 1923–1942* (London: Heath Cranton, 1945); and Forrest Capie, *Depression and Protectionism: Britain between the Wars* (London: Allen & Unwin, 1983).

[37]Estimates of the average rate of British protection during the 1920s vary widely. Frederick E. Kip, in a report prepared for Senator McCumber, chairman of the Senate Finance Committee and introduced into the *Congressional Record*, estimated that the British tariff was approximately 15 percent in 1920. This figure is clearly too high, especially since the Safeguarding of Industry Act was not yet passed at the time the calculations were made. Yet this estimate was the only substantive information provided on tariff policies abroad during the Fordney-McCumber debates and it was not challenged by other members of Congress.

[38]*Congressional Record*, 67th Cong., 2d sess., 1922, pp. 6055–56.

Emergency Tariff Act of 1921. Immediately after the passage of this bill, Congress began work on a new omnibus tariff act, which was finally passed in September 1922.

In the Fordney-McCumber Act the level of duty on all imports was raised from 8.8 to 13.9 percent. Similarly, the average rate on dutiable imports was increased from 26.8 to 38.2 percent. Finally, the free list of the Fordney-McCumber Act was reduced from 67.5 to 63.5 percent. Although it is often claimed that the Republicans merely readopted the Payne-Aldrich Act of 1909, this was clearly not the case. In the previous Republican tariff the duty on all imports was 20.0 percent, more than 6 percent higher than the 1922 measure. Likewise, the Fordney-McCumber Act, described inaccurately by Frank W. Taussig as "a tariff with rates higher than any in the long series of protective measures,"[39] appears moderate by comparison with tariff levels in the 1890s, when the average rates of duty were approximately 23.5 percent on all imports and 45.7 percent on dutiable imports.

The instability of the international economy clearly played a major role in the desire for a new higher tariff in the United States and was a continually recurring theme in the debates on the Fordney-McCumber bill. Both Joseph W. Fordney (R.-Mich.), chairman of the House Ways and Means Committee, and Porter J. McCumber (R.-N.D.), chairman of the Senate Finance Committee, opened the debates in their respective chambers by calling attention to the pervasive instability facing the United States. "Mr. President," McCumber declared at the outset, "never before in times of peace have such difficult and such serious problems confronted the country, its industries, and its whole social fabric as those which challenge its attention to-day." Of particular concern to the legislators were the drastically depreciated currencies of the European belligerents, which they feared would give America's trade rivals an unfair advantage not only in foreign markets but in the United States as well. The solution to this condition of instability, McCumber argued, was to raise the tariff. "Of all times in the history of the country," he stated, "this is the time in which a protective tariff is most needed to sustain our American industries and our millions of people dependent upon them."[40]

Despite the desire of Congress to raise duties as a means of insulating the United States from the vagaries of the international economy, tariff rates continued to be constrained by America's position within the struc-

[39]Frank W. Taussig, *The Tariff History of the United States*, 8th ed. (New York: Putnam's, 1931), p. 453.
[40]*Congressional Record*, 67th Cong., 2d sess., 1922, p. 5763. See also Fordney's remarks, ibid., 1st sess., 1921, pp. 3476–78.

ture of bilateral opportunism. Although aware of the desire to shield the country from external instability, President Harding argued that the United States could not adopt a reclusive trade policy in 1922 any more than it could in 1913. The country was too large and important a factor in the international economy to pursue such a strategy successfully. Sounding remarkably like his Democratic predecessor in 1913, Harding stated in his Inaugural Address, "We must understand that ties of trade bind nations in closest intimacy, and none may receive except as he gives. . . . Today, as never before, when people are seeking trade restoration and expansion, we must adjust our tariffs to the new order. We seek participation in the world's exchanges. . . . We know full well we cannot sell where we do not buy."[41] Discussing the pending Fordney-McCumber Act during his Annual Message to Congress in 1921, Harding elaborated on this argument:

> Again comes the reminder that we must not be unmindful of world conditions, that people are struggling for industrial rehabilitation and that we can not dwell in industrial and commercial exclusion and at the same time do the just thing in aiding world reconstruction and readjustment. We do not seek a selfish aloofness, and we could not profit by it, were it possible. We recognize the necessity of buying wherever we sell, and the permanence of trade lies in its acceptable exchanges. In our pursuit of markets we must give as well as receive.[42]

This recognition of the link between imports and exports was much less clear in Congress, yet it manifested itself as an ill-defined fear of retaliation. Retaliation was most commonly discussed through denials by the Republican congressional leadership that the proposed rates of duty in the Fordney-McCumber bill were so onerous as to warrant such a reaction,[43] yet this fear clearly placed constraints on how high the tariff walls could be safely built. Thus, though the higher rates of the Fordney-McCumber Tariff were adopted as a response to increased international economic instability, the higher duties were nonetheless influenced and shaped by the constraints exerted by the structure of bilateral opportunism.

In addition to managing instability through a general increase in the

---

[41]*Inaugural Addresses of the Presidents of the United States from George Washington 1789 to Richard Nixon 1969* (Washington, D.C.: U.S. Government Printing Office, 1969), pp. 209–13.

[42]*Foreign Relations of the United States, 1921*, 2 vols. (Washington, D.C.: U.S. Government Printing Office, 1936), 1: xxiv–xxv.

[43]See Fordney's remarks, *Congressional Record*, 67th Cong., 1st sess., 1921, p. 3477; and those of William M. Calder (R.-N.Y.), ibid., 2d sess., 1922, p. 11262.

tariff, a limited amount of administrative flexibility was also introduced into the Fordney-McCumber Act as a more direct mechanism of adjustment. Section 315 authorized the president to raise or lower all or any duties by up to 50 percent to equalize the costs of production. The Tariff Commission, created in 1916 under President Wilson, was charged with conducting the necessary investigations into production costs and recommending any changes the president might find necessary.[44] The importance of this provision was recognized by many. Even Oscar Underwood, author of the Democratic Tariff Act of 1913 and now senator from Alabama, cited this section as the most important part of the bill.[45]

Section 315 was clearly intended to lead to a reduction in duties once international economic conditions were stabilized. Smoot, who introduced the provision, believed that there would be "'many more occasions' when the President would exercise his authority 'in lowering rates than in increasing them,' and if conditions became normal, he expected that the President would lower 'the majority of rates.'"[46] In practice, however, Section 315 was more often used to increase rates of duty as a result of the mandate for equalizing the costs of production. Between 1922 and 1929 more than 600 applications covering 375 items were filed with the Tariff Commission.[47] Of these, only 47 investigations covering 55 items were completed, 38 of which resulted in a change of duty. Thirty-three of these changes increased and five decreased tariff rates.[48] Over the course of the 1920s, many of Section 315's original supporters became disillusioned with the flexibility concept and opposed a similar provision in the Smoot-Hawley Act of 1930 (see Chapter 6).[49]

Coupled with this moderately higher flexible tariff was an attempt by the United States to expand its exports through a more active trade policy. Central to this effort was Section 317 of the Fordney-McCumber Act, which authorized the president to retaliate against countries that discriminated against American goods, and the adoption of the unconditional form of the MFN principle by the United States in 1923.

The United States maintained its commitment to nondiscrimination

[44]For a brief history of the origins and early years of the Tariff Commission, see John M. Dobson, *Two Centuries of Tariffs: The Background and Emergence of the U.S. International Trade Commission* (Washington, D.C.: U.S. Government Printing Office, 1976), pp. 83–93.

[45]*Congressional Record*, 67th Cong., 2d sess., 1922, p. 11205.

[46]William B. Kelly, Jr., "Antecedents of Present Commercial Policy, 1924–1939," in Kelly, ed., *Studies in United States Commercial Policy* (Chapel Hill: University of North Carolina Press, 1963), p. 16.

[47]See Dobson, *Two Centuries of Tariffs*, pp. 83–93; and J. R. Snyder, "Coolidge, Costigan and the Tariff Commission," *Mid-America* 50 (April 1968): 131–48.

[48]Kelly, "Antecedents of Present Commercial Policy," pp. 18–22.

[49]Joan Hoff Wilson, *American Business and Foreign Policy, 1920–1933* (Boston: Beacon, 1971), p. 86.

in international trade throughout the war and the 1920s. In response to the European allies' desire to organize the international economy around regional trading blocs as announced in Paris in 1916,[50] President Wilson recommitted the United States to the principle of nondiscrimination. In the third of his fourteen points, Wilson set forth as an explicit goal of the United States "the removal, so far as possible, of all economic barriers and the establishment of an equality of trade conditions among all nations consenting to the peace and associating themselves for its maintenance." Wilson carried this commitment to nondiscrimination into both the Treaty of Versailles and the League of Nations Charter.[51]

The principle of nondiscrimination continued to receive support from the Republicans after they took office in 1920. As Secretary of State Charles Evans Hughes stated, "We are not seeking special privileges anywhere at the expense of others. We wish to protect the just and equal rights of Americans everywhere in the world. We wish to maintain the equality of commercial opportunity; as we call it, the open door."[52] Section 317 of the Fordney-McCumber Act was designed to put this commitment to the open door into action.[53] It empowered the president to impose penalty duties against "any empire, country, dominion, colony or protectorate" which "discriminates in fact against the United States."[54] Unlike the maximum-minimum provision of the Payne-Aldrich Act of 1909, Section 317 gave the president absolute discretion over the goods against which the penalty duties could be assessed and the magnitude of the penalty duties so long as they did not exceed 50 percent *ad valorem*. If after these sanctions the foreign country continued to discriminate against the United States, the president was further empowered to prohibit all imports from that country.

Section 317 is often interpreted as a congressional endorsement of the

---

[50]Parrini, *Heir to Empire*, p. 16.

[51]Quoted in Wallace McClure, "A New Commercial Policy: As Evidence by Section 317 of the Tariff Act of 1922," *Columbia University Studies in History, Economics and Public Law* 114 (1924): 261, see also pp. 262–67; and Melvyn P. Leffler, *The Elusive Quest: America's Pursuit of European Stability and French Security, 1919–1933* (Chapel Hill: University of North Carolina Press, 1979), pp. 3–39.

[52]Quoted in James W. Gantenbein, *The Evolution of Our Latin-American Policy: A Documentary Record* (New York: Oxford University Press, 1950), p. 108.

[53]The United States also employed other nontrade instruments to obtain the open door, including loans and war debts. See Wilson, *American Business and Foreign Policy*, pp. 104 and 118; and Michael J. Hogan, *Informal Entente: The Private Structure of Cooperation in Anglo-American Economic Diplomacy, 1918–1929* (Columbia: University of Missouri Press, 1977), p. 28.

[54]U.S. Congress, House of Representatives, *The Tariff Act of 1922 (with Index)*, 67th Cong., 2d sess., 1922, House Doc. 393, pp. 97–98.

unconditional MFN principle. Although this principle follows logically from the section, the senators in charge of the provision clearly believed it was consonant with the conditional interpretation of the MFN principle which the United States had traditionally adhered to. In a colloquy between Senators McCumber and Henry Cabot Lodge (R.-Mass.), chairman of the Foreign Relations Committee, the latter noted that "reciprocal arrangement[s] never [have] been held, and can never be held, to be a violation of the favored-nation clause."[55]

Section 317 did, however, evince a strong congressional commitment to the principle of nondiscrimination. In 1923, and without a specific congressional mandate, the president adopted the unconditional MFN principle as the basis for all United States commercial relations and abandoned its single remaining reciprocity agreement (except for those with Cuba, the Philippines, and the Panama Canal Zone, which it declared as exempt from this policy because of the close political and economic ties of these areas with the United States). It encouraged other nations to do likewise. Since 1904, the United States had, upon its request, received preferential treatment on several products in Brazil, the most important of which was wheat flour. In 1923, the United States declined to seek renewal of these preferences. Brazil accepted the American decision but asked why the United States had given up advantages it already possessed. In reply, the State Department noted that the unconditional MFN principle is "the policy best calculated to be of the maximum advantage in furthering relations of amity and commerce" and that Brazil would surely recognize "how inconsistent it would be for . . . the United States to enter into any arrangement involving . . . special customs treatment."[56]

Whereas in the second phase of American trade strategy examined in Chapter 4, unconditional MFN had been inconsistent with the policy of continued domestic protection, and was rejected in favor of bilateral bargaining for that reason, it now accorded with the United States's desire for freer trade abroad and willingness to accept limits on its protectionist policies at home. Between 1923 and 1929, the United States concluded twenty-two unconditional MFN treaties or agreements, including ones with Germany, Spain, and many of the small or newly independent European countries.[57] Despite its efforts, the United

[55]Quoted in Kelly, "Antecedents of Present Commercial Policy," p. 41.
[56]*Foreign Relations of the United States, 1923*, 2 vols. (Washington, D.C.: U.S. Government Printing Office, 1938), 1:124–25.
[57]Unconditional MFN treaties were reached with Germany (1923), Hungary (1925), Estonia (1925), Salvador (1926), and Honduras (1927). Other treaties containing unconditional MFN clauses were reached with Turkey (1923) and Panama (1926). Finally, modus

States was unable to negotiate similar agreements with Great Britain or France.[58] Even the successful agreements were not easily concluded in all cases. During talks with at least Spain, Romania, and Venezuela, the United States explicitly threatened to invoke the penalty duties provided for in Section 317 of the Fordney-McCumber Act. In each case, an agreement was reached and the threat was withdrawn.[59]

The United States also sought to gain broader support for the unconditional MFN principle through multilateral negotiations, the most important of which occurred at the World Economic Conference held in Geneva in 1927. There, at American insistence, the final declaration of the conference recognized the unconditional MFN principle as the most desirable basis on which to organize international trade, although few expected any results to follow from this effort.[60]

The United States was not entirely successful in its pursuit of non-

---

vivendi recognizing the unconditional MFN principle were obtained with Albania (1923), Brazil (1923), Dominican Republic (1924), Greece (1924), Guatemala (1924), Nicaragua (1924), Poland (1925), Lithuania (1925), Finland (1925), Romania (1926), Haiti (1926), and Latvia (1926).

[58]Franco-American trade relations were acrimonious throughout the decade of the 1920s. France often accused America's high tariffs of being one of the most important sources of international economic instability. The United States responded that its imports were growing faster than its exports and that, in actuality, the discriminatory tariff practices of countries such as France were the key impediments to international trade. After the war, France had abandoned the unconditional MFN principle in favor of the conditional variant. In July 1919 it sanctioned tariff rates, to be set through negotiation, between its maximum and minimum schedules, thus creating "a dozen schedules instead of two." France raised all tariffs by 30 percent on an emergency basis in April 1926 and by a second 30 percent five months later. In August 1927 it granted Germany de facto MFN status. One month later, France raised its minimum tariff; set its maximum tariff approximately 400 percent above the minimum rate; placed many American goods—which had previously entered under France's intermediate rates—on the maximum schedule; and, noting its adherence to only the conditional MFN principle, demanded considerable concessions on its exports in return for a less harsh treatment of American products. The United States replied that under its current tariff laws it was not able to offer special concessions but that if France continued upon its present course it would not be possible for the United States to "avoid using Section 317 and increasing the rates against French goods." As tension escalated and a tariff war appeared imminent, the United States and France concluded a modus vivendi by which the former agreed to begin investigations of the duties on French exports under Section 315 (the flexibility provision) of the Fordney-McCumber Tariff, while the latter, in return, would levy duties on American goods no higher than those existing in August 1927 before the conflict began, except if the new minimum duties were higher, in which case they would take precedence. See *Foreign Relations of the United States, 1927*, 3 vols. (Washington, D.C.: U.S. Government Printing Office, 1942), 2: 472–73 and 693–703. The quotation is on p. 473.

[59]For negotiations with Spain, see *Foreign Relations of the United States, 1923*, 2:849–50; for negotiations with Romania and Venezuela, see *Foreign Relations of the United States, 1927*, 3:635 and 822, respectively.

[60]League of Nations, *The World Economic Conference: Final Report* (Geneva, 1927); Parrini, *Heir to Empire*, pp. 270–71 and 274–75.

discrimination abroad through a more active trade strategy. Although it obtained its goal in many cases, it was not influential enough to secure this result in all instances. Despite this only partial success, however, the United States did, contrary to the arguments of some scholars, try to lead other countries toward a more liberal trading regime during the 1920s.[61] Its leadership was more limited in origin, scope, and purpose than that exercised by either the United Kingdom in the nineteenth century or the United States itself after World War II, but it was leadership.

The Harding Administration and the Domestic Policy Process

Warren G. Harding was an unlikely supporter of restrained protection, flexibility, and equality of treatment—the central principles of commercial policy which came to characterize his administration. Although he had been a lifelong advocate of protection, the president "made no pretense at being an expert on the tariff."[62] Regardless (or perhaps because) of his lack of knowledge, Harding's high-tariff views earned him the support of the protectionist lobby, and he more than repaid his benefactors by declaring in the closing weeks of the presidential campaign his desire for upward tariff revision.[63] Harding also backed the movement for the "American selling price," a nationalistic appeal that would have substituted the price of equivalent domestic products for the exported price as the basis for calculating the *ad valorem* duty, thereby raising the real rate of protection while allowing tariffs themselves to drop or remain the same.[64]

Initially siding with the protectionists and later continuing to lend them his support, Harding gradually moved toward a more liberal position on trade policy during his first year in office. By late 1921, the president began to recognize the need to maintain import levels so as to promote exports and fell increasingly under the sway of his secretary of commerce, Herbert Hoover, a moderate protectionist and highly respected member of the cabinet.[65] As with McKinley in 1897, holding the office of president altered the former protectionist's views.

[61]Charles P. Kindleberger, *The World of Depression, 1929–1939* (Berkeley: University of California Press, 1973).

[62]Robert K. Murray, *The Harding Era: Warren G. Harding and His Administration* (Minneapolis: University of Minnesota Press, 1969), p. 206.

[63]Harding's hotel bill at the 1920 Republican National Convention was paid by the American Protective Tariff League. See Randolph C. Downes, *The Rise of Warren Gamaliel Harding, 1865–1920* (Columbus: Ohio State University Press, 1970), p. 661.

[64]Murray, *Harding Era*, p. 273.

[65]See ibid.

During this same period, William S. Culbertson of the Tariff Commission and Wallace M. McClure and Stanley K. Hornbeck of the State Department clearly and persuasively articulated the importance of flexibility and equality as principles of commercial policy. A moderate Republican protectionist appointed by Wilson to the Tariff Commission and later reappointed by Harding, Culbertson was the key figure in gaining support for these principles in both Congress and the administration. Culbertson emerged as the spokesman for this platform for two reasons. As Melvyn P. Leffler writes, "He successfully integrated prevailing ideas and developed a clear vision of the types of administrative machinery that might resolve the conflicting demands for protection and expansion and reconcile the divergent needs of the national and international economy." More important, his colleagues in the State Department—wary of "interfering" in legislative affairs—believed that Culbertson, operating under the guise of the nonpartisan Tariff Commission, could obtain their shared goals more effectively.[66]

Having cultivated the friendship of the congressional delegation from his home state of Kansas, Culbertson used these contacts to gain access to the president and the Senate Finance Committee. As economic adviser for the Washington Disarmament Conference, Culbertson also developed cordial relations with Secretary of State Hughes, through whom he impressed his views on the secretary and urged him to do the same with the president.[67] Culbertson's efforts paid off: in his 1921 Annual Message to Congress (quoted above), Harding called for a moderate and flexible tariff; and Smoot proposed Sections 315 and 317, drafted by Culbertson, as committee amendments to the Fordney bill. Under the active lobbying of Culbertson and support of Harding and Hughes, Smoot's amendments were adopted by the Senate and accepted by the conference committee, which struck the 1890s-style bilateral reciprocity provision included in the House version.

Harding had clearly called for moderation in raising the tariff rates, but the executive focused its attention on Sections 315 and 317 rather than on specific duties during the congressional deliberations on the Fordney-McCumber bill. This more narrow emphasis appears to have occurred for two reasons. First, lacking Wilson's strong conception of presidential leadership, Harding and his subordinates accepted their weakness relative to the legislature and lobbyists in the setting of specific rates of duty.[68] Whereas Wilson had charged into the tariff fray, the

---

[66]Leffler, *Elusive Quest*, pp. 48–49.
[67]Ibid., p. 47.
[68]Ibid., p. 49.

Harding administration followed Taft's example and chose not to interfere. Second, regardless of the shape of the bill eventually enacted by Congress, flexibility held out the promise of subsequent presidential adjustment to remove whatever inequities remained. On this score, Harding followed McKinley's 1897 example, preferring not to fight in Congress and hoping to rewrite unsatisfactory portions of the bill by executive action.

Having succeeded in enacting a tariff bill containing their suggestions, Culbertson and his colleagues at the State Department then turned their attention to the unconditional MFN principle. Although it was specifically disavowed in the Senate debate, Culbertson argued that unconditional MFN followed logically from Section 317. In light of the demand of the United States for equal treatment abroad, Culbertson wrote that "consistency . . . requires that we do not ourselves initiate discriminatory rates." Conversely, he continued, "when all countries follow the unconditional [MFN] practice, equality of treatment is guaranteed generally and tendencies are set in motion contributing to commercial stability, simplicity and uniformity of rates, mutual confidence and international good will." With support from Hughes, Culbertson's arguments persuaded Harding, who subsequently endorsed the unconditional MFN principle. "I am well convinced," Harding wrote, "that the adoption of the unconditional favored-nation policy is the simpler way to maintain our tariff policy in accordance with the recently enacted law and is probably the surer way of effectively extending our trade abroad."[69] This executive decision to abandon the conditional MFN principle was later validated by legislative ratification of treaties containing the new unconditional language—with one important reservation (see below).

The strategy of flexibility and equality adopted by the Harding administration, though promising to reconcile pressures for protection and incentives for moderation and export expansion, proved less successful than hoped. For reasons examined in the next section, the United States and the United Kingdom were unable to negotiate an unconditional MFN treaty. In addition, hopes of using the flexibility provision for lowering duties were undermined by early presidential appointments and the anomalous position of the Tariff Commission between the executive and legislature.

At the outset of his administration and in an attempt to maintain the support of Republican protectionists, Harding appointed three high-tariff advocates to the Tariff Commission: Thomas O. Marvin (chair-

[69]*Foreign Relations of the United States, 1923,* 1:124–25, 129.

man), secretary of the Boston Home Market Club and editor of the *Protectionist*; William Burgess, a lobbyist for the pottery industry; and, Henry M. Glassie, a Democrat with connections to the Louisiana sugar industry.[70] Having "packed" the commission with protectionists, it subsequently recommended more increases in duty than decreases—to no one's surprise.

Regardless of its personnel, however, the work of the Tariff Commission was hampered by the competing pressures placed upon it by the executive-legislative struggle for control over trade policy. Created by Congress following a recommendation by Wilson in 1916, the commission was designed as an independent "fact-finding" or investigatory agency "capable of looking at the whole economic situation of the country with a dispassionate and disinterested scrutiny."[71] Free to investigate a broad range of issues, the commission was charged with collecting and presenting data to Congress and the president for use in making trade policy. Its recommendations, however, were not binding on either.

Section 315 of the Fordney-McCumber Act expanded the duties of the Tariff Commission, making it the principal agent for investigating and recommending changes in the tariff. Yet, as a result of the battle for continued control over trade policy, the commission was rendered largely ineffective. Although Culbertson, Smoot, and others had convinced Congress of the need for a flexible tariff to respond to the international economic instability confronting the United States, the legislators were hesitant to yield their tariff-making prerogative to the president. Consequently, they placed a 50 percent *ad valorem* cap on all tariff changes and, more important, mandated that all duties should be set to equalize differences in the costs of production in the United States and the principal competing country.[72] By seeking to limit the discretion of the president, Congress saddled the Tariff Commission with the unworkable formula central to the Payne-Aldrich Act of 1909, thereby limiting its ability to reach clear conclusions and allowing for multiple interpretations of any set of findings. Thus the distribution of power within the decentralized structure of the American state blocked the reform of the trade policy-making machinery and dashed any hopes of using flexibility either to rewrite the tariff once it was passed by Congress or to respond to changes in the unstable international economic environment.

Even though protectionists in Congress thwarted the use of flexibility to adjust the tariff, the Harding administration's accomplishments were

[70]Murray, *Harding Era*, p. 392.
[71]Dobson, *Two Centuries of Tariffs*, p. 87.
[72]Ibid., p. 94.

substantial. The increase in the tariff, though still larger than desired by many, was restrained by the fear of retaliation and a recognition that America's national trade interest would be best served by openness abroad. The administration also adopted an active trade strategy designed to expand the number of countries adhering to the liberal principle of nondiscrimination. In both these areas and in the push for flexibility, the foreign policy executive of the Harding administration pursued a relatively coherent liberal and active trade strategy.

The postwar period lends partial support to both interest-group and political-party explanations of American trade strategy. Wilson's veto and Harding's support of the Emergency Tariff Act of 1921 highlight the differences between the two major parties on the tariff question. Yet, as argued above, in a longer historical perspective this explanation contains important anomalies, although it is supported in this case.

Joan Hoff Wilson and other interest-group theorists have argued that the trade strategy of the Harding administration was fundamentally confused and that this state arose from the political standoff between the nationalists, who received the higher duties they desired, and the internationalists, who obtained flexibility and unconditional MFN.[73] Although this analysis of the Fordney-McCumber Act is persuasive, a comparison of the 1913 and 1922 tariffs fails to support it. As Table 2.1 indicates, American industry was far more export-dependent in 1919 than at any other time in the period covered by this study. Moreover, American industry and finance greatly expanded their overseas assets during the war, which should have further inclined the leading sectors of the American economy toward a more liberal policy. Only agriculture, which previously had been unsuccessful at realizing its interests, became more protectionist after the war. Yet in 1913 a less "internationalized" United States adopted a more liberal tariff than in 1922.

This interest-group explanation of the early 1920s also depends on a conception of American trade strategy as deeply at odds with itself, the product of too many ad hoc compromises demanded by competing groups. The analysis presented here, however, finds a greater coherency in American strategy. Seeking to insulate itself from increased international economic instability, the United States raised its tariff and compensated for this protectionist move by adopting a more active policy designed to maintain American exports. This strategy may have satisfied various groups within the United States, as all past strategies

[73]Wilson, *American Business and Foreign Policy*, pp. 65–100; and Jeff Frieden, "Sectoral Conflict and U.S. Foreign Economic Policy, 1914–1940," *International Organization* 42 (Winter 1988).

had done as well. But it is also consistent with the response of a relatively unified foreign policy executive to the constraints and opportunities of an international economic structure of bilateral opportunism beset by widespread economic instability.

This is not to deny that interest groups played an important role in the setting of American trade policy, only that they provide no more than a partial explanation of that outcome. As in 1909, protectionists in Congress thwarted the effective implementation of executive strategy. The high duties of the Payne-Aldrich Act hindered Taft's ability to wield the weapon provided by the maximum-minimum schedules. Likewise, congressional mandates limited the effectiveness of the flexibility provisions of the Fordney-McCumber Act. Yet a focus on interest groups alone provides a distorted picture of American policy and ignores the very real strategic interests created by the structure of the international economy.

ANGLO-AMERICAN COOPERATION IN THE 1920S

The rise, decline, and partial success of Anglo-American cooperation is central to an understanding of the international economy during the 1920s. It is also important for the theory developed in Chapter 1 and is of direct policy relevance today (see the Conclusion).

The postwar period was plagued, as I have argued, by severe international economic instability. As for a hegemonic power, the theory set forth in Chapter 1 hypothesizes that two or more opportunists will jointly seek to reduce instability and lead the international economy toward greater free trade. Success is not assured, however. Just as Britain failed to regulate the international economy effectively during the Great Depression of 1873–96, the success of joint Anglo-American attempts in the 1920s were not guaranteed. Indeed, given the magnitude of the disruption—the overnight rise of the United States as a net creditor, the wartime destruction of the European economies, the elimination of Germany as a central economic actor, the fracturing of historical trade patterns—successful regulation would have been highly unlikely under any circumstances. Nonetheless, significant and important Anglo-American cooperation did occur and the two opportunists met at least partial success.

Anglo-American cooperation underwent three phases in the postwar era.[74] The first stage, immediately after the war, was a period of compe-

[74]Considerable cooperation occurred between the United States and the United Kingdom outside the trade area. See Parrini, *Heir to Empire*, and Leffler, *Elusive Quest*, for a general discussion of Anglo-American efforts in the areas of general political and financial stabilization.

tition. The most divisive issue was Britain's attempt to revive its prewar commercial network emanating from its financial services center in London. Threatened by America's wartime inroads into the dominions and Latin America, the United Kingdom desired to integrate the United States into the British system, offering access to its well-developed information-gathering network in exchange for a promise that the United States would not create a global trading/financial system of its own. Although the American business community was far from unanimous on this issue, with the House of Morgan advocating collaboration with the British so as to dominate the system from within and the National City Bank seeking to construct its own network, Britain's offer was finally rejected in favor of the development of a wholly American system.[75]

This competition reflects two different conceptions of the appropriate postwar international economic regime. The United Kingdom advocated a "closed-door" approach to reconstruction and trade wherein international exchange would be loosely governed by an international consortium. This was reflected in its recent adoption of imperial preferences. The United States, on the other hand, as the most productive country within the international economy and expecting to be the victor in any equal struggle for world markets, desired an "open-door" regime.[76]

After Britain had recovered from the immediate disruptions of the war and as a result of pressure placed by the United States on its fellow opportunist through government control over private lending to foreign countries,[77] Great Britain acquiesced in the United States's position on several key issues and considerable Anglo-American cooperation began to emerge. In this second stage, beginning in the early 1920s, cooperation was most evident in efforts to stabilize the international economy and preserve the open door in the developing regions. Between 1924 and 1926, the London Conference and the Dawes Plan temporarily settled the reparations issue, the Locarno Treaty helped stabilize the European political order by resolving several outstanding points of disagreement between France and Germany, and the Mellon-Berenger Agreement settled the war debt problem (again temporarily). In each of these cases, Anglo-American cooperation was central to the final outcome.

Believing they had resolved some of the key political issues dividing Europe, the United States and the United Kingdom then turned their

---

[75]Parrini, *Heir to Empire*, pp. 40–71.
[76]Ibid., p. 142.
[77]Ibid., pp. 171–211.

attention toward stabilizing international exchange markets. The Dawes Plan funded Germany's return to gold in 1924. Assistance from the Federal Reserve Bank of New York enabled Great Britain to stabilize its currency and resume convertibility into gold in 1925. Similar efforts facilitated France's return to gold in 1927. Returning to gold, many believed, was the single most important means of alleviating the pervasive instability then confronting the international economy and plaguing relations between the opportunists.

In the trade and investment arenas, Anglo-American cooperation focused on the developing regions. In the Second China Consortium and the Washington Conference of 1921 and 1922, Britain and the United States joined together to restrain Japanese efforts to secure a "special" position in China. Under American pressure, Britain agreed to honor the open door in Middle East petroleum development. The United States, in turn, became willing to allow foreign participation in its domestic oil industry. Finally, the United Kingdom also accepted the open-door principle and American participation in the cable and communications systems it had previously developed in Latin America and elsewhere.[78]

During the third stage, from the mid-1920s to 1930, the loosely woven fabric of Anglo-American cooperation began to unravel. As Britain's position in the international economic structure declined further, and in particular as the United Kingdom found it increasingly difficult to stabilize its overvalued pound and domestic economy while preserving London's central position within the international financial network, new conflicts emerged that weakened the "Atlantic partnership" formed in the first half of the decade. Britain and the United States continued to cooperate in the maintenance of the open door in developing regions, but the two opportunists now came to differ on war debts—with a British attack on American policy sparking a brief but bitter debate, European recovery, and the limitations to be placed on armaments at the Geneva Naval Disarmament Conference in 1927.[79]

Despite their substantial cooperation in the early to mid-1920s, the United States and the United Kingdom never confronted the central problem of reducing protection between themselves in the postwar period. Each opportunist was individually aware of the dangers of retaliation and restrained its own tariff levels accordingly. But the two

[78]Hogan, *Informal Entente*, pp. 84–96, 105–85; and Wilson, *American Business and Foreign Policy*, pp. 184–218. Both Hogan and Wilson note that Anglo-American cooperation often took the form of bilateral monopoly rather than a strict adherence to the open-door principle.

[79]Hogan, *Informal Entente*, p. 218.

opportunists did not attempt to reduce their tariffs in a mutual or reciprocal manner. Indeed, the only explicit agreement reached between them was illiberal, when the United States agreed not to challenge Britain's imperial preferences despite their contravention of the open door, perhaps because of its own preferences granted to the American "colonies" of Cuba, the Panama Canal Zone, and the Philippines.

The most important example of the lack of cooperation in bilateral trade relations was the failure of the United States and the United Kingdom to negotiate an unconditional MFN treaty. The war and its aftermath had increased America's determination to create an independent shipping industry. Throughout the 1920s, this industry received both direct subsidies and protection. In the ratification of the unconditional MFN treaty with Germany, the Senate—despite considerable opposition from within the executive—attached a reservation granting the United States the right to exempt shipping from the terms of the treaty upon very short notice. It was recognized at the time that because of the importance of shipping to Great Britain, this reservation would most likely block the negotiation of a similar treaty between the two opportunists.[80] Indeed, negotiations were never formally begun.[81]

Cooperation between two or more opportunists is paradoxical. Just when it becomes more essential, it is rendered more difficult. As instability increases, the present value of free riding relative to future cooperation also increases. This paradox colored all attempts at Anglo-American cooperation in the 1920s, resulting in what might be called "segmented cooperation." The two opportunists cooperated most readily in stabilizing the international economy as a whole and maintaining openness in third parties. In these areas, their interests overlapped and did not directly conflict. Both opportunists could clearly gain. Cooperation on reducing barriers to trade between themselves proved more difficult. Here, each opportunist sought to free ride to a limited extent on the other.

Does this paradoxical situation indicate that closure within an international economic structure of bilateral opportunism is inevitable? Although openness is always problematic, its demise was by no means certain in the 1920s. The United States and the United Kingdom did engage in substantial cooperation designed to stabilize the international economy, thus mitigating some pressures threatening liberalism. Their failure to eliminate instability is not surprising in light of the magnitude

[80]See Parrini, *Heir to Empire*, pp. 242–43; and *Foreign Relations of the United States, 1924*, 2 vols. (Washington, D.C.: U.S. Government Printing Office, 1939), 2:188–89.
[81]No correspondence or internal memorandum appears in the *Foreign Relations of the United States* series indicating that negotiations had taken place.

of the disruption they faced. Although we cannot know for certain, their cooperative attempts might have been sufficient under conditions of lower instability. Additionally, Anglo-American cooperation was undermined in the late 1920 not by its own failure but by the continued decline of Britain within the international economic structure, as discussed in Chapter 6. Had the transformation of Great Britain from an opportunist into a spoiler not been imminent, limited or segmented Anglo-American cooperation might have persisted.

CONCLUSION

With the change in the international economic structure from hegemony to bilateral opportunism, the United States adopted a radically new trade strategy centering on lower tariffs at home and freer trade abroad. In the Underwood Act of 1913, domestic protection was compromised in favor of export expansion or free trade abroad for the first time. Although the international economic instability that followed World War I raised protection in both the United States and the United Kingdom, the same tension between protection and export expansion existed as in 1913. As a consequence, tariff increases were restrained for fear of retaliation abroad. Correspondingly, the United States adopted a more active trade strategy designed to alter the interests and behavior of other countries and, in particular, to gain general adherence to the unconditional MFN principle. Recommitting itself to the goal of nondiscrimination abroad, the United States finally adopted the instruments necessary to negotiate credibly with other nations to obtain this objective.

The United States had eagerly accepted a free ride on British hegemony during the first two phases examined here, but it now had little choice but to accommodate the interests of its fellow opportunist. Throughout these first three phases of American trade strategy, the trade preferences of the United States had not changed. Even after 1913, the United States still preferred protection at home and free trade abroad (P/FT), to universal free trade (FT/FT), which was preferred, in turn, to universal protection (P/P). Yet, immediately before the war its national trade interest changed dramatically toward freer trade as the international economic structure was transformed from hegemony to bilateral opportunism.

In both the Underwood and Fordney-McCumber acts, officials within the foreign policy executive were most clearly aware of the constraints and opportunities of the international economic structure. And although they did not receive everything they desired from the more protectionist Congress, these officials clearly initiated and forcefully advocated the change in policy designed to accommodate the new demands of bilateral opportunism. Recognizing the new international environment facing the United States and realizing that continued exports required freer trade at home, Wilson almost single-handedly pushed the Underwood Act through a resistant Congress. Although President Harding did not undertake a leadership role similar to Wilson's and the resulting policy was more constrained by congressional protectionism, flexibility, unconditional MFN, and the restraints on tariff increases all clearly originated with and were promoted by foreign policy officials.

CHAPTER SIX

Protection, Retaliation, and Response, 1930–1939

In the Smoot-Hawley Act of 1930, perhaps the most infamous tariff on record, American trade strategy took a dramatic turn toward protectionism. Four years later, the United States adopted the liberal and extremely active Reciprocal Trade Agreements Act (RTAA). Seldom has a country reversed its trade strategy so quickly and extensively.

The early 1930s are commonly seen as the last gasp of an old protectionist system that had outlived its usefulness and, simultaneously, as the formative years of American hegemony. Because their respective attributes have often been exaggerated, it is important to place both the Smoot-Hawley Tariff and the RTAA into perspective. The Smoot-Hawley Act did contain the highest rates of duty in American history, but these rates were assessed on a comparatively small range of goods. As a result, the level of duty on *all* imports was lower in the Smoot-Hawley Act than in any of the four tariffs passed during the first two phases of American trade strategy examined in this book. Similarly, although the RTAA did constitute a significant shift in policy by delegating more tariff-making authority to the president than ever before and reversing the trend toward higher tariffs, the United States did not abandon protectionism in 1934 nor did it contemplate acting in the long-term interests of the international economy. Rather, American trade strategy remained narrow and explicitly self-seeking. The RTAA was seen as a complement to protection through which the United States could reopen foreign markets to its exports. Moreover, the accomplishments of the RTAA were modest. By 1939, the end of this fourth phase of American trade strategy and the beginning of World War II, the level of protection in the United States, though significantly lower than under the 1930 tariff, had been reduced to approximately the same level obtained under the Fordney-McCumber Act of 1922.

The short, rapid swing of the tariff pendulum between 1930 and 1934, however, remains a historical conundrum and is most often explained by a variety of ad hoc or idiosyncratic factors. While recognizing the limitations of the theory outlined in Chapter 1, I argue that the evolution of American trade strategy during this phase—as in the past—was ultimately rooted in the changing international economic structure.

In approximately 1932, the United Kingdom evolved from an opportunist into a spoiler, transforming the international economic structure from bilateral into unilateral opportunism. The impending change of the international economic structure altered the constraints and opportunities facing the United States as early as the late 1920s. In particular, three analytically distinct factors, increased international economic instability, the forthcoming termination of bilateral opportunism, and the emerging structure of unilateral opportunism, incited the United States toward a modest increase in trade protection, particularly in the agricultural and basic commodity schedules of the tariff. And in a proposal consistent with the new constraints and opportunities of the emerging international economic structure, President Herbert Hoover, soon after taking office in 1929, called for a limited upward revision of the agricultural schedule of the tariff.

As part of this ongoing transformation of the international economic structure, the dominant trade strategies of other countries rendered American policy less interdependent or contingent, creating conditions under which the preexisting congressional propensity for logrolling—a nonsystemic factor—could flourish. As foreign protectionism increased and promised to expand even further irrespective of American actions, the need for the United States to act "responsibly" by limiting tariffs at home was reduced. In other words, as foreign protectionism appeared imminent and inevitable, the fear of foreign retaliation, which had played an important role in restraining protectionist pressures within the United States after 1912, could no longer exert its moderating influence. The tariff was once again defined as a "domestic" issue, and the protectionist forces in Congress were unleashed. The Smoot-Hawley Tariff of 1930 was the result.

Between 1930 and 1934, as a result of retaliation against the Smoot-Hawley Act, the depression, and motivations internal to various countries, the level of protection within the international economy rose precipitously. Even the United Kingdom, under pressure from its empire and protectionist forces at home, adopted its first general system of protection since the mid-nineteenth century. Most important, the unconditional most-favored-nation principle broke down under the pressure of rising tariffs. Trade was, in some cases, explicitly balanced on a bilateral basis and, in nearly all instances, heavily influenced by bilateral tariff agreements negotiated between trading partners.

Higher tariffs and the growing depression led to a decline in world trade to 70 percent of its 1929 volume and 35 percent of its value by 1933. American exports suffered disproportionately, declining to 52 percent of their 1929 volume and 32 percent of their value.[1] With the drop in world trade, the United States could hope to regain its export markets only by reversing the trend toward higher tariffs and exclusive bilateral agreements abroad. Because of extensive foreign protection, the potential rewards for reopening the international economy now appeared to exceed the costs of leadership. The United States sought to accomplish this liberalization while maintaining modest domestic protection through the extremely active RTAA of 1934.

JUMPING OFF THE PRECIPICE

The International Economic Structure

In approximately 1932, the United Kingdom evolved from an opportunist into a spoiler, leaving the United States as the only middle-sized and highly productive country and transforming the international economic structure from bilateral into unilateral opportunism (see Table 1.1 and Figure 1.5). This was only the second change of the international economic structure since the mid-nineteenth century. Britain's changing position was entirely the result of its continuing slide in relative productivity. The rate of decline in its share of world trade slowed after World War I and was reversed during the 1930s.

The transformation of the international economic structure from bilateral into unilateral opportunism altered the constraints and opportunities facing the United States, enhancing the attractiveness of protection and reducing the fear of foreign retaliation. In the late 1920s, three systemic factors conspired to raise the incentives for protection in the United States.

First, the level of international economic instability within the existing structure of bilateral opportunism, so important in the early 1920s, increased again after 1927. Exchange rates, stabilized between 1924 and 1927 in Germany, Great Britain, and France, remained relatively steady. By 1925–26, instability in wheat prices had also declined to less than half the immediate postwar rate. After 1927, however, commodity prices

---

[1]Asher Isaacs, *International Trade: Tariff and Commercial Policies* (Chicago: Irwin, 1948), p. 244.

Table 6.1. International economic instability,
Phase IV: Wheat price fluctuations (average to
good quality at Liverpool average spot)

Period	Level of instability
1913	.0189721
1919–1922	.1289417
1925–1926	.0500649
1927–1930	.0953094

For methods and sources see Table 5.2.

began to fluctuate more widely, with the instability of wheat prices rising between 1927 and 1930 to the midpoint of their postwar high and low (see Table 6.1). Though still below its immediate postwar levels and confined to commodity prices, international instability was nonetheless on the rise again.

As in the early 1920s, increased international economic instability served to stimulate pressure for protection within the United States in two ways (see Chapter 5). Nearly all countries, including opportunists, seek to insulate themselves through protection from international instability. Additionally, by making future interactions between opportunists less likely or predictable, instability increases the value of present returns relative to future returns, also increasing the attractiveness of protection. Because of the relatively narrow nature of international economic instability in the late 1920s, it is reasonable to expect that higher tariffs would be targeted at the agricultural products and other basic commodities experiencing the greatest fluctuations.

The second systemic factor was Britain's impending evolution from an opportunist into a spoiler, which created an end point to the iterated prisoner's dilemma faced by that country and the United States, reducing both the incentives for cooperation and restraints on protectionism. As discussed in Chapter 1, each party can gain by defecting (adopting protection) on the last move of an iterated prisoner's dilemma game. Knowing this, each player then has an incentive to defect on the next to the last move, and so on. An end point to the game leads cooperation to unravel up to the present moment in play.[2]

The changing structure of British interests, and thus the payoff structure of the game, was signaled early in the 1920s by the slow accretion of protection in the United Kingdom. The McKenna duties, first imposed

[2]For the effects of introducing an end point into an iterated prisoner's dilemma, see Robert Axelrod, *The Evolution of Cooperation* (New York: Basic Books, 1984).

in 1915, were repealed in 1924 and then reimposed in 1925. Commercial motor cars were added in 1926 and rubber tires in 1927. The Key Industry duties, imposed by the Safeguarding of Industry Act of 1921 and covering over sixty-five hundred articles, were renewed in 1926 for ten more years. New duties, important mainly for their symbolism, were imposed between 1925 and 1928 in accordance with the recommendations of the safeguarding committees on lace and embroidery, cutlery, gloves, gas-mantles, packing and wrapping paper, pottery, enameled hollowware, and buttons. Special duties were imposed on silk and hops in 1925. The Merchandise Marks Act, designed to encourage consumption of British products by requiring all goods to be labeled by country of origin, was passed in 1926. Finally, the Cinematographic Films Act, intended to limit the number of foreign (that is, American) films shown in Britain, was enacted in 1927.[3] These individual duties, though not necessarily important in themselves, were part of a larger political trend that questioned the value of free trade. As contemporary observer Frederic Benham wrote, "Faith in free trade had been weakening during the post-war years. This had very little to do with logical reasoning. It was simply that Great Britain was obviously lagging behind her rivals."[4]

The problem of increasing British protectionism was compounded by the breakdown of the "segmented cooperation" between the United Kingdom and the United States formed over the first part of the 1920s. As the two opportunists clashed over war debts, European recovery, and armaments, hopes of ever resolving the contentious trade issues separating them, and especially the question of unconditional MFN, steadily diminished.

The trend toward increased British protection and imperial preferences was duly noted by American foreign policy officials. After arguing that European-American trade rivalries had become more intense since the war, Julius Klein, director of the Bureau of Foreign and Domestic Commerce and a close personal friend and adviser of President Hoover, wrote in 1929 that "another phase of these international trade rivalries is the inevitable tendency toward preferment within colonial and imperial groups for the products of their various members." Similarly, Charles G. Dawes, then ambassador to Great Britain, noted on October 5, 1930, that "Britain is being inexorably driven toward the policy of protection and away from that of free trade." It is the inevitable and inexorable movement of British policy that is important here. As the United Kingdom edged ever closer to a general system of protection, the United

[3]Deryck Abel, *A History of British Tariffs, 1923–1942* (London: Heath Cranton, 1945), p. 47.
[4]Frederic Benham, *Great Britain under Protection* (New York: Macmillan, 1941), p. 22.

States lost its incentive to restrain protection at home. It no longer had to fear British retaliation, for protection and imperial preferences were growing of their own accord.[5]

These expectations were soon fulfilled as the United Kingdom took a dramatic turn toward protection in the early 1930s, apparently as a result of pressures internal to the empire rather than in reaction to America's Smoot-Hawley Tariff.[6] The protective duties adopted after the war had been gradually expanded over the 1920s, but Britain adopted in relatively quick succession the Abnormal Importations Act (1931), the Horticultural Products Act (1931), and the Import Duties Act (1932–subsuming the first two measures), creating the first general system of tariff protection in the United Kingdom in nearly a century.[7] Also, at the Ottawa Conference of 1932, Britain—under pressure from its empire—greatly expanded its discriminatory imperial preferences, agreeing not to impose the Import Duties Act upon imperial products, to levy duties on wheat, corn, copper, and linseed oil to expand the basis for imperial preference, to raise duties from 10 to 33.3 percent on a variety of agricultural products, to impose quotas on meats and dairy products to be administered in favor of imperial producers, and to refrain from reducing existing preferences.[8]

[5]Julius Klein, *Frontiers of Trade* (New York: Century, 1929), p. 48; and Charles G. Dawes, *Journal as Ambassador to Great Britain* (New York: Macmillan, 1939), p. 245. The logic here is somewhat paradoxical. A threat by B can influence A's behavior only if that threat is conditional upon A's performing some desired action. A mugger has more influence over his victim's actions if he says, "Give me your wallet or I will kill you" than if he states that "I am going to kill you whether you give me your wallet or not." A threat that becomes a certainty stops being a threat. American decision makers were certainly aware of increasing foreign protectionism and the likelihood of retaliation against the Smoot-Hawley Act. Yet, as the quotes from Klein and Dawes indicate, this protectionism was seen as inevitable. Consequently, foreign protectionism was no longer contingent upon American tariff restraint at home; it was now analogous to the mugger's second statement. The United States, in other words, no longer needed to fear foreign protectionism because it appeared to be a virtual certainty. To complicate the paradox further, American protectionism most likely reinforced tendencies toward protectionism abroad, indicating the possible presence of a vicious cycle of mutual protectionist expectations.

[6]Barry Eichengreen writes, "While there is some disagreement over the precise reasons for Britain's adoption of the General Tariff, there is no dispute that retaliatory motives rank low on the scale of motivations. There is little evidence in Parliamentary debate, ministerial correspondence or discussions among economic advisors that retaliation played much role in British discussion" ("The Political Economy of the Smoot-Hawley Tariff," Harvard Institute of Economic Research, Discussion Paper 1244, May 1986, p. 51).

[7]For a brief summary of these measures, see National Institute of Economic and Social Research, *Trade Regulations and Commercial Policy of the United Kingdom* (Cambridge: Cambridge University Press, 1943), pp. 21–26; and Isaacs, *International Trade*, pp. 358–60.

[8]Joseph M. Jones, "Tariff Retaliation: Repercussions of the Hawley-Smoot Bill," (Ph.D. diss., University of Pennsylvania, 1934), pp. 236–37; and Isaacs, *International Trade*, p. 360.

The third incentive for U.S. protectionism was the emerging structure of unilateral opportunism. As discussed in Chapter 1, a single opportunist can gain in the short term, defined as the period until others retaliate, by adopting protection before competing countries do, thereby approximating an opportunist's first choice of protection at home and free trade abroad (P/FT). By doing so, the opportunist diverts imports from its own market to the most open market, in this case Britain, while its own exports remain at or near prior levels.[9] This strategy must be implemented preemptively. Once other countries have raised their tariff levels, the opportunist will gain little by raising its own level of protection. The opportunist benefits only until other countries retaliate. Nonetheless, it is an attractive strategy, particularly if there is a lag before others respond. It is even more attractive if imports are rapidly increasing in sensitive sectors, as they were in the case of American agriculture.[10]

Basic commodity and agricultural prices, which had been declining since the war, began to plummet after mid-decade. Expanded farm production in Argentina, Canada, and Australia during the war coupled with postwar agricultural protection in the United States, Britain, France, and Germany—after the latter's return to tariff autonomy in 1925—created a desperate situation for farmers. Using 1923–25 as a base (that is, 1923–25 = 100), a condition of oversupply compared to 1913, world stocks of agricultural commodities rose to 146 in 1927, and agricultural prices declined to 81. Abundant harvests in 1928 and 1929 further undermined agricultural markets, pushing stocks to 193 and prices to 64.[11] The United States had become a net agricultural importer in 1922 for the first time in its history. By 1929, as a result of these adverse trends within the world economy, agricultural imports into the United States were nearly twice as large as agricultural exports.[12] Diverting this rising tide of agricultural commodities to other markets promised to relieve the precarious position of American farmers.

Moreover, the time was ripe in 1930 to take advantage of the short-

---

[9]As might be expected, Britain was the target of significant export "dumping" in the early 1930s. See Dawes, *Journal*, pp. 337 and 386.

[10]See Murray Benedict, *Farm Policies of the United States, 1790–1950* (New York: Twentieth Century Fund, 1953).

[11]J. B. Condliffe, *The Commerce of Nations* (New York: Norton, 1950), p. 481; see also League of Nations, *World Economic Survey, 1931–32* (Geneva: League of Nations, 1932), pp. 277–81.

[12]See Robert E. Lipsey, *Price and Quantity Trends in the Foreign Trade of the United States* (Princeton: Princeton University Press, 1963), p. 158; and David A. Lake, "Export, Die, or Subsidize: The International Political Economy of American Agriculture, 1875–1939," paper presented at the 1986 Annual Meeting of the American Political Science Association, Washington, D.C., August 28–31, 1986.

term benefits of preemptive protection. In the four years before the passage of the Smoot-Hawley Act, forty-five countries had undertaken major alterations in their tariffs, and many, particularly in central and eastern Europe, were specifically designed to reduce agricultural imports.[13] In fact, a tariff war then raging in Europe was so serious that all of the major countries except Russia agreed to attend the customs truce conference in Geneva in February 1930, five months before the Smoot-Hawley Act was finally adopted by the United States.[14] Had the United States delayed longer, even higher American tariffs might not have diverted the ever-increasing surplus of agricultural commodities from its shores.

All three of these factors—renewed instability, the termination of bilateral opportunism, and the emergence of unilateral opportunism—served to incite the United States toward a moderate increase in protection in the late 1920s. Indeed, in light of the impending transformation of the international economic structure from bilateral into unilateral opportunism, there was little reason for the United States not to adopt modest protection, and it might actually benefit from such action, at least in the short term.

These three factors, and particularly the end point created in the structure of bilateral opportunism, also combined to reduce the constraints on American trade strategy imposed by the fear of foreign retaliation. Protection itself was now more attractive, and to the extent that the closure of foreign markets was now perceived as inevitable the United States found it easier to be swept along with the tide. In the third phase of American trade strategy examined in Chapter 5, both Wilson and Harding explicitly linked the need for tariff restraint in the United States to the fear of foreign retaliation. In 1929 and 1930, while the Smoot-Hawley bill was under consideration, no one in the Hoover administration voiced similar fears despite clear evidence that other countries would respond with new and more painful duties if the United States raised its tariff. Instead, as Melvyn Leffler writes, "the president and his supporters emphasized that France and other major nations had raised their tariffs repeatedly throughout the 1920s and had therefore set precedents for the American action."[15]

The Republican leadership in Congress, which had accepted if not supported Harding's call for restraint in 1922, now refused to recognize

[13]Eichengreen, "Political Economy of the Smoot-Hawley Tariff," pp. 47–48.
[14]Harris Gaylord Warren, *Herbert Hoover and the Great Depression* (New York: Oxford University Press, 1959), p. 95.
[15]Melvyn P. Leffler, *The Elusive Quest: America's Pursuit of European Stability and French Security, 1919–1933* (Chapel Hill: University of North Carolina Press, 1979), p. 199.

the link between imports and exports or even to consider the possibility of retaliation. These concerns were raised by the small minority of free traders in Congress. Representative Cordell Hull (D.-Tenn.), one of the most vocal members of this minority, persuasively argued for a more liberal trade policy:

> Instead of a new policy of moderate tariffs with fair and liberal commercial or trade policy, based on the favored-nation doctrine in its unconditional form, it is now proposed further to build all our economic policies around the doctrine of extreme nationalism or isolation, with discrimination or retaliation as our chief commercial policy, ignoring the patent fact that the future progress and prosperity of the country requires expanding production and expansion of foreign markets.

Hull concluded, "Our economic imperialism and isolation to-day are more unpopular than Germany's military imperialism in 1914." Indeed, the probable reactions of foreign countries to the Smoot-Hawley bill were known early in the debate. On September 13, 1929, more than seven months before the Senate finally passed the bill, Senator Pat Harrison (D.-Miss.) stated,

> I hold in my hand—and I want to call it to the attention of the chairman of the Finance Committee [Smoot]—a book of 255 pages of small type that contains the protests of practically every government in the world against some provision of this tariff bill. Retaliations are threatened, confusion ensues. . . . Such proposals as this tariff do not bring people closer to us nor make them more friendly with us. Distrust and suspicion inevitability attends such a policy.[16]

Yet the Republicans in Congress never explicitly addressed the arguments raised by Hull, Harrison, and others. Nor did they examine the question of exports. Rather, Smoot and his Republican colleagues implicitly denied that a relationship between imports and exports existed and explicitly redefined the tariff as a "domestic" political issue. In a direct fashion not heard since the opening stages of debate on the McKinley Tariff of 1890, Smoot declared that "the tariff is a domestic matter, and an American tariff must be framed and put into force by the American Congress and administration. No foreign country has a right to interfere." This sentiment was also prevalent in the House, as noted by Edward E. Browne (R.-Wisc.): "I agree perfectly with the distinguished chairman of the Committee on Ways and Means [Mr. Hawley]

[16]*Congressional Record*, 71st Cong., 1st sess., 1929, pp. 1201, 1203, 3592–93.

192

that the markets of the United States are for the producers of the United States, and that this is a domestic question. No matter what foreign countries think about our tariff and the tariff duties, it is a question for the people of the United States to decide."[17]

Despite the vociferous denunciations of a few, the majority in Congress appeared to agree with the Republican leadership that the tariff was a domestic issue. In passing the bill, Congress intentionally disregarded the international consequences of its actions. And Hoover, who was in a position to advocate international responsibility, failed to challenge Congress. If he did not support it, Hoover at least accepted Congress's view of the situation and the final outcome. During the third phase of American trade strategy a clear conception of the importance of exports and a fear of retaliation guided American policy in a more liberal direction. The changing international economic structure negated this fear in 1930. In American eyes, the tariff really did appear as a domestic issue. This intentional disregard of the possibility and consequences of foreign retaliation helped create the conditions under which congressional logrolling could take hold and allowed the United States to return to a policy of high protection.

The Smoot-Hawley Act and American Trade Strategy

There was no electoral mandate for reforming the tariff in 1930. The Republican platform of 1928 reaffirmed the party's "belief in the protective tariff as a fundamental and essential principle of the economic life of the Nation" but made no pledge for the reform of existing duties.[18] The Democrats also declared in favor of protection, although in "pleasingly ambiguous language," further obscuring the differences between the two parties.[19] Nevertheless, upon taking office in March 1929, President Herbert Hoover called Congress into special session to revise the agricultural schedule of the tariff. He also raised the possibility of limited reforms of other schedules, declaring that "the test of necessity for revision [should be] . . . whether there has been substantial slackening of activity in an industry during the past few years, and a consequent decrease of employment due to insurmountable competition in the products of that industry."[20]

[17]Ibid., pp. 3548, 1562.
[18]Isaacs, *International Trade*, p. 228.
[19]The phrase is Lawrence Chamberlain's, quoted in Robert A. Pastor, *Congress and the Politics of U.S. Foreign Economic Policy, 1929–1976* (Berkeley: University of California Press, 1980), p. 77.
[20]*Public Papers of the Presidents of the United States, Herbert Hoover, March 4 to December 31, 1928* (Washington, D.C.: U.S. Government Printing Office, 1974), p. 79.

Table 6.2. Levels of duty by tariff act, Phase IV*

Year of tariff act	Level of duty on all imports	Level of duty on dutiable imports	Percentage of all imports on free list
1922	13.9	38.2	63.5
1930	19.0	55.3	65.5
RTAA**	14.4	37.3	61.3

*Average rates of duty and average percentage of imports on free list computed for all complete years tariff act in effect.
**Because of the continually changing nature of the tariff under the RTAA, duties are calculated for 1939 only.
SOURCE: *Statistical Abstract of the United States* (Washington, D.C.: U.S. Government Printing Office, selected years).

What little guidance this principle provided was largely ignored by Congress, which redefined its mandate as a general revision of the tariff.[21] Even the Republican leadership in Congress exhibited little concern for logic or the principles upon which the revision should be founded. It had become tradition that the first days of debate in the House and the first weeks of debate in the Senate on any tariff bill were devoted to general issues and principles: duty-free raw materials (1894), equalizing the costs of production (1909 and 1922), or a competitive tariff (1913), for instance. Yet in the Smoot-Hawley debate the Republican leadership in the House confined the discussion to individual items in the bill almost from the start. Similarly, the Senate leadership began amending the bill soon after its introduction.

The bill was under debate on the floors of the House and Senate for a total of eight months. The Senate attached 1,253 amendments to the House bill, which had already been expanded beyond the limited revision initially proposed by Hoover. Despite the obvious influence that logrolling exerted on the legislative process, the Smoot-Hawley Act, though it established higher rates of duty, was not as extreme as commonly thought.[22] As finally passed and signed into law in June 1930, the Smoot-Hawley Act raised the average rate on dutiable imports from 38.2 to 55.3 percent, the highest level in American history (see Table

[21]The Ways and Means Committee, according to Taussig, made a "half-hearted" attempt to obtain the "limited revision" requested by the president. But even here, he notes, there were large increases on manufactured goods. The full revolt occurred on the floor of the House and Senate (Frank W. Taussig, *The Tariff History of the United States*, 8th ed. [New York: Putnam's, 1931], pp. 494–95).

[22]John D. Hicks writes that the Smoot-Hawley Act "raised American import duties to an all-time high" (*Republican Ascendancy, 1921–1933* [New York: Harper & Row, 1960], p. 221).

Table 6.3. Average rates, by schedules, in the tariff acts of 1922 and 1930 (in percentages)*

Category	1922	1930	Increase
Chemicals, oils, and paints	29.22	31.40	2.18
Earths, earthenwares, and glassware	45.62	53.62	8.00
Metals and manufactures of	33.71	35.01	1.30
Wood and manufactures of	7.97	10.49	2.52
Sugar, molasses, and manufactures of	67.85	77.21	9.36
Tobacco and manufactures of	63.09	64.78	1.69
Agricultural products and provisions	19.86	33.62	13.76
Spirits, wines, and other beverages	36.48	47.44	10.96
Manufactures of cotton	40.27	46.33	6.06
Flax, hemp, jute, and manufactures of	18.16	19.14	0.98
Wool and manufactures of	49.54	59.83	10.29
Manufactures of silk	56.56	59.13	2.57
Manufactures of rayon	52.68	53.62	0.94
Paper and books	24.72	26.06	1.34
Sundries	21.97	27.39	5.42

*Calculated on the basis of 1928 imports.

SOURCE: Frank W. Taussig, *The Tariff History of the United States* (New York: Putnam's, 1931), pp. 518–19.

6.2). The free list, however, was expanded from 63.5 to 65.5 percent. In other words, only 34.5 percent of all imports paid any duty at all. Only the Underwood Act of 1913 allowed more goods to enter duty-free into the United States than did the Smoot-Hawley bill. Because of the large free list, the average rate of duty on all imports was increased only from 13.9 to 19.0 percent. This was the third lowest average rate of duty on all imports of the seven tariff acts examined in this study: only the Underwood and Fordney-McCumber acts were lower. Thus, although the duties were higher than ever before, they were applied to relatively few goods. Nonetheless, the act still constituted a substantial upward revision of the tariff.

Despite the general increase in duties and the apparent lack of a guiding principle in the tariff debates, the final bill did reflect, in part, Hoover's original design. Table 6.3 presents a comparison of the fifteen tariff schedules in the 1922 and 1930 tariff bills (with rates calculated on the basis of 1928 imports). With the exception of wool and manufactures thereof, which groups the raw material produced by the farmer together with the finished product, the largest increases in rates are found in the agricultural and processed food schedules. Specifically, agricultural products and provisions were raised by 13.76 percent *ad valorem*, spirits, wines, and other beverages (which because of prohibition was largely "other") by 10.96 percent, and sugar by 9.36 percent.

The Smoot-Hawley Act also reenacted the retaliatory and flexibility provisions of the Fordney-McCumber Tariff. Section 338 authorized the president to impose retaliatory duties of up to 50 percent *ad valorem* on the goods of countries that discriminated against American products. As in Section 317 of the 1922 act, Section 338 further authorized the president to prohibit all imports from the offending country if the initial penalty duties did not lead to the removal of discriminations. This section, which had generated much support in 1922, was not subjected to an extensive debate in Congress, and few appeared to consider it an important component of the Smoot-Hawley bill.[23] Whereas in 1922 the penalty provision had been expected to be immensely successful in freeing up foreign markets for American producers, in 1930 it was passed with few apparent expectations and without distinct enthusiasm.

The flexibility provision, formerly Section 315 and renumbered as Section 336, engendered considerably more controversy.[24] This provision had originally been supported in 1922 by the foreign policy decision makers in the White House and the liberal or internationalist faction in Congress. Its passage was widely perceived as a significant victory for a liberal American trade policy. Over the 1920s, as Section 315 was more often used to raise than to lower tariffs, the supporters of the flexibility provision became disillusioned. In 1930 the liberal internationalists opposed the inclusion of the flexibility provision in the Smoot-Hawley bill and the moderate protectionists supported it.[25] President Hoover, maintaining his faith in the ability of the bipartisan Tariff Commission to get the "tariff out of politics," strongly supported Section 336 and threatened to veto the legislation if the flexibility provision was not included. Thus, though the Smoot-Hawley Act contained the same potential for international activism as did the Fordney-McCumber Act, few had strong expectations that this result would be obtained.

Hoover, Congressional Logrolling, and the International Economic Structure

Hoover was the only president in the period covered by this book to initiate and advocate an upward revision of the tariff. In all other cases,

[23]Breaking with tradition, the Senate considered the administrative provisions of the Smoot-Hawley bill first rather than last. In the several weeks during which these sections were under active debate, Section 338 was touched upon only briefly.

[24]This controversy is discussed in Joan Hoff Wilson, *American Business and Foreign Policy, 1920–1933* (Boston: Beacon, 1971), pp. 74–87; and J. Marshall Gerstin, *The Flexible Provisions in the United States Tariff, 1922–1930* (Philadelphia: University of Pennsylvania Press, 1932).

[25]Wilson, *American Business and Foreign Policy*, p. 86.

the party platform had already been determined before the candidate was chosen, as in 1920, or the president sought to lower duties, as in 1909 and 1913. In 1928, however, it was Hoover who first called for a limited revision of the agricultural schedule of the Fordney-McCumber Act and opened the possibility of more extensive changes.

Despite Hoover's role in initiating the revision of the tariff, congressional logrolling is the most striking aspect of the domestic political process leading up to the Smoot-Hawley Act. The bill was debated longer on the floors of the House and Senate and amended more than any other tariff bill in American history. The Ways and Means Committee attempted to hold to Hoover's suggestion but was not sorry to see the House amend the bill on the floor. All restraint disappeared in the Senate.

Though supporting only a moderate upward revision, Hoover intervened only twice in the legislative deliberations over rates. In May, shortly before the House passed the Hawley bill, Hoover met with several leaders from the lower chamber and urged them to "get changes on farm products and reject industrial changes."[26] And on July 2, 1929, almost a year before the Senate finally passed the Smoot bill, Hoover caucused with Senators David A. Reed (R.-Pa.), Reed Smoot (R.-Utah), and Walter Edge (R.-N.J.), who agreed to reduce some of the rates set forth in the House bill.[27] Neither of these efforts significantly affected the final result.

Hoover and other key foreign policy makers in his administration did not fully support the final version of the Smoot-Hawley bill.[28] Hoover

[26]Edgar E. Robinson and Vaughn Davis Bornet, *Herbert Hoover: President of the United States* (Stanford: Hoover Institution Press, 1975), p. 110.

[27]William S. Myers and Walter H. Newton, *The Hoover Administration: A Documentary Narrative* (New York: Scribner's, 1936), p. 396.

[28]Hoover possessed a well-developed and articulated tariff philosophy. William J. Barber provides an excellent summary: "Hoover steadfastly denied that there was any incompatibility between his advocacy of export promotion, on the one hand, and his support of U.S. tariff policy on the other. In his view, the world—not just the United States—had a stake in American prosperity. High incomes and high wages increased the demand for imported raw materials which, for the most part, entered the country duty free. In addition, prosperity in the United States tended to swell the flow of dollars abroad through tourism and remittances. In short, the reinforcement to American income levels provided by the right kind of tariff program created the conditions that would permit foreigners to acquire more dollars. A skeptic could readily point out that other countries might be tempted to use similar arguments to justify protectionist measures of their own. As Hoover developed the case, however, the argument was not generalizable. The circumstances of the American economy, it was suggested, made it special. By virtue of its structure, demand for imports in the United States was highly elastic with respect to national income, but not particularly sensitive to changes in the prices of imported goods" (*From New Era to New Deal: Herbert Hoover, the Economists, and American Economic Policy, 1921–1933* [New York: Cambridge University Press, 1985], p. 35).

Perhaps because of his peculiar view of the tariff, Hoover does not appear to have been was keenly aware that it went far beyond the limited revision he had originally proposed. The State Department, led by Henry L. Stimson, supported Hoover's original suggestion but feared that any greater increase would undercut efforts to negotiate additional unconditional most-favored-nation treaties.[29] Yet Stimson "remained aloof from the tariff discussions" until the very end, according to Elting E. Morison, when he "fought like mad" for two days attempting to persuade Hoover to veto the bill.[30]

Hoover was not involved in the deliberations over specific rates, but he did lobby hard for reenactment of the flexibility provision contained in the Fordney-McCumber Act and eventually signed the bill because it included this authority. Like nearly all of his predecessors, Hoover desired to expand executive power in the tariff arena. When the flex-ibility provision proved of limited utility and was used to raise duties more often than to lower them, many of its original supporters turned against the provision. Hoover retained a perhaps naive faith that he could effectively mobilize the machinery contained in the provision to set duties "scientifically." Thus, like McKinley in 1897, Hoover re-mained safely aloof from the tariff-writing process confident that he could later use his executive authority to remake the legislation in line with his own desires. In 1930 Democrats and progressive Republicans opposed flexibility because they did not believe Hoover could succeed where others had failed. Conservative Republicans opposed the provi-sion for the opposite reason: they feared Hoover would make good on his promise to use flexibility to lower duties. Despite this double-sided opposition, Hoover continued to push for flexibility. He succeeded only by threatening to veto the entire bill if it was not included. "No provision for flexible tariff," Hoover told Republican leaders, "then no tariff bill."[31]

---

particularly sensitive to the constraints and opportunities of the international economic structure. Hoover's lack of activity on the tariff is thus overdetermined and explicable both by the redefinition of the tariff as a domestic issue and the consequent handicapping of the president and by ideology.

[29]Leffler, *Elusive Quest*, pp. 196–97.

[30]Elting E. Morison, *Turmoil and Tradition: A Study of the Life and Times of Henry L. Stimson* (Boston: Houghton Mifflin, 1960), p. 312.

[31]David Burner, *Herbert Hoover: A Public Life* (New York: Knopf, 1979), p. 298. Hoover's views on the flexible tariff and his role in getting the provision adopted are described in *The Memoirs of Herbert Hoover: The Cabinet and the Presidency, 1920–1933* (New York: Macmillan, 1952), pp. 291–99. The flexible provision was used more actively under Hoover than before. During the first year of Section 336's operation, thirty-two investiga-tions were completed, of which eight resulted in no change, eighteen in decreases, and six in increases (see Jones, *Tariff Retaliation*, p. 23). Hoover claims that under Section 336 "250 industrial items were reviewed by the [Tariff] commission, and the rates changed in about 75 of them, most downward," between 1930 and 1932 (*Memoirs*, p. 299).

Had Hoover demonstrated similar resolve on the overall level of duties early in the legislative process, he might have achieved the moderate upward revision he proposed.[32] Yet he took no such action. Congress was effectively given a free hand in setting tariff rates. As a result, the congressional logrolling process was set in motion.

Following E. E. Schattschneider's classic study of the tariff, the Smoot-Hawley Act is often cited as an ideal-typical case of logrolling or distributive politics.[33] Although logrolling was clearly important to the final outcome, its causal significance diminishes in comparative perspective. As recognized by several contemporary observers, logrolling had been an essential element in the passage of nearly every tariff bill in American history and certainly in all of the bills enacted since 1887.[34] Tariff rates, as seen in previous chapters, varied widely.

Though the changing international economic structure was not the direct cause of the congressional logrolling that pushed duties far beyond Hoover's original proposal, it did create the conditions under which the log could be rolled more easily than before. The diminished fear of foreign retaliation removed the principal restraint on higher duties. Whereas in 1913 and 1922 the executive had urged tariff restraint and Congress acquiesced to avoid antagonizing America's trading partners, no such limitation was perceived as necessary in 1930.

Also, as American trade policy became less contingent and as other countries adopted dominant strategies of protection at home the influence of the president relative to the socially mobilized groups in Congress was reduced. From Grover Cleveland on, American presidents had attempted to increase their political leverage over the tariff by defining it, at least in part, as a foreign policy issue. By appealing to his position as the principal foreign policy decision maker, each president increased his legitimate authority in the tariff-making process. Faced with dominant strategies of protection abroad against which United States trade strategy could have only a limited impact, however, the tariff once again appeared as a "domestic" issue, as indicated in the quotes from Smoot and Brown above. Whereas Wilson and Harding had linked the tariff to exports and larger issues of foreign policy, Hoover remained uncharacteristically silent.

[32]Taussig, *Tariff History*, p. 500.
[33]E. E. Schattschneider, *Politics, Pressures, and the Tariff* (New York: Prentice-Hall, 1935). See also Theodore J. Lowi, "American Business, Public Policy, Case-Studies, and Political Theory," *World Politics* 16 (July 1964): 667–715; and William B. Kelley, Jr., "Antecedents of Present Commercial Policy, 1922–1934," in Kelley, ed., *Studies in United States Commercial Policy* (Chapel Hill: University of North Carolina Press, 1963), p. 12.
[34]Taussig, *Tariff History*, p. 481. In his classic study of the Smoot-Hawley Tariff, Schattschneider clearly believed that he was examining a case typical for its era rather than a unique event (*Politics, Pressures, and the Tariff*, pp. 13–17 and 283–93).

The international economic instability generated by fluctuations in the prices of basic commodities and the incentives for preemptive protection created by the emerging structure of unilateral opportunism and the increasing agricultural surplus focused tariff increases on primary products, particularly agriculture. It is nearly impossible, however, to limit tariff increases to basic commodities. Such changes raise prices to manufacturers, who can be expected to demand compensating tariffs of their own. Higher tariffs on basic commodities, in other words, set off a chain reaction, culminating in increased pressures for protection at all higher stages of processing.[35] The truly surprising result of the Smoot-Hawley bill is that the final tariff increases were weighted toward agriculture.

With this confluence of circumstances, the protectionist forces in Congress were given free rein, and the logrolling process was set in motion. Thus, although the changing international economic structure cannot be indicted as the direct cause of the high and extensive duties found in the Smoot-Hawley Act, it did provide the conditions under which the preexisting congressional propensity for logrolling could become more prominent than usual.

The outcome of the tariff deliberations of 1930 cannot be easily explained solely by reference to domestic politics. Political parties played only a peripheral role in the passage of the Smoot-Hawley Act. The tariff issue was not central to the presidential campaign of 1928. And the Democratic party had moved closer to the Republican position, further minimizing the differences between the two parties on this issue. More important, the Republican party, which enacted the more restrained Fordney-McCumber Tariff of 1922, was still in power.

The Great Depression, which accentuated pressures for protection, is also cited as a possible cause of the high level of protection contained in the final bill.[36] The Wilson-Gorman Act of 1894, however, which marginally lowered the tariff, was also passed by Congress in the opening months of a severe economic downturn.[37] Moreover, the House ap-

---

[35]Raising tariffs on manufacturing inputs lowers the "effective" rate of protection.

[36]The link between the depression and the Smoot-Hawley bill is more of a popular than a scholarly myth. See "Reagan Denounces 'Bunker Mentality' of Protectionism," *Washington Post*, March 4, 1983. Yet several academics have also focused on this relationship, among them Timothy J. McKeown, "Firms and Tariff Regime Change: Explaining the Demand for Protection," *World Politics* 36 (January 1984): 215–33; and G. M. Gallarotti, "Toward a Business Cycle Model of Tariffs," *International Organization* 39 (Winter 1985): 155–87.

[37]For the timing of the "first Great Depression," see W. Arthur Lewis, *Growth and Fluctuations, 1870–1913* (London: Allen & Unwin, 1978); and Charles Hoffman, *The Depression of the Nineties: An Economic History* (Westport, Conn.: Greenwood, 1970).

proved the Hawley bill on May 28, and it had already been under debate in the Senate for two months when the stock market crashed in October 1929. The final shape, or lack thereof, of the new tariff had already been settled before the depression began. To the extent that the depression is important, its effects were more likely felt through the mechanisms of international economic instability and preemptive protection discussed above.

The most persuasive domestic explanation of the Smoot-Hawley Act links the distributive nature of the tariff and underlying changes in the structure of societal interests.[38] Although American industry was less internationalized in 1929 than in previous decades (see Table 2.1), the farm community is more often singled out as the social group whose changing interests stimulated the process of logrolling in 1930. Barry Eichengreen has argued that farmers located along America's borders and coastlines, beset by heavy agricultural imports throughout the postwar period, allied themselves with the business nationalists—typically from smaller, more labor-intensive, and traditionally protectionist industries—and traded reciprocal support for higher tariffs. Yet this alliance was formed not in 1929, as a focus on the Smoot-Hawley Act might suggest, but in 1921 with the passage of the Emergency Tariff Act and solidified in 1922 by the Fordney-McCumber Tariff. This coalition may be the most proximate cause of higher duties found in the Smoot-Hawley Act, but the important difference between 1922 and 1930 remains unexplained.

An examination of the changing international economic structure is necessary for understanding the results of 1930. As argued above, increased international economic instability, the impending termination of bilateral opportunism, and the emerging structure of unilateral opportunism incited the United States to adopt a modest upward revision of the tariff. These factors also reduced the fear of foreign retaliation, constrained the executive's ability to appeal to foreign policy concerns, and—by focusing attention on increased tariffs for basic commodities—increased pressures for protection at higher stages of processing, thereby creating the conditions under which congressional logrolling could flourish. Thus, although the international economic structure may not have directly caused the extreme aspects of the Smoot-Hawley Act, the changing constraints on the United States allowed the societally generated process of logrolling to go forward. In other words, the difference between 1922 and 1930 lies not so much in domestic conditions as in the changing structure of the international economy.

[38] See Eichengreen, "Political Economy of the Smoot-Hawley Tariff," for an elaboration of this argument.

RETURN FROM THE ABYSS

The International Economic Structure

Justified and stimulated in part by foreign tariff increases, the Smoot-Hawley Act served as a catalyst for higher protection within the international economy and retaliation against the United States. Thirty-three countries filed formal protests against the Smoot-Hawley Tariff. Even before the bill was passed, Canada increased its duties on certain American products and widened the margin of preference accorded British goods. This was soon followed by an "emergency tariff" in September 1930. In July 1930 Spain raised its tariff and, in November of that same year, entered into bilateral treaties with France and Italy which effectively withdrew most-favored-nation status from the United States. Italy increased its duties on automobiles in July 1930 and, in September 1931, raised nearly all duties by 15 percent *ad valorem* and those on radios and radio equipment to virtually prohibitive levels. Italy also quietly began to balance trade on a bilateral basis. Soon after the passage of the Smoot-Hawley Act, Switzerland began a public boycott of American products. Beginning in July 1931, France gradually placed quotas on 1,131 formerly dutiable items, or one-seventh of all goods subject to tariffs. Great Britain returned to general protection in 1932. In short, after 1930 government barriers to trade increased and trade flows came to be organized on a bilateral basis.

It is difficult to establish the precise role of the Smoot-Hawley Act in stimulating this outbreak of protectionism. The increased international instability of the late 1920s and the growing depression are, in many cases, sufficient explanations of the protectionist reaction. Moreover, with the threat of additional penalty duties under Section 338 on their exports if they discriminated against the United States, few countries were willing to single out the Smoot-Hawley Act as the cause of their own tariff increases. Republican politicians within the United States also attempted to ignore or downplay the retaliatory nature of these foreign measures so as not to burden an already unpopular tariff with further opprobrium. Despite its various disguises, retaliation clearly did occur. Other countries increased their tariffs and, more important, disproportionately raised duties on typically American products.[39]

Although some countries reacted almost immediately, most retaliations occurred only after a substantial period of time had passed. These

---

[39]On retaliation against the Smoot-Hawley Act see Jones, *Tariff Retaliation*; and Percy Wells Bidwell, "The New American Tariff: Europe's Answer," *Foreign Affairs* 9 (October 1930): 13–26.

lags provided a significant period in which the United States—reaping the fruits of preemption—was effectively insulated from imports while its export markets remained at essentially the same level of openness that had existed before 1930.

Once retaliation had pushed tariff levels to prohibitive levels, the national trade interest of the United States shifted from preemptive protection to modest protection coupled with the rebuilding of export markets. The upward spiral of protection within the international economy, in conjunction with depressed growth rates, reduced American exports from $5,157 million in 1929 to a low of $1,576 million in 1932.[40] This decline was much steeper than the reduction in world trade as a whole. As trade shrank, the pressure for export expansion grew within the United States.

Facing an increasingly closed international economy, the United States chose to lead other countries unilaterally back to a modicum of openness. Once tariff levels were high enough virtually to halt the wheels of international commerce, any reduction in duties then benefited the United States. Stated more formally, as countries directly and indirectly retaliated against the Smoot-Hawley Act, the game-theoretic outcome moved to the far corners of the southeast cells of Figure 1.4. From this position, the United States would prefer any increase in free trade by others. It is important that the costs of international leadership did not change between 1930 and 1934, only the potential gains. This case demonstrates that if foreign tariffs are high enough, and the gains from free trade large enough, leadership by a single opportunist is indeed possible.

As noted in Chapter 1, tariff reductions sought by a single opportunist will not be associated with general principles of liberalism. An opportunist will continue to desire protection for its domestic economy. And because a single opportunist has limited influence and resources, tariff reductions—to the extent that they are possible—will be the result of pragmatic bargaining and the exchange of tangible concessions. Specifically, the United States could be expected to bargain away its own tariffs, at least some of which were superfluous, to induce others to lower theirs. Again, because the resources available to a single opportunist for influencing other countries are relatively modest, it would not be expected that a situation of universal free trade (FT/FT) could be obtained. The final result would most likely lie somewhere between free trade and extreme protection.

[40]Real exports (constant 1913 dollars) declined from $3,873 million in 1929 to $1,993 million in 1932, a significantly smaller drop (Lipsey, *Price and Quantity Trends*, p. 155).

The Reciprocal Trade Agreements Act and American Trade Strategy

The RTAA proposed by Franklin D. Roosevelt in March 1934 and passed by Congress three months later was not a repudiation of protection in the United States. Nor does it indicate that the country desired to adopt the policies of a hegemonic leader. Protection at home remained an important goal of American trade strategy, as would be expected of an opportunist. Given the widespread increase in global protection after 1930, the RTAA simply reflected a recognition within the United States that lower tariffs abroad and an ability to bargain bilaterally for such reductions were necessary for the restoration of its export markets. It was a tactical and pragmatic response to the international closure precipitated in part by its own earlier actions. The RTAA demonstrated only the willingness of the United States to trade limited reductions in its own tariff wall in return for substantial reductions by others.

The RTAA was intended to achieve two central goals. The first purpose of the bill was to restart the wheels of international commerce or, as Secretary of State Cordell Hull explained during testimony before Congress, to expand "foreign markets for the products of the United States as a means of assisting in the present emergency."[41] Roosevelt declared in a speech before the New York State Grange in February 1932 that it was time "for us to sit down with other nations and say to them: 'This tariff fence business, on our part and yours, is preventing world trade. Let us see if we can work out reciprocal methods by which we can start the actual interchange of goods.'"[42]

The second objective of the RTAA, stimulated by the growth of bilateralism and the attendant expansion of executive authority over trade issues abroad, was to sharpen America's own weapons of economic warfare.[43] If it was to lower foreign tariffs, the American executive now required the capacity to bargain effectively with other countries. In his special message to Congress, Roosevelt set forth the argument that would later become the central theme of the bill's supporters: "If American agricultural and industrial interests are to retain their deserved place in [the trade of the world], the American Government must be in a position to bargain for that place with other Governments by rapid and decisive negotiation based upon a carefully considered program, and to grant with discernment corresponding opportunities in the American market for foreign products supplementary to our own."[44] Hull echoed

[41]Quoted in Pastor, *Congress and the Politics of U.S. Foreign Economic Policy*, p. 88.
[42]Quoted in Raymond Moley, *After Seven Years* (New York: Harper, 1939), p. 12.
[43]Henry J. Tasca, *The Reciprocal Trade Policy of the United States: A Study in Trade Philosophy* (Philadelphia: University of Pennsylvania Press, 1938), p. 45.
[44]Reprinted in Sidney Ratner, *The Tariff in American History* (New York: VanNostrand, 1972), p. 146.

the president but narrowed the proper negotiator from "government" to "executive," effectively placing the locus of decision making squarely within his own department. Because other governments were concluding trade agreements among themselves, Hull declared, "It is manifest that unless the Executive is given authority to deal with the existing great emergency somewhat on parity with that exercised by the executive departments of so many other governments for purposes of negotiating and carrying into effect trade agreements, it will not be practicable or possible for the U.S. to pursue with any degree of success the proposed policy of restoring our lost international trade."[45]

The RTAA was, in actuality, an amendment to the Smoot-Hawley Act of 1930. Under its provisions the president was authorized "whenever he finds as a fact that any existing duties or other import restrictions of the United States or any foreign country are unduly burdening and restricting the foreign trade of the United States . . . to enter into foreign trade agreements with foreign governments" within three years after the passage of the act.[46] All changes in duties were to be generalized to all countries possessing unconditional most-favored-nation agreements with the United States. No agreement, however, could raise or lower duties by more than 50 percent or transfer any good between the free and dutiable schedules. Finally, as a concession to the protectionists within Congress, the act provided that public hearings should be held before any agreement was concluded and that the Tariff Commission and Departments of State, Agriculture, and Commerce were to be consulted. No additional congressional approval was required for any agreement negotiated under the RTAA.

In its individual provisions, the RTAA contained little that had not already been enacted into previous tariff acts.[47] The president had been authorized to enter into reciprocity agreements in the acts of 1890, 1897, and 1913. The reciprocity agreements negotiated under the act of 1890 and section three of the act of 1897 did not require subsequent congressional approval. The authority to negotiate over any and all duties was granted to the president in section four of the act of 1897 and in the act of 1913. The discretion to alter rates by up to 50 percent was granted to the president in Section 315 and 317 of the Fordney-McCumber Tariff and Sections 336 and 338 of the Smoot-Hawley Tariff. Finally, the unconditional most-favored-nation principle was adopted by the United States in 1923. The RTAA is unique, however, in delegating all of these various powers to the president simultaneously. As a result,

[45]Pastor, *Congress and the Politics of U.S. Foreign Economic Policy*, pp. 88–89.

[46]Isaacs, *International Trade*, p. 251.

[47]Some of the similarities between the RTAA and past tariff measures are recognized in Tasca, *Reciprocal Trade Policy*, pp. 38–44.

the executive possessed considerably more control over trade policy under the RTAA than ever before. Despite this sweeping grant of authority, Congress nonetheless kept a tight leash on the president by limiting his authority to only three years. If the executive abused this grant, it would most likely not be renewed.

The RTAA was not intended to overturn the American system of protection. In his special message to Congress requesting the RTAA, Roosevelt included several key phrases designed to comfort protectionists. "You and I know, too," he wrote, "that it is important that the country possess within its borders a necessary diversity and balance to maintain a rounded national life, that it must sustain activities vital to national defense and that such interests cannot be sacrificed for passing advantage." Moreover, Roosevelt continued, "The successful building up of trade without injury to American producers depends upon a cautious and gradual evolution of plans."[48] The protectionist nature of the measure was even more clearly stated by Roosevelt's supporters in Congress. Representative Fred M. Vinson (D.-Ky.), in the closing Democratic speech on the bill, argued that the RTAA was not a free trade measure: "Occasionally our friends in their desperation refer to the Democratic tariff policy as tending toward free trade. Since I have been in Congress, I have never seen or heard of a free trader. I know of no one on the Democratic side of the House who does not believe that American industry, labor, and agriculture should be protected against a flood of foreign-made goods."[49] In its implementation, the RTAA was also guided by the principle of protection. Though it specified that any provision of the Smoot-Hawley Act inconsistent with it was to be repealed, the RTAA did not automatically lower the high tariffs contained in the 1930 measure. Any article not covered in an agreement with a foreign country, as a result, would remain dutiable at the rate set by Congress. In the actual negotiations, moreover, the Roosevelt administration, holding true to its initial request for authority to consider reductions in the American tariff "for foreign products supplementary to our own,"[50] attempted to limit its concessions to goods that did not compete with domestic producers.[51]

[48]Ratner, *Tariff in American History*, p. 146.
[49]*Congressional Record*, 73d Cong., 2d sess., 1934, p. 5775.
[50]Ratner, *Tariff in American History*, p. 146.
[51]Raymond F. Mikesell, *United States Economic Policy and International Relations* (New York: McGraw-Hill, 1952), p. 66. Rexford G. Tugwell, *The Democratic Roosevelt: A Biography of Franklin D. Roosevelt* (New York: Doubleday, 1957), p. 325, agrees with this assessment of the modest ambitions of the RTAA. See also Robert M. Hathaway, "1933–1945: Economic Diplomacy in a Time of Crisis," in William H. Becker and Samuel F. Wells, Jr., eds., *Economics and World Power: An Assessment of American Diplomacy since 1789* (New York: Columbia University Press, 1984), p. 287.

Nor did the United States emphasize the long-term health of the international economy or the necessity of lowering protection at home regardless of the actions of other countries. In 1934 the United States considered neither unilaterally lowering its own tariff in hopes that others would follow suit, as Britain did in the mid-nineteenth century, nor ignoring some elements of protection or discrimination against its exports so as to obtain at least partial free trade, as it would itself do after World War II.[52] Rather, in the RTAA the United States adopted a short-term strategy in which the lowering of American tariff barriers was acceptable only insofar as this action lowered foreign tariffs and expanded American exports.

Between June 12, 1934, when Roosevelt signed the RTAA into law, and the outbreak of World War II, the United States signed twenty-two agreements and three supplementary agreements.[53] The RTAA was renewed for a second three years in 1937 although by a narrower margin than obtained in its first passage. By 1939, when nearly all of these agreements had been implemented, the average tariff on dutiable imports in the United States had dropped from 55.2 to 37.3 percent, or approximately 1 percent below the rate of the Fordney-McCumber Act of 1922. Likewise, the level of duty on all imports declined from 19.0 to 14.4 percent, about one-half of 1 percent above the Fordney-McCumber rates. Although these reductions were considerable, the RTAA—at

[52]For a review of British trade strategy during the nineteenth century, see Robert Gilpin, *U.S. Power and the Multinational Corporation: The Political Economy of Foreign Direct Investment* (New York: Basic Books, 1975), pp. 79–98; Condliffe, *Commerce of Nations*, pp. 203–36; Albert H. Imlah, *Economic Elements in the Pax Britannica: Studies in British Foreign Trade in the Nineteenth Century* (Cambridge: Harvard University Press, 1958); Robert J. A. Skidelsky, "The Evolution of British Economic Foreign Policy, 1870–1939," in Benjamin M. Rowland, ed., *Balance of Power or Hegemony: The Interwar Monetary System* (New York: New York University Press, 1976), pp. 147–92; and A. A. Iliasu, "The Cobden-Chevalier Commercial Treaty of 1860," *Historical Journal* 14 (March 1971): 67–98. For American trade strategy after World War II, see Richard N. Gardner, *Sterling-Dollar Diplomacy in Current Perspective: The Origins and Prospects of Our International Economic Order* (New York: Columbia University Press, 1980); and David P. Calleo and Benjamin M. Rowland, *America and the World Political Economy: Atlantic Dreams and National Realities* (Bloomington: Indiana University Press, 1973).

[53]Trade agreements reached under the RTAA before 1939 were as follows (date effective): Cuba, September 3, 1934; Belgium, May 1, 1935; Haiti, June 3, 1935; Sweden, August 5, 1935; Brazil, January 1, 1936; Canada, January 1, 1936; Netherlands, February 1, 1936; Switzerland, February 15, 1936; Honduras, March 2, 1936; Colombia, May 20, 1936; Guatemala, June 15, 1936; France (including all colonies except Morocco), June 15, 1936; Nicaragua, October 1, 1936; Finland, November 2, 1936; El Salvador, May 31, 1937; Costa Rica, August 2, 1937; Czechoslovakia, April 16, 1938; Ecuador, October 23, 1938; United Kingdom (including all Empire and Newfoundland), January 1, 1939; Canada (supplementary), January 1, 1939; Turkey, May 5, 1939; Venezuela, December 16, 1939; Cuba (supplementary), December 23, 1939; Canada (supplementary), January 1, 1940; Argentina, November 15, 1941 (Isaacs, *International Trade*, p. 257).

least in its first five years—did not constitute free trade or even a return to the liberal trade strategy adopted in the Underwood Tariff of 1913. Yet the RTAA did achieve its objective of expanding American exports. By 1939 sales of American goods abroad had approximately doubled from their 1933 level, although they remained significantly less than in 1929. In addition, Asher Isaacs calculates that exports to countries with which the United States possessed trade agreements increased by 62.8 percent between 1934–35 and 1938–39, but exports to nonagreement countries increased by only 31.7 percent.[54]

Of all the agreements reached before 1939, the negotiations between the United States, Great Britain, and Canada—successfully concluded on November 17, 1938—were the most important.[55] The United States reduced 446 duties, froze 44, and agreed to maintain 65 more items of concern to Great Britain on the free list. In addition, it reduced 22 rates, bound 3 against increases, and bound 41 items on the free list in the interests of the British colonies and Newfoundland. The reductions covered a broad range of agricultural and manufactured commodities.[56]

Great Britain, in return, granted the United States reductions on 236 agricultural and manufactured products and bound 918 items.[57] Canada, as an important trading partner of the United States and the leading advocate of preferential trading arrangements within the British Empire, played an essential role in facilitating the agreement between the United States and Great Britain.[58] Having already concluded an extensive trade agreement in 1935, the United States and Canada further agreed to lower duties on a broad range of commodities, including both agricultural and manufactured goods.

The RTAA was significant for two reasons. First, as part of a worldwide trend, it granted the president considerably greater authority to negotiate trade agreements with other countries than ever before. Second, it reduced the levels of duty contained in the Smoot-Hawley Act and stimulated American exports. But the RTAA did not constitute a

---

[54]Ibid., p. 273.

[55]The negotiations leading up to these agreements and their importance are discussed in detail in Carl Krieder, *The Anglo-American Trade Agreement: A Study of British and American Commercial Policies, 1934–1939* (Princeton: Princeton University Press, 1943); and Richard N. Kottman, *Reciprocity and the North Atlantic Triangle, 1932–1939* (Ithaca: Cornell University Press, 1968).

[56]Isaacs, *International Trade*, p. 265; and Krieder, *Anglo-American Trade Agreement*, p. 176.

[57]Ibid., p. 266.

[58]Kottman, *Reciprocity and the North Atlantic Triangle*, pp. 10–12. Developing the role played by Canada in facilitating the agreement between the United States and the United Kingdom is the major contribution of Kottman's study to the understanding of the Anglo-American agreement already set forth in Krieder, *Anglo-American Trade Agreement*.

major break with past American trade strategy. It did not institute free trade nor was it ever intended to. In fact, as can be seen in the agreement with Great Britain, as much emphasis was placed on halting further tariff increases as in reversing the trend. Nor did the RTAA indicate a concern by the United States for the health of the international economy as a whole. Rather, it was simply designed to increase American exports by halting and reversing the movement toward higher tariffs initiated by the Smoot-Hawley Act. This was to be accomplished through the negotiation of specific and tangible bargains with the aim of securing at least equal if not favorable tariff reductions abroad.

Roosevelt, Hull, and the Passage of the Reciprocal Trade Agreements Act

Roosevelt "was, in theory, a low-tariff man."[59] This view accorded well with the ideas of his secretary of state, who had been a prominent congressional advocate of lowering tariffs through reciprocal agreements for almost two decades. In a 1929 letter to Hull, Roosevelt applauded the future secretary's tariff stand. Speaking before the New York State Grange in 1932, the presidential candidate blamed the Smoot-Hawley Act for the widespread retaliation against the United States and called for "reciprocal methods" to negotiate mutually beneficial tariff reductions at a "trade conference with the other Nations of the world." Roosevelt also endorsed the tariff plank in the 1932 Democratic platform written by Hull and A. Mitchell Palmer, Woodrow Wilson's former attorney general, which called for both a "competitive tariff" and "reciprocal trade agreements with other nations."[60]

Despite these low-tariff views, Roosevelt as president was initially under the sway of the economic nationalists in his "brains trust" and particularly Raymond Moley and George Peek.[61] "Our international trade relations, though vastly important," Roosevelt stated in his first Inaugural Address "are in point of time and necessity secondary to the establishment of a sound national economy. I favor as a practical policy the putting of first things first."[62]

This policy of domestic primacy scuttled Hull's desires for the early adoption of reciprocal trade agreements. A bill for such purposes, en-

[59]Quoted in Moley, *After Seven Years*, p. 12. See also Wayne S. Cole, *Roosevelt and the Isolationists, 1932–45* (Lincoln: University of Nebraska Press, 1983), p. 96.

[60]Cole, *Roosevelt and the Isolationists*, p. 96.

[61]Cordell Hull, *The Memoirs of Cordell Hull*, 2 vols. (New York: Macmillan, 1948), 1:353; and Cole, *Roosevelt and the Isolationists*, pp. 98–99.

[62]Text reprinted in Raymond Moley, *The First New Deal* (New York: Harcourt, Brace and World, 1966), p. 123.

abling the United States to enter into multilateral negotiations, was drafted under Hull soon after the Roosevelt administration came to power. Hull clearly hoped that Roosevelt would submit this bill during the first special session of Congress along with the other important legislative acts of the first New Deal. Indeed, the secretary of state set off for the International Economic Conference in London early in 1933 with a copy of the bill in his pocket, which he planned to use as evidence of America's good intentions in the area of international trade and—by publicly committing America to this new course—to bind his fellow policy makers in the United States. At home, however, Roosevelt desired to obtain full discretionary authority to fix the tariff at any height necessary for the successful operation of the Agricultural Adjustment Act and the National Recovery Act.[63] While Hull was at sea en route to the London conference, Roosevelt torpedoed his hopes, radioing that the closing days of the special session of Congress were "so full of dynamite that immediate adjournment is necessary. Otherwise bonus legislation, paper money inflation, etc., may be forced." Under these circumstances, Roosevelt continued, "tariff legislation seems not only highly inadvisable, but impossible of achievement."[64]

Gradually shifting away from this nationalistic position, a move facilitated by the rising influence of Hull within the administration, Roosevelt encouraged the drafting of reciprocal trade legislation early in 1934. The final proposal, written by a committee in the White House composed of Hull, Peek (the secretary of state's principal antagonist and chair of a temporary committee to reorganize the government's trade policy-making machinery), several members of Congress, and others, "was the product of many minds."[65] Yet, for the first time, a major piece of trade legislation was drafted by the executive, not Congress.

The passage of the RTAA by large majorities in both houses of Congress and with few amendments did not resolve the conflict between the "internationalists" and "nationalists" within the Roosevelt administration. In late 1934, Peek negotiated a bilateral barter agreement with Germany which would have traded raw cotton for American dollars and cut-rate German products.[66] Inclined to accept the agreement, Roosevelt vetoed it only under pressure from Hull, thereby undermining the position of Peek within the administration. With Peek's resignation in July 1935, Hull emerged as the dominant voice on trade within the Roosevelt administration. The series of trade agreements discussed

---

[63]Hull, *Memoirs*, 1: 353.
[64]Quoted in Cole, *Roosevelt and the Isolationists*, p. 96.
[65]Ibid., p. 102.
[66]Ibid., p. 104.

above soon followed. Thus by 1935, the Roosevelt administration had shed its economic nationalism and fully embraced a program designed to open up international markets by limited tariff reductions at home. In the process, the executive expanded and consolidated its power over trade strategy.

The RTAA has been examined by numerous scholars and has often been cited in support of both political-party and interest-group explanations of American trade policy. Neither can be easily dismissed. In political-party explanations, however, the usual cautionary notes already sounded in previous chapters also apply here. In a comparative perspective, changes in political-party dominance do not always correlate with changes in trade strategy. Likewise, just as the various Republican tariffs differed substantially, the Wilson-Gorman Act of 1894, Underwood Act of 1913, and RTAA of 1934 also differed in their substantive provisions. Knowing which party controls the government may indicate the direction of policy change, but it cannot explain the specifics of the various tariff acts.

Interest-group arguments also have limitations. As exports declined more rapidly than imports between 1930 and 1934, American manufacturers were, most likely, less export-dependent at the time the more liberal and active RTAA was passed than before. In a more sophisticated version of this approach, however, Thomas Ferguson has argued that the depression broke apart the old protectionist coalition and allowed a new free-trade alliance between internationally competitive, high value-added industries and labor to rise to dominance.[67] Although this explanation also correctly predicts the direction of policy change, it cannot account for the substance of the RTAA, and particularly why it took the form of bilateral negotiated reductions dependent upon executive authority rather than a "free-trade" omnibus tariff similar to the Underwood Act of 1913.

Finally, the RTAA is also seen by many as the triumph of economic rationality and the culmination of the tariff reform movement begun in the early twentieth century; with effective tariff-setting power in the hands of the president, the United States could now enjoy the benefits of a "scientific tariff."[68] Though partially correct, this "state-building" ar-

[67]Thomas Ferguson, "From Normalcy to New Deal: Industrial Structure, Party Competition, and American Public Policy in the Great Depression," *International Organization* 38 (Winter 1984): 41–94.

[68]See Cynthia A. Hody, "The Failure of American Trade Policy in the 1920s: Institutional Change and the Requisites of Trade Liberalization," paper presented at the 1986 Annual Meeting of the American Political Science Association, Washington, D.C., August 28–31, 1986.

gument is misleading. Neither Roosevelt nor Hull approached reform in these terms. The Tariff Commission, the reformers' preferred body of experts, was not involved in the negotiating process. Indeed, it was only one of the agencies that the president was mandated to consult before concluding negotiations. Rather, the RTAA is better explained as part of a worldwide trend toward executive tariff making driven by the expansion of bilateralism in the early 1930s. Expanded executive authority derived not from legislative failure but from the need to bargain effectively with other countries. International closure, in other words, led to the final reconceptualization of the tariff as a wholly foreign policy issue, the consequent augmentation of presidential power in the international commerce issue area, and the extremely active and liberal RTAA.

CONCLUSION

American trade strategy was dramatically altered by the change of the international economic structure from bilateral to unilateral opportunism. In the late 1920s, increased international economic instability, the impending termination of bilateral opportunism, and the emergence of unilateral opportunism all conspired to prompt a modest upward revision of the tariff, a systemic incentive consistent with Hoover's original proposal to Congress. The new constraints and opportunities of the international economic structure, however, reduced the fear of foreign retaliation, which had played such an important role in restraining protection between 1912 and 1930; undermined the influence of the foreign policy executive; prompted a "ratchet"-like tariff increase for manufactured goods by focusing attention on higher duties for basic commodities and agricultural products; and, as a result, created the conditions under which legislative logrolling could prosper.

Thus though the new constraints and opportunities of the structure did not directly cause congressional logrolling to rise to a new extreme, they did allow this process to be untethered. Consequently, domestic political processes become more important in explaining the Smoot-Hawley Tariff than in previous cases. The conception of process outlined in Chapter 2 does not assert that the foreign policy executive will always succeed in realizing the systemically derived national trade interest. Its partial success in this case, however, highlights the limitations of a structural theory of trade strategy. Systemic incentives can be subverted by domestic political processes, and when this occurs a structural theory will fall short. But these domestic political processes alone cannot explain the tariff act of 1930. The same political party and societal coalition were in power in both 1922 and 1930. And logrolling was an essential part of every American tariff bill. The shifting constraints and opportunities of the international economic structure must be appreciated to explain the Smoot-Hawley Act.

As other countries retaliated against the new American strategy and world trade slowed under the pressure of sharply increased tariffs throughout the international economy, the national trade interest of the United States shifted from emphasizing protection at home to pursuing free trade abroad. The benefits of international leadership, in other words, now appeared relatively larger. In the RTAA of 1934, the United States sought to exert a measure of unilateral leadership and restore its export markets by reducing foreign trade barriers. This highly active trade strategy did not reflect a new commitment to free trade or hegemonic leadership. Throughout this period, the United States remained an opportunist. It continued to desire protection at home and free trade abroad and to act in its narrow self-interest with little regard for the health of the international economy as a whole. Although tariffs were significantly reduced between 1934 and 1939, free trade was not contemplated. By the close of this phase, tariff levels in the United States had been reduced only to levels obtained in 1922.

As in the earlier cases examined in Chapters 3 through 5, the foreign policy executive played a key role in the formulation of the RTAA. Appealing to the need to expand exports and to negotiate with foreign powers, the RTAA was written by the executive and most forcefully advocated by Secretary of State Cordell Hull, who persuaded a president under competing pressures and, later, Congress itself. As before, the domestic policy-making process readily responded to the highly salient constraints and opportunities of the international economic structure.

The United States is often faulted for not leading the international economy more effectively during the 1920s and early 1930s. As Charles P. Kindleberger concludes, "The world economic system was unstable unless some country stabilized it, as Britain had done in the nineteenth century and up to 1913. In 1929, the British couldn't and the United States wouldn't. When every country turned to protect its national private interest, the world public interest went down the drain, and with it the private interests of all."[69] Similarly, other analysts date the beginnings of America's hegemonic leadership from the passage of the RTAA in 1934.[70] Such arguments both belittle and exaggerate the leadership

---

[69]Charles P. Kindleberger, *The World in Depression, 1929–1939* (Berkeley: University of California Press, 1973), p. 292.

[70]Gilpin, *U.S. Power and the Multinational Corporation*, pp. 100–101; and Joan Edelman Spero, *The Politics of International Economic Relations*, 2d ed. (New York: St. Martin's, 1981), p. 66.

role played by the United States in the interwar period. In short, they fundamentally misunderstand the nature of American trade strategy during the third and fourth phases examined here.

It is true that the United States at this time did not attempt to lead the international economy by example as Great Britain did in the nineteenth century or by accepting discriminations against its exports so as to encourage a measure of free trade in other areas as the United States itself would do after World War II. But throughout the third phase and the second half of the fourth, the United States did exercise leadership within the international economy. With the publication of the Open Door notes in 1899, the United States developed an explicit commitment to the principle of nondiscrimination which became more firmly entrenched with time. This commitment was exhibited for the first time in a tariff bill in the Payne-Aldrich Act of 1909. It became the cornerstone of America's active trade strategy through the Fordney-McCumber Tariff of 1922 and the adoption of the unconditional most-favored-nation principle in 1923. Even the Smoot-Hawley Act, which was in many ways a temporary abdication of leadership, did not violate the rule of nondiscrimination and, indeed, contained the same provision found in the 1922 act. In addition, the United States, under the conditions of relative international economic stability before World War I, also adopted a mechanism with which to pursue free trade abroad in the Underwood Act of 1913. During the 1920s and in tandem with Great Britain, the United States also acted to preserve the open door in much of the developing world. In short, the United States did seek to influence the policies of other countries and, when it did so, the effort was largely in a more liberal direction. Although this was not the same kind or degree of leadership undertaken by Great Britain or the United States at their hegemonic zeniths, it was leadership nonetheless.

The international economy might have been more stable and liberal if American trade strategy had been less protectionist in the 1920s. Yet American policy during this period as well as the policies of the other major trading countries were rational, self-interested responses to the international economic structure of bilateral opportunism and the widespread international economic instability created by the war. Similarly, the increase in global protectionism between 1930 and 1933 might have been less severe if the United States had not adopted the Smoot-Hawley Act. In this measure the United States chose to abandon whatever leadership role it had previously possessed. It did not attempt to influence the policies of other countries and in fact denied that it could. The country, in effect, turned inward upon itself. It did so not because the United States "wouldn't," as Kindleberger suggests, but as the result of

America's preemptive protection during the transition of the international economic structure from bilateral to unilateral opportunism. As international instability increased and its fear of retaliation diminished, the United States adopted greater protection because it promised at least a short-term relative benefit. To understand why the United States adopted the Smoot-Hawley Act, it is insufficient to examine only domestic political will, political leadership, and the depression. It is necessary to understand the constraints and opportunities of the international economic structure which confronted the United States in 1930.

Conversely, too great a leadership role can be attributed to the United States in the RTAA. Although that act did constitute a reversal of policy and a significant change in the policy-making process, it was not a radical break with past practice. It was not adopted in the pursuit of free trade nor was this goal entertained. At that time, the United States neither accepted the burdens nor sought the rewards of hegemonic leadership. Throughout this fourth phase, the United States remained an opportunist.

Conclusion

The four preceding chapters have argued that American trade strategy responded not only to a domestic political logic but to a systemic
logic generated by the constraints and opportunities of the international
economic structure as well. Despite the country's low level of dependence on the international economy, large domestic market, isolationist
ideology, and permeable political process dominated by domestic pressure groups, the trade strategy of the United States was influenced in
important ways by the structure of the international economy. Explanations focusing on domestic politics and processes thus capture only part
of the dynamics behind trade strategy. They highlight the role of interest groups and Congress but overlook the importance of the national
trade interest and the foreign policy executive.

The constraints and opportunities of the international economic
structure facing the United States changed considerably over the period
1887 to 1939. As I attempt to demonstrate in Part II, American trade
strategy evolved and, at several points, was sharply transformed in
response. In this period, four different international economic structures and, correspondingly, four phases of American strategy can be
identified. These phases are summarized graphically in Figure C.1. The
placement of the phases in relation to one another is approximate, and
therefore represented by broken lines, but the overall pattern is clear.

During the first phase of American trade strategy, from 1887 to 1897,
discussed in Chapter 3, the international economic structure of British
hegemony and America's increasing relative labor productivity combined to create an era of opportunity for the United States: Britain's
commitment to free trade remained secure and the United States could
easily obtain an opportunist's first policy preference of protection at

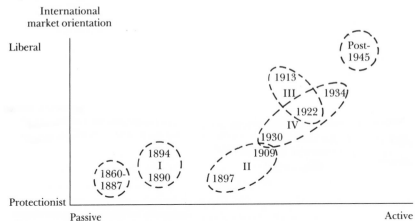

Figure C.1. American trade strategy, 1887–1939

home and free trade abroad (P/FT). The United States could both protect its domestic economy and expand its exports, thereby undercutting Britain's, without fear of retaliation from its principal trading partner. It could, in other words, free ride on free trade.

As a result, the tariff—previously an instrument of protection—was internationalized and transformed into a tool for both protection and export expansion. It continued to protect American industries at home, but under the new, more activist policies of bilateral reciprocity and duty-free raw materials exports to Latin America were also expanded. Between 1887 and 1890, both political parties adopted identical trade strategies despite the severe electoral competition and deep rhetorical differences that divided them. This simultaneous Republican backing for reciprocity and Democratic advocacy of duty-free raw materials is, perhaps, one of the strongest cases of support for the systemic theory developed in Chapter 1.

In the second phase, a new international economic structure of declining hegemony emerged. In approximately 1897, the United States surpassed Great Britain in relative labor productivity, creating a significant change within the international economic structure. Despite this change, Britain remained committed to free trade, thereby creating an incentive for the United States to pursue policies similar to those found in the first phase. America's increasing relative labor productivity, on the other hand, broadened the country's export horizons and stimulated a desire for greater access to foreign markets. At the same time, and perhaps because of America's increasing competitiveness, many Europeans increased their tariff barriers and specifically sought to exclude goods exported from the United States.

Torn between the desire to free ride on Britain and the need to preserve and expand its markets on the Continent, the United States adopted more active but nonetheless protectionist policies designed to differentiate between trading partners. Using first an expanded form of reciprocity in the Dingley Tariff of 1897 and later maximum-minimum tariff schedules in the Payne-Aldrich Act of 1909, the United States maintained protection at home and its policies of export expansion in Latin America while arming itself with the bilateral tools necessary to counter continental trade restrictions.

During the third phase of American trade strategy, from 1912 to 1930, the international economic structure imposed greater constraints on the United States than faced in any other period between 1887 and 1939. In approximately 1912, the United Kingdom evolved from a hegemonic leader into an opportunist, transforming the international economic structure from hegemony into bilateral opportunism. With this structural change, the trade policy preferences of the United States and the United Kingdom became mirror images of each other: the two opportunists could agree to adopt mutual free trade or mutual protection, but they could not simultaneously realize their preferred strategies of protection at home and free trade abroad.

Given the iterative nature of international trade relations, whether two or more opportunists will settle at mutual free trade, mutual protection, or some point in between is determined largely by the level of instability present in the international economy. Instability increases incentives for protection within a structure of bilateral opportunism in two ways. First, opportunists—like all countries—desire stability and will use protection to insulate themselves from international disruptions. Second, instability undermines the ability of opportunists to cooperate in the adoption of mutual free trade by increasing the value of present returns for protection (or defection) relative to the value of future returns for free trade.

Before World War I and under conditions of relative international economic stability, the United States adopted a liberal, freer-trade policy. The Underwood Tariff of 1913 drastically reduced tariff levels and explicitly endorsed the goal of free trade within the international economy. The war, however, created widespread international economic instability. Both the United States and the United Kingdom responded with higher protection, and cooperation between the two opportunists became difficult. The United States compensated for this decrease in liberalism with a more active trade strategy, threatening retaliation for discriminations against American exports and adopting the unconditional most-favored-nation principle.

The fourth phase, from 1930 to 1939, saw a pendulumlike swing in American trade strategy. In approximately 1932, the United Kingdom evolved from an opportunist into a spoiler, creating a second change of the international economic structure from bilateral to unilateral opportunism. The impending transformation of the international economic structure altered the constraints and opportunities facing the United States as early as the late 1920s. Three factors, increasing international economic instability, the forthcoming termination of bilateral opportunism, and the emerging unilateral opportunism all conspired to push the United States toward a strategy of preemptive protection. In particular, these factors reduced the fear of foreign retaliation, important in restraining protectionism in 1913 and 1922; rendered American policy less contingent or interdependent, thereby allowing the tariff to be redefined as a domestic political issue and weakening the foreign policy executive; and prompted tariff increases on agricultural and primary commodities, increasing pressures for protection at all higher levels of processing. Thus the evolving international economic structure created not only systemic incentives for a modest increase in the tariff but also conditions under which congressional logrolling could flourish. The Smoot-Hawley Act of 1930, a highly protectionist and moderately active tariff, was the result.

The Smoot-Hawley Act unleashed a wave of protectionism in the international economy directed, in part, against the United States. As its export markets closed, the United States could once again gain only by exerting a measure of leadership and reversing this trend, which it sought to do through the Reciprocal Trade Agreements Act of 1934. This was an extremely active and potentially liberal amendment to the Tariff Act of 1930 designed to counter the growing trend toward bilateralism in international trade. The United States did not abandon protectionism in the RTAA. Nor did the single opportunist perceive itself as acting in the long-term interests of the international economy. The RTAA was, at least in contemporary American eyes, a complement to protection through which the country could reopen foreign markets. By 1939, the United States had returned to the level of protection it had maintained during the 1920s.

The theory developed here also highlights the importance of the foreign policy executive as the agent that transforms the constraints and opportunities of the international economic structure into trade strategy. In each of the four phases examined here, the major innovations in American trade strategy designed to respond to the changing incentives of the international economic structure were initiated and most forcefully advocated by individuals in positions of authority within the foreign policy executive. The efforts of Presidents Grover Cleveland and Benjamin Harrison and Secretary of State James G. Blaine to internationalize the tariff between 1887 and 1890, President William McKinley's transformation from a protectionist into an advocate of reciprocity in 1897, President Woodrow Wilson's push for tariff reform in 1913, and Secretary of State Cordell Hull's crusade for the RTAA of 1934 are perhaps the clearest examples of trade strategy leadership by foreign policy executives. Yet Presidents Warren G. Harding and Herbert Hoover also played central though perhaps less dramatic roles in the formulation of trade strategy during their respective administrations. Although he appointed strong protectionists to the Tariff Commission, Harding called for restraint in 1922 by raising the fear of retaliation. He also adopted the unconditional MFN principle in 1923. Hoover initiated an appropriate revision of the tariff in 1930 but failed to restrain the protectionists in Congress. Although the foreign policy makers may not have achieved everything they desired, they generally recognized and pursued the national trade interest as derived from the international economic structure (the important exceptions are discussed below). And in most cases the principal objectives of the foreign policy executive were met.

This relative success can be attributed to two factors. Although society and Congress, on one hand, and the foreign policy executive, on the other, consistently possessed different trade agendas and objectives, throughout most of this period little fundamental conflict existed between society's demand for continued protection and the foreign policy executive's trade strategy initiatives. As noted in Chapter 2, the actors possessed different but seldom irreconcilable goals. Given Britain's commitment to free trade, American policy makers could easily reconcile protection with export expansion in the early 1890s. This is only slightly less true for the strategy of protection and market preservation pursued between 1897 and 1912. Likewise, in light of the impending change of the international economic structure, Hoover was generally in accord with the higher protection desired by Congress, although he did not support the final bill. And many members of Congress recognized the need for lowering duties through international negotiations and were willing to follow the lead of the Roosevelt administration in 1934.

Only in the period 1912–30 was there a gap between Congress and the executive which could not be easily bridged. The executive's desire to reduce tariffs in the first instance, and to moderate revisions in the second, fundamentally conflicted with society's continued desire for protection. Yet Wilson accomplished his proposed reform despite deep-seated congressional opposition. And although the widespread international economic instability created by the war lessened the gap between the interests of the executive and society, Harding nonetheless emerged as the successful advocate of moderation.

Foreign policy leaders were also successful because of the bargaining strategies adopted to a greater or lesser extent by every executive. As argued in Chapter 2, two strategies follow from the executive's need to penetrate the otherwise closed congressional tariff-making process and the unique position of the foreign policy executive at the intersection of the domestic and international political economies. First, the foreign policy executive can mobilize societal groups with complementary interests into the policy-making process, thereby gaining access to the legislature. This strategy, for example, was effectively used by Blaine in 1890 to mobilize farmers into the tariff-making process for the first time and by Wilson in 1913 to incite his progressive supporters to political action directed at the legislature.

The second strategy is for the foreign policy executive to use its role as the sole authoritative maker of foreign policy to redefine issues and bind the government through international agreements. Cleveland was the first to redefine the tariff debate through his 1887 Annual Message. Nearly every president who followed also highlighted the foreign policy dimension of trade policy and sought to expand the legitimate role of the executive in the trade policy-making process. Blaine effectively used the strategy of international linkage in the first International American Conference to build support for export expansion and reciprocity. Hull, although thwarted by his own president, sought to use this same strategy to build support for the RTAA at the London Economic Conference in 1933.

To highlight the success of the foreign policy executive is not to argue that the individuals involved always and everywhere obtained their goals. Despite his later praise for the Payne-Aldrich Act of 1909, Taft had originally desired a more substantial reduction in the tariff. A smoother transition in policy might otherwise have been expected, but the president's widely cited political ineptitude most likely contributed to the sharp break in strategy between 1909 and 1913. Similarly, McKinley had staked much of his trade strategy in 1897 on the successful passage and implementation of reciprocity. Subsequent congressional resistance and President Theodore Roosevelt's acquiescence limited the effectiveness of the assassinated leader's program. Finally, with a naive faith in the ability of the independent Tariff Commission to determine appropriate duties scientifically, Hoover stoked up the tariff locomotive only to watch Congress overheat the engine and steam off out of control.

In conclusion, American trade strategy did largely conform to the constraints and opportunities of the international economic structure throughout the period 1887–1939; the results are summarized in Table C.1. The theory of international economic structures is supported in seven out of the eight tariff acts passed between 1887 and 1939. The Smoot-Hawley Act, which only partially supports the theory, is the exception. Although the timing and direction of the 1930 tariff bill are generally correct, the magnitude of the upward revision is not predicted by the theory. Even this is partly explicable, however. The changing constraints and opportunities of the international economic structure appear to have acted as a spur to the preexisting congressional propensity for logrolling.

In addition, the foreign policy executive generally pursued the expected role in the policy-making process. Out of a total of ten presidential administrations that had an important bearing on American trade strategy between 1887 and 1939, six confirm the framework set forth in Chapter 2.[1] In these cases, the president or secretary of state recognized and actively pursued policies consistent with the constraints and opportunities of the international economic structure. Presidents Theodore Roosevelt and Taft are disconfirming cases. Roosevelt laid the groundwork for subsequent revision, but he allied himself with the protectionist wing of Congress while in office and did not vigorously pursue the policy of reciprocity set forth in the Dingley Act of 1897. Taft appears to have been particularly insensitive to the constraints and opportunities of the international economic structure and, following Roosevelt's preset course, was outmaneuvered by the protectionists in Congress. Finally, the cases of Harding and Hoover are ambiguous. Harding worked hard to restrain increases in the tariff in 1922 and readily adopted the unconditional MFN principle in 1923. Yet he also appointed staunch protectionists to the Tariff Commission, undercutting the effectiveness of the flexibility provision of the Fordney-McCumber Act. Hoover's initial call for tariff revision conformed well with the constraints and opportunities of the international economic structure, as did the later advice given him by his secretary of state, Henry L. Stimson. But like Taft, Hoover appeared not to understand the changing systemic constraints confronting him and failed to restrain the protectionists in Congress. Despite these

[1] McKinley and Wilson each served two consecutive terms in office but are counted as one administration. The only president not considered in this analysis is Calvin Coolidge. No tariff bills were passed under his administration, and he did not appear to play any role in shaping the approach of Hoover, his successor. Theodore Roosevelt is included even though no tariff bills were enacted between 1901 and 1908. As argued in Chapter 4, Roosevelt played a key role both in undermining the success of reciprocity and in setting the stage for Taft and the Payne-Aldrich Act of 1909.

Table C.1. American trade strategy, 1887–1939

Phase	Structure	Trade strategy	Foreign policy executive
I 1887–1897	British hegemony	Free riding on free trade; tariff transformed into tool for both protection and export expansion, particularly to Latin America; *confirms.**	Cleveland initiated debate in 1887; *confirms.* Secretary of State Blaine and Harrison lobbied for reciprocity despite congressional opposition; *confirms.* Cleveland also championed duty-free raw materials in 1894; *confirms.*
II 1897–1912	Declining British hegemony	U.S. continued to free ride on British free trade, pursuing protection and export expansion to Latin America; U.S. export horizons expanded, increasingly focused on rising European tariff walls; *confirms.*	McKinley took passive role in congressional deliberations but strongly supported reciprocity; *confirms.* Roosevelt allied with congressional protectionists, although he set basis for future revision; *disconfirms.* Taft failed to recognize incentives of international economic structure, outmaneuvered by protectionists; *disconfirms.*
III 1912–1930	Bilateral oportunism, U.S. & U.K.	Dramatic turn toward freer trade at home and abroad in 1913; under greater international instability, tariff raised modestly in 1922 and compensated by greater activism and unconditional MFN; *confirms.*	Wilson, strong advocate of tariff reform; *confirms.* Harding worked to restrain tariff increase in 1922 and adopted unconditional MFN in 1923, but his efforts were partially offset by support for protectionist tariff commissioners; *ambiguous.*
IV 1930–1939	Unilateral oportunism, U.S.	Preemptive protection in 1930, but final bill higher than expected as a result of congressional logrolling; *partially supportive.* Turn toward greater liberalism and activism in 1934; *confirms.*	Hoover initiated call for appropriate reform but failed to understand international economic structure or restrain Congress; Secretary of State Stimson urged restraint to Hoover; *ambiguous.* Secretary of State Hull, strong advocate of RTAA, Roosevelt less clear but supportive over time; *confirms.*

*In other words, this case confirms the theory of international economic structures. Other summaries are self-explanatory.

anomalies and ambiguities, however, the results are generally supportive of the theory.

The case study of American trade strategy also reveals two important
and more general limitations of the theory. First, the theory is underdetermining at the level of specific policy choices. This is most clearly
revealed in the first phase of American trade strategy discussed in Chapter 3. Although the theory of international economic structures explains
the trade strategy adopted by both the Harrison and Cleveland administrations, it cannot explain the specific policies they pursued. In this
case, at least two (and perhaps more) policies were consistent with the
constraints and opportunities of the international economic structure,
national trade interest, and final trade strategy adopted by the United
States. Similarly, the theory of international economic structures cannot
explain the pattern of protection across industries or sectors. Nor can it
explain the rate of protection on a single article over time. Such phe-
nomena are best explained by the interest-group or public-choice approaches discussed in Chapter 2.[2]

This lack of specificity is shared by other theories in the social sciences.
As a rule, the more general the theory, the less specific are its predictions
and, hence, explanations. Likewise, the higher the level of analysis from
which the theory is drawn, the less detailed and refined are the dependent variables it can explain. This limitation should not, in my opinion,
lead scholars to reject systemic-level theories. We should, instead,
choose theories appropriate to the question at hand and not expect
more of a theory than it can reasonably deliver.

As a second limitation of the theory, the level of protection in the
United States between 1887 and 1939 was often higher than in France
or Germany, the two spoilers of the system. This raises an empirical
anomaly for the theory of international economic structures. Despite
their desires for free riding on the hegemonic power and the effects of
international economic instability, the theory predicts that opportunists
will have a weaker preference for protection than countries of relatively
low labor productivity. This anomaly does not, I believe, falsify the
theory because the substance, direction, and timing of changes in American trade strategy are still correctly predicted. Rather, it indicates the
presence of other factors affecting national trade strategies.

[2]See Jonathan J. Pincus, *Pressure Groups and Politics in Antebellum Tariffs* (New York:
Columbia University Press, 1977); Bennett D. Baack and Edward John Ray, "The Political
Economy of Tariff Policy: A Case Study of the United States," *Explorations in Economic
History* 20 (January 1983): 73–93; Robert Baldwin, *The Political Economy of U.S. Import
Policy* (Cambridge: MIT Press, 1985); and Real P. Lavergne, *The Political Economy of U.S.
Tariffs* (New York: Academic, 1983).

Specifically, two national-level variables appear to be important for explaining the higher than expected level of American protection. The first factor is domestic market size. The smaller the domestic market of a country the higher the opportunity costs of closure and the more likely it is that a country will adopt free trade. This is a central tenet of international trade theory.[3] As argued in Chapter 1, moreover, increasing returns protection is more effective in countries with large domestic markets. With the world's largest Gross National Product in the period examined here, the United States could better afford and gain more from protection than either France or Germany. It could, in other words, more readily give in to protectionist demands from society.

The second factor, discussed in Chapter 3 and incorporated into the conception of the policy-making process developed there, is state structure. This structure conditions the access and influence societal groups have in the policy-making arena. The more decentralized the state, the greater access societal groups are likely to have, and the more likely the policy process will be to respond to societal demands for protection. Both France and pre–World War II Germany possessed more centralized state structures than did the United States. Their comparative insulation from domestic pressures may have enabled them to resist producers' demands more effectively.[4]

Despite these limitations and the empirical anomalies summarized in Table C.1, this study provides relatively strong support for the theory of international economic structures developed in Chapter 1 and the framework for understanding the trade policy-making process outlined in Chapter 2. Together they provide a relatively powerful and parsimonious explanation of the substance and changes in American trade strategy during the late nineteenth and early twentieth centuries, the goals and policies pursued by the foreign policy executive, and the principal political cleavages within the trade policy-making process.

As discussed in Chapter 1, American trade strategy during the period 1887 to 1939 approximates a "hard" or least likely crucial case study for the systemic-level theory of international economic structures. The country's large domestic market, low level of international economic interdependence, isolationist ideology, and permeable political process

[3]The political implications of smallness have been discussed by Peter J. Katzenstein, *Small States in World Markets* (Ithaca: Cornell University Press, 1985).

[4]See, among others, Barrington Moore, Jr., *Social Origins of Dictatorship and Democracy: Lord and Peasant in the Making of the Modern World* (Boston: Beacon, 1967); Alexander Gerschenkron, *Economic Backwardness in Historical Perspective: A Book of Essays* (Cambridge: Belknap Press of Harvard University Press, 1962), pp. 1–30; and Peter Gourevitch, *Politics in Hard Times: Comparative Responses to International Economic Crises* (Ithaca: Cornell University Press, 1986).

dominated by domestic interest groups should vitiate the constraints and opportunities of the international economic structure. The explanatory power of the theory in this case suggests that it will also be able to explain, at least in part, other "softer" cases.

The theory of international economic structures, however, has never been intended as a monocausal explanation of national trade strategy and, specifically, American trade strategy. From the outset, I have attempted only to discover how far this one variable could be pursued without presuming that it could explain all or even most of American trade strategy. Clearly, detailed prediction or, more important, explanation requires both better and more refined theory and, ultimately, attention to more than one causal factor. In seeking to move beyond the more simplistic versions of the theory of hegemonic stability, I have emphasized the former task. Before examining the interaction of several independent variables we must first understand their individual effects. This has been the limited ambition of this book.

INTERNATIONAL AND DOMESTIC EXPLANATIONS

As noted in the Introduction, the dominant explanation of American trade strategy between 1887 and 1939 focuses on interest-group pressures and party politics. The interpretation of American trade strategy presented in Part II, however, raises important anomalies for this approach.

Changes in the export dependence of American industry do not correlate strongly with alterations in tariff levels. The tariff was internationalized between 1887 and 1890, when few industries were export-dependent; here, action by the foreign policy executive clearly preceded societal demands. Export dependence then increased sharply in the 1890s, yet average tariffs remained relatively constant. Conversely, with only a slight increase in export dependence during the first decade of the twentieth century, tariffs were lowered modestly in 1909 and dramatically in 1913. Finally, export dependence and foreign investment increased during the war, but tariffs were actually raised in 1922. In only the Smoot-Hawley Act of 1930 did the export dependence of American industry have the predicted effect: as export dependence declined the tariff was raised. But increased foreign investment may have offset this decline in the expected liberalism of American industry. Perhaps a more disaggregated measure of export dependence would provide stronger support for this approach. And other sectors of the American economy were of obvious importance, but adding agriculture, finance, labor, and consumers only obscures the predictions of the interest-group model even further (see Chapter 2). Competition between the political parties also receives only mixed support as an explanation. It is true that whenever the Democrats captured the presidency and Congress tariffs were lowered, slightly in some cases and more so in others. Likewise, Republicans raised tariffs, with the exception of the Payne-Aldrich Act of 1909. Yet, as is most clearly demonstrated in the early 1890s, significant commonalities in trade strategy existed despite changes in party. And important changes occurred in party platforms over time. The Wilson-Gorman Act of 1894, Underwood Act of 1913, and RTAA of 1934 are more different than similar; the same holds for the five Republican tariffs passed during this period. Although interest-group pressure and party competition no doubt played important roles in the formulation of American trade strategy, the simple causal relationships typically posited in the existing literature appear inadequate.

Two debates have been central to the fields of political science and international political economy for at least the past decade: the first concerns the relative efficacy of domestic and international explanations of policy, the second the comparative importance of the state and society. The traditional explanation of American trade strategy focuses on domestic society. The theory of international economic structures, on the other hand, is international and state-centered. Taken as a whole, however, this study suggests that these debates, though helpful in their early stages for clarifying the issues, have ultimately proved to be based on false distinctions.

The systemic theory of international economic structures developed here appears best at explaining the broad contours of national trade strategy, including the overall level of protection, changes in that level, and the degree of international activism or passivism. Conversely, a focus on domestic interest groups and political parties performs less well at this broader level. Yet domestic political pressures remain the best explanation of the pattern of protection across industries and the specific rates of duty established for each industry. The alternative strengths of domestic theories and the theory of international economic structures indicates a disjuncture between the levels of analysis. The international and domestic levels do not lie on a continuum from which alternative theories can be chosen at will to explain a single phenomenon. Rather, theories from each level explain different parts of the puzzle. Moreover, domestic and international factors may exert a synergistic effect on politics. This is seen most clearly in the Smoot-Hawley Act of 1930, when the changing constraints and opportunities of the international economic structure interacted with the existing con-

227

gressional propensity for logrolling to create some of the highest duties on record. Likewise, to the extent that the framework for understanding the domestic political process set forth in Chapter 2 is helpful in explaining trade strategy, it suggests that both the state and society are important and, indeed, interactive. Rather than being starkly defined alternatives, these various approaches to understanding politics are actually complementary. The task still before us is to integrate domestic and international, statist and society-centered explanations. A first step was taken in this direction in Chapter 2, but at this stage it remains only suggestive.

POSTSCRIPT: LESSONS FOR THE PRESENT

The arguments developed in this book suggest that protection is not necessarily a sign of domestic political failure, as many economic and domestically oriented explanations imply. Both protection and free trade are legitimate and effective instruments to be used in the pursuit of national advantage. We should not allow an economic ideology, or a concern with cosmopolitical economy as Friedrich List termed it, to blind us to this historical and deeply political reality.

Nonetheless, current policy, classical international trade theory, and the theory of international economic structures all agree that universal free trade is still in the national trade interest of the United States. Drawing upon the decline of the Pax Britannica in the late nineteenth century and the interwar period, however, current variants of the theory of hegemonic stability predict that America's declining hegemony will lead to increased economic instability, international conflict, and national protectionism. Robert Gilpin, in particular, argued in 1975 that there are three possible scenarios for the present and future international economy.

> The first is that the original core [that is, the United States] somehow manages to retain or reassert its dominant position relative to the emergent cores; it continued to set the rules. . . . The second possibility is a shift from a hierarchically organized international economic system to one composed of relatively equal cores; the several cores together negotiate the rules governing trade, money, and investment. . . . Finally, the system can break down and fragment into conflicting imperial systems or regional blocs. . . . Although none of these possibilities is inevitable . . . the third is most likely.[5]

[5]Robert Gilpin, *U.S. Power and the Multinational Corporation: The Political Economy of Foreign Direct Investment* (New York: Basic Books, 1975), p. 72.

Two years later, Gilpin reflected on this same point: "Drawing parallels between the contemporary period and past eras is obviously a risky undertaking. . . . Yet, the strains and tensions of the present are there, and the experience and lessons of the past indicate cause for concern over the future of the international economic order in an era of weakened international and domestic leadership."[6] Both Stephen D. Krasner and Charles P. Kindleberger echo Gilpin's apparent pessimism for the future of the liberal international economy constructed under the Pax Americana.[7]

The "1930s analogy," however, is inaccurate. The present evolution of the international economic structure is quite different from that experienced in the period studied above. Whereas the structure of British hegemony first evolved into bilateral opportunism and then unilateral opportunism, the current direction has been toward a proliferation of opportunists.

In the mid-1960s, the United States evolved from a hegemonic leader into an opportunist (see Table 1.2 and Figure C.2). The Federal Republic of Germany was also transformed from a spoiler into an opportunist in approximately 1965. France followed West Germany's path, evolving into an opportunist in the mid-1970s. By 1975, as a result, a clear structure of multilateral opportunism had emerged. If present trends in productivity growth continue, Japan is likely to join these nation-states within the next decade.

Consequently, the present evolutionary trend within the international economy is not toward unilateral opportunism as occurred during the decline of the Pax Britannica. Rather, the Pax Americana has evolved into multilateral opportunism and is likely to remain so into the foreseeable future. It will be quite different from its historical predecessor. If the theory developed above is correct, the international economy will remain relatively open and liberal despite the decline of American hegemony. The international economy will resemble that which existed between 1912 and 1930, but we are unlikely to see a repetition of the economic conflicts of the 1930s. Indeed, considerable potential for international economic cooperation presently exists.

Four structural threats to the liberal international economy are apparent, however. First, any evolution of the international economic struc-

[6]Robert Gilpin, "Economic Interdependence and National Security in Historical Perspective," in Klaus Knorr and Frank N. Trager, eds., *Economic Issues and National Security* (Lawrence: Regents Press of Kansas, 1977), p. 61.
[7]Stephen D. Krasner, "State Power and Structure of International Trade," *World Politics* 28 (April 1976): 317–47; and Charles P. Kindleberger, *The World in Depression, 1929–1939* (Berkeley: University of California Press, 1973).

Figure C.2. The international economic structure, 1950–1977

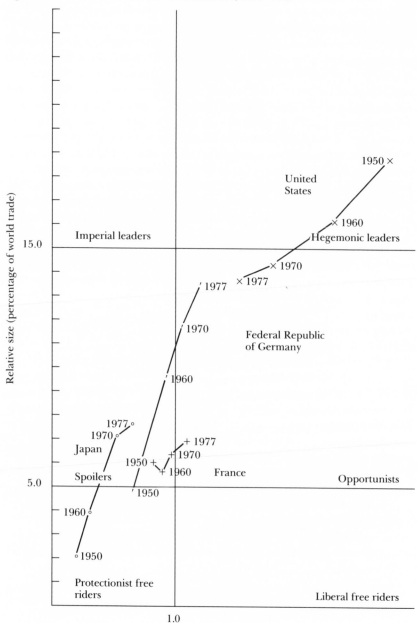

ture away from bilateral or multilateral opportunism is likely to prompt preemptive protection or defection. As in the Smoot-Hawley Act of 1930, any impending transformation of the international structure reduces incentives for cooperation among opportunists and encourages protection. This is an unlikely possibility in the near term. The structure is likely to remain relatively stable at least for the foreseeable future.

Second, although a change of structure may be unlikely, changes within the structure of multilateral opportunism are already under way. The last decade has seen a leveling or equalization of productivity rates among the advanced industrialized countries.[8] As the number of opportunists and near opportunists within the structure proliferates, the problem of free riding once again becomes important. Opportunists restrain protectionism in one another through the threat of retaliation. As the number of opportunists expands, the probability that any one opportunist will punish or retaliate against "cheating" at the margin declines. Each may hope that others will ignore its own violations while otherwise strictly enforcing the trade rules. Thus, rather than being a positive development, the expansion of the number of opportunists is actually a potential threat to the liberal international economy. It is not clear how many opportunists are necessary before the politics of mutual restraint breaks down. The problem is complicated by the differences in relative size between the opportunists. Even as an opportunist in the late 1970s, France was approximately half the size of the United States or the Federal Republic of Germany and could potentially free ride better than either. Cooperation and mutual restraint clearly become more difficult as the number of opportunists expands.

Third, employing a "tit-for-tat" strategy to induce international cooperation or universal free trade is not without risks. As seen in the early 1920s, actual or feared protectionism in one opportunist will stimulate similar action by others in return. Given the fragility of universal free trade under a structure of multilateral opportunism, policy makers should resist any actions which threaten or imply that they will defect from their current commitment to free trade. A tit-for-tat strategy, however, must be retaliatory to be effective. The danger here is that retaliation may be misperceived by the target as protection, and vice versa.[9] Statesmen should not be reluctant to retaliate against cheating,

---

[8]Historically, labor productivity has correlated strongly across sectors within a country. Thus a country that was on average more productive than others typically dominated all manufacturing sectors. With the introduction of so-called "industrial targeting" strategies, this relationship may be breaking down. See Appendix.

[9]Even low levels of misperception can undermine the utility of tit-for-tat as a cooperation-inducing strategy. See George W. Downs, David M. Rocke, and Randolph M. Siver-

but they must strive to maintain the distinction between retaliation and protection.

Finally, as in the 1920s, the level of international economic instability has an important effect upon the trade strategies of nation-states in a structure of bi- or multilateral opportunism. Despite the oil shocks of the 1970s, the present international economy remains relatively stable. The patterns of trade and finance have been altered, but the disruptions have generally not been as large as those that followed World War I. Indeed, the success of the advanced industrialized countries in regulating the oil shocks may demonstrate the potential of a structure of multilateral opportunism. This is a hopeful sign for the liberal international economy.

It is this level of instability, however, which policy makers can most directly affect. Countries must actively stabilize exchange rates at realistic levels. They must carefully monitor trade patterns and price levels to ensure gradual and steady evolution. A renewed emphasis on growth will also help mitigate instability. As noted in Chapters 1 and 5, instability renders cooperation more difficult just when it is most necessary. All involved should realize that restabilizing an international economy is much more difficult than safeguarding existing levels of stability. This is, indeed, the lesson of the 1920s.

---

son, "Arms Races and Cooperation," in Kenneth A. Oye, ed., *Cooperation under Anarchy* (Princeton: Princeton University Press, 1986), pp. 118–46. The tariffs on Japanese products imposed by the Reagan administration in April 1987, in retaliation for Japanese violations of an earlier agreement on semiconductor chip pricing, are an excellent example of the type of retaliation proposed here. The tariffs are contingent on specific Japanese behavior and imposed upon products in which there is substantial foreign competition, thereby reducing the protection that would otherwise be provided to American industry.

Relative Labor Productivity: Definitional and Operational Considerations

Relative labor productivity can be used as a summary measure for many aspects of a country's economy, but it is used here primarily as an indicator of internal and external returns to scale. Returns to scale, in turn, are defined as increasing if equiproportionate increases in all factors give rise to more than proportionate increases in output, constant if increases in output are proportionate, and decreasing if increases in output are less than proportionate.

Increasing returns tend to be associated with industries that intensively use physical and human capital. As a result, labor productivity in these industries will be relatively high, as it will be for a country specializing in such industries, and increasing rapidly.

Other possible measures of increasing returns to scale would be plant size, length of production runs, and the like. Unfortunately, consistent cross-national data for the late nineteenth and early twentieth centuries do not exist for these indicators. More important, these measures reflect only internal economies of scale. Only relative labor productivity captures both internal and the more diffuse external economies.

The limited sectoral data that do exist tend to confirm the validity of relative labor productivity as an indicator of national specialization in increasing returns industries and production techniques. In 1924–25, 1969, and 1976, the United States was found to be consistently more productive than the United Kingdom across all industries studied. In only 1947–48 and in only two sectors (beet sugar and manufactured ice) was Great Britain found to be more productive.[1] Similarly, in 1968 and

[1]A. W. Flux, "Industrial Productivity in Great Britain and the United States," *Quarterly Journal of Economics* 48 (November 1933): 1–38; Marvin Frankel, "Anglo-American Pro-

1976, Germany was found to be more productive than the United Kingdom in all but one sector.[2] Other studies have found similar patterns.[3]

With the rapid spread of technology and the practice of industrial targeting, however, this clustering of sectoral productivity levels may be breaking down. In a recent study of sixty Japanese and American industries, six Japanese industries were found to be more productive than their American counterparts despite an aggregate level of Japanese labor productivity less than half that found in the United States.[4] Thus, relative labor productivity may now be a less valid indicator of national specialization in constant or increasing returns industries than it was in the past. If present trends continue, it may be even less valid in the future, especially as differentials in labor productivity between countries decline, although large differences—as, say, between the United States and Argentina or Brazil—will still be telling.

As described in Chapter 1, relative labor productivity is defined as national output per worker-hour relative to the average national output per worker-hour in the other middle- and large-sized countries. In restricting the comparison group to the middle- and large-sized countries, it is implicitly assumed that countries compare their gains from trade only against the largest and most prominent members of the international economy. There is considerable indirect evidence to validate this assumption. Before World War I and during the interwar period, for instance, the United States, United Kingdom, France, and Germany appear to have perceived each other as their principal trade rivals and not the often more productive but smaller European nation-states.[5] Nonetheless, Table A.1 presents relative labor productivity calculations on a base of sixteen countries (column 1) and a base of the four middle- and large-sized nations (column 2) for 1913. From these comparisons, it is evident that France and Germany would be classified as

---

ductivity Differences: Their Magnitude and Some Causes," *American Economic Review* 45 (May 1955): 94–112; and A. D. Smith et al., "International Industrial Productivity: A Comparison of Britain, America, and Germany," *National Institute Review*, no. 101 (August 1982), pp. 13–25.

[2]Smith et al., "International Industrial Productivity."

[3]These studies are reviewed in Angus Maddison, *Phases of Capitalist Development* (New York: Cambridge University Press, 1982), p. 103.

[4]Cited in ibid., p. 103.

[5]See Ross J. S. Hoffman, *Great Britain and the German Trade Rivalry, 1875–1914* (Philadelphia: University of Pennsylvania Press, 1933); Matthew Simon and David E. Novack, "Some Dimensions of the American Commercial Invasion of Europe, 1871–1914; An Introductory Essay," *Journal of Economic History* 24 (December 1964): 591–605; and Frank A. Vanderlip, "The American 'Commercial Invasion' of Europe," *Scribner's Magazine* 31 (January–March 1902): 3–22, 194–213, and 287–306.

Table A.1. Relative labor productivity compared by base, 1913

Country	1 (16 countries)	2 (Middle- and large-sized countries only)
Australia	1.79	
Austria	.83	
Belgium	1.23	
Canada	1.41	
Denmark	.95	
Finland	.61	
France	.85	.68
Germany	.90	.73
Italy	.62	
Japan	.33	
Netherlands	1.16	
Norway	.77	
Sweden	.78	
Switzerland	.96	
United Kingdom	1.30	1.15
United States	1.65	1.56

SOURCE: Angus Maddison, "Long Run Dynamics of Productivity Growth," *Banca Nazionale de Lavoro Quarterly Review* 128 (March 1979): 43. Recomputed by author.

spoilers and the United Kingdom and United States as opportunists at this time regardless of which method was adopted.

In addition to the problem of external validity, there are two problems of internal validity in the measurement of relative labor productivity. First, there is large debate on the utility of output measured by monetary value of production as compared to output measured by physical volume of production.[6] The difficulty of matching actual goods produced and their quality over time and across countries clearly precludes the use of physical output for this study, whatever the merits of the measure.

Second, even productivity comparisons across countries based on monetary values of output are fraught with statistical and methodological problems. These have been discussed elsewhere in the literature and need not be reviewed here.[7] I recognize that a considerable margin of error may exist in the data; they should be taken to indicate only general magnitudes and trends.

[6]See Jean Fourastie, *Productivity Prices and Wages* (Paris: Organization of European Economic Cooperation, 1957).
[7]See International Labour Office, *Measuring Labour Productivity* (Geneva: International Labour Organization, 1969); and Franz-Lothat Altmann et al., eds., *On the Measurement of Factor Productivities: Theoretical Problems and Empirical Results* (Göttingen: Vandenhoeck and Ruprecht, 1976).

Table A.2. Relative labor productivity compared by source, 1913

Country	Clark	Maddison	Clark/Maddison
United States	1.70	1.56	1.09
United Kingdom	1.21	1.15	1.05
France	.44	.68	.65
Germany	.86	.73	1.18

SOURCES: See text.

Most studies of labor productivity are concerned with intranational comparisons over time. Only two sources present their results in the form required here. The first, Colin Clark's *The Conditions of Economic Progress*, last rewritten in 1957, is largely out of date.[8] The second, Angus Maddison's "Long Run Dynamics of Productivity Growth,"[9] presents national productivity estimates in 1970 U.S. dollars and is used here. For comparison, Clark's "real output per man-hour" was recalculated as relative real output per worker-hour and compared to the recalculations of Maddison's estimates presented in the text. The results for 1913 are presented in Table A.2. The two sources are relatively consistent for the United States and the United Kingdom. Clark's estimates are considerably lower for France and higher for Germany. Nonetheless, the categorizations of these four nation-states as opportunists and spoilers would remain the same regardless of which source was used.

[8] 3d ed. (New York: St. Martin's, 1957).
[9] *Banca Nazionale de Lavoro Quarterly Review* 128 (March 1979): 3–43.

Index

Library of Congress Cataloging-in-Publication Data

Lake, David A.
  Power, protection, and free trade.
  (Cornell studies in political economy)
  Includes index.
  1. United States—Commercial policy—History. 2. International economic relations.
3. Free trade and protection—History. I. Title. II. Series.
HF1455.L34   1988   382'.3'0973   87–47869
ISBN 0–8014–2134–9 (alk. paper)